Gaining by Losing is a call and challenge to return to what matters most as Christians—to go and make disciples. Whether a church or marketplace leader, sending and planting is in our job description as followers of Jesus. And J.D. is calling us to a higher standard and level of commitment. This is a challenge to leaders everywhere to take up the flag and mantle of going and doing, not just staying and sitting. Many of us need to be shocked from our comfortable church recliners and out into our neighborhoods, communities, and cities. Come on! Movements are about moving, and we are each part of the movement of God, the church, to scatter and be sent. I'm fired up after reading this book! And you will be too!

—BRAD LOMENICK, Speaker, leadership advisor; author of *The Catalyst Leader* and *H3 Leadership*; former president and key visionary, Catalyst and Catalyst Conferences

Faithfulness to the Great Commission means a commitment to church planting—both locally and globally. J.D. Greear understands this well. His new book, *Gaining by Losing*, argues on clear biblical grounds that healthy churches plant other churches, even at great cost to themselves and their resources. Church leaders who care about fidelity to Christ's commission to his church will be encouraged and equipped by this book.

—R. ALBERT MOHLER JR., President of the Southern Baptist Theological Seminary

Gaining by Losing is a challenging and essential message for the church.

—LOUIE GIGLIO, Passion City Church/Passion Conferences, Atlanta, GA

J.D. Greear is my friend. I respect him, and I love the ministry of Summit Church. He's done us all a huge favor by writing *Gaining by Losing*. Like J.D., this book is a theological, gospel driven, Great Commission-shaped jewel. I can't wait for you to read this book!

—DERWIN L. GRAY, Lead Pastor of Transformation Church, South Carolina; author of *The High Definition Leader*

With raw and compelling honesty, J.D. Greear shares with us his story of coming to terms with what Jesus considers "success"—namely, our *sending capacity*, not our *seating capacity*. He then helpfully walks us through the risky business of keeping our individual and corporate lives centered on discipleship, planting, and sending. Yes, it is a risky business, but it's God's business into which he invites us, and it's a business that will produce a harvest for the fame of Christ and the good of our churches and our souls. Get it. Read it. Do it!

—STEVE TIMMIS, Executive Director of Acts 29

Wow! I rarely finish a book and feel like it took my breath away, but *Gaining by Losing* by J.D. Greear is nothing short of incredible. Healthy churches are sending churches. Healthy Christians are going Christians. I truly believe that all the concerns about the health of our churches could be alleviated if we practice the biblical truths in this book. It's just that powerful.

—THOM S. RAINER, President and CEO of LifeWay Christian
Resources, www.ThomRainer.com

Christians are often tempted to forget that the greatest call we have upon our lives is to lose those lives for the sake of the gospel. In *Gaining by Losing*, J.D. Greear challenges us to remember that those who wish to truly live should be willing to lose; those who truly want to gain should start by giving away. This book is a timely and convicting reminder for us all.

—ED STETZER, Conference and seminar leader, prolific author,
www.edstetzer.com

For the church in North America to fulfill its calling to reach our continent and the nations with the gospel, we need tens of thousands of new congregations—and the leaders to start them. To do that, we need churches to take the challenge that J.D. lays before them in this book, to generously send out their best to start new churches elsewhere. I urge pastors throughout North America to read this book, internalize its message, and let it become a guide for their churches' disciple-making efforts.

—KEVIN EZELL, President, North American Mission Board, SBC

If every pastor could allow these truths to take root in their hearts and capture their ministries, the church just might begin to win again.

—SHAWN LOVEJOY, Lead Pastor, Mountain Lake Church,
Georgia; author of *Be Mean: Relentlessly Protecting the Vision*

This is a book that inspires and informs—inspiring to pastors who want to see gospel-centrality spill over into Great Commission passion, informative to leaders who want to know how to create a sending culture in their churches. *Gaining by Losing* is a game changer.

—TREVIN WAX, Managing Editor of The Gospel Project; author
of *Gospel-Centered Teaching* and *Clear Winter Nights*

This year Northwood celebrates twenty years of working in Vietnam. During that time we have mobilized 2,500 members, raised millions of dollars, hosted over 100 exchange students, and literally impacted millions of lives. Northwood went out into the world to change the world, not realizing how much we would be changed and transformed as a church. What we have experienced there changed us here. Some of the things that I've learned and come to believe I find in this book. I'm excited that J.D. has written about them. How I long for a new generation that not only sees the Western church through different eyes, but can see the world through fresh eyes. J.D. gives so many practical things and fresh ways of thinking about how we engage the world.... Now do it!

—BOB ROBERTS JR., Senior Pastor and Chief Missionary of
Northwood Church, Texas; author of *Bold as Love*

J.D. offers a challenging and thoroughly biblical vision for the church of how we actually gain by losing. It is truly exciting to think about what could happen in the global church if this message is taken seriously by Christians.

—MATT CARTER, Pastor of Preaching, Austin Stone Community
Church, Texas; coauthor of *The Real Win*

J.D. Greear casts great vision for becoming a sending church and then shows us how it is done! In *Gaining by Losing*, the vision challenges each follower of Jesus to understand they are sent and asks every church to see them as a sending agent for new churches. If you long for the church to become the commissioned people of God, you need to read this book!

—DAVE FERGUSON, Lead Pastor of Community Christian
Church, Naperville, IL; author of *Finding Your Way Back to God*

This book desperately needed to be written, and I'm so glad that my friend, J.D. Greear, took on the challenge to write it. *Gaining by Losing* will challenge you to the core to change the scorecard for how you gauge success in ministry. It takes us back to the emphasis of the New Testament. We are called to make disciples and send them out to expand God's kingdom, rather than capture them, count them, and keep them in their seats. Read this book slowly. Soak it in, and let it reshape the way you measure faithfulness in God's kingdom.

—BRIAN BLOYE, Pastor of West Ridge Church, Atlanta, GA;
coauthor of *It's Personal*

Warning! J.D.'s transparency in *Gaining by Losing* will cause you to look in the mirror of Scripture to identify and surrender the hidden idols of your heart! J.D. preaches here what he practices and does well in allowing the reader into the inner corridors of his heart. Glean from his timely wisdom. This book is a MUST have!

—D. A. HORTON, Executive Director of ReachLife Ministries

I encourage you to read and share this new book by J.D. Greear. It is a modern-day, pragmatic application of the revolutionary teachings of our Lord Jesus that encourages us to live selfless lives, on mission for him. The principles that J.D. outlines could revolutionize our understanding of mission work, domestically and internationally, and provide resources to see the Great Commission accomplished in our lifetime.

—FRANK S. PAGE, Ph.D., President and CEO,
Southern Baptist Convention Executive Committee

With a like-minded passion to send our members to the nations, married to a passion for church planting, this book reads and challenges my soul. You will love the urgency and guidance *Gaining by Losing* presents to your life. Commend to your people; they will get it.

—JOHNNY HUNT, Senior Pastor, First Baptist Church,
Woodstock, GA

In *Gaining by Losing*, J.D. Greear helps us focus on the simple, yet profound concept that Christ's kingdom is multiplied when churches give away our resources—our people, our time, our money, ourselves—for his work. This is a thought-provoking, convicting, and inspiring look at how to do missions. Any pastor or lay leader who is serious about taking the gospel to the ends of the earth will benefit from J.D.'s insight.

—BRYANT WRIGHT, Senior Pastor, Johnson Ferry Baptist Church,
Marietta, GA

Mission hype from the stage is everywhere, but the practice of mission in the local church is often missing. Summit Church and Greear do not merely talk about mission; they have been living out the mission of God for more than a decade. *Gaining by Losing* lays out a clear game plan for mission and coaches us in succinct but powerful "plumb lines" toward the future of the church. God sends to bring himself glory, to grow us into the image of Christ, and to fulfill the Great Commission. Read this book and begin the adventure of obedience to God's vision for the world.

—DANIEL MONTGOMERY, Lead Pastor of Sojourn Community
Church, Louisville, KY; founder of the Sojourn Network;
author of *Faithmapping* and *PROOF*

GAINING

BY

LOSING

GAINING

BY LOSING

WHY THE FUTURE BELONGS TO CHURCHES THAT SEND

J. D. GREEAR

ZONDERVAN

ZONDERVAN

Gaining by Losing
Copyright © 2015 by J.D. Greear

This title is also available as a Zondervan ebook.

This title is also available in a Zondervan audio edition.

Requests for information should be addressed to:
Zondervan, 3900 Sparks Dr. SE, Grand Rapids, Michigan 49546

This edition: 978-0-310-53395-5 (softcover)

The Library of Congress Cataloged the hardcover edition as follows:

Greear, J. D., 1973-
    Gaining by losing : why the future belongs to churches that send / J.D. Greear.
      pages cm
    ISBN 978-0-310-51524-1 (hardcover, jacketed)
    1. Church development, New. 2. Missions. 3. Evangelistic work. 4. Mission of the church. I. Title.
    BV652.24.G74 2015
    269'.2—dc23
                                   2015004624

Published in association with Yates & Yates, www.yates2.com

Cover design: *Dual Identity Design*
Interior design: *Denise Froehlich*

Printed in the United States of America

---

16 17 18 19 20 21 22 /DHV/ 20 19 18 17 16 15 14 13 12 11 10 9 8 7 6 5 4 3 2 1

DEDICATION

To the people of the Salem Baptist Church in Winston-Salem, NC, who taught me, from childhood, to love missions and the spread of the gospel among the nations, and that seemingly endless string of missionaries from there whose slide shows mystified, entertained, and enlightened me. What I now see comes from standing on your shoulders.

———

To the more than 500 Summit Church members who have left our church in pursuit of the goal of "planting 1,000 churches in our generation" on both international and domestic church planting teams. Thanks to you, we are 113 churches closer to our goal. Only 887 to go. Thank you for living out the mission and vision of our church. You are God's fulfillment of Psalm 2:8 to us.

———

To Carl Scott, Chris Gaynor, and Rick Langston, who led the way in reshaping this congregation to believe that gaining comes by losing.

———

To Kharis, Allie, Adon and Ryah: You are arrows God has given your mother and me to send out for his kingdom. Jesus will send you places where your mother and I cannot go. Most of all, *the future*. You are the inheritance we leave behind for future generations, Lord permitting (Ps. 127:1–4). May you know the joy of receiving him who was sent from heaven for you and being sent by him for others.

CONTENTS

FOREWORD

When I was a young boy, my dad taught me to play a game he called "Giveaway Checkers."

It was a simple game. The goal was to "give away" all of your checkers by putting them in a position to be jumped and captured by the other player. The first one to "give away" all of his checkers was declared the winner. In essence, you won by losing.

I didn't know it at the time, but my dad was teaching me a powerful lesson about the marketplace, marriage, and ministry — because in each of these important arenas, those who give away the most end up gaining the most.

In the following pages, J.D. Greear shows how this simple but profound principle of gaining by losing applies to church life. With solid theology, unassailable logic, and a host of real-life examples he shows us how to play "Giveaway Church."

It's a game we all need to learn to play, because in God's economy the church that *sends* the most *wins* the most. Yet few pastors or churches actually play "Giveaway Church" or have a desire to do so.

It's easy to see why. Our culture at large doesn't celebrate those who grow their fruit on someone else's tree. We may praise kingdom impact, but we reward church growth. We may talk a lot about kingdom priorities, but more often than not our success is measured by how many people we keep, not by how many we send. In the church world, the pastor or church with the most checkers wins.

So what's gone wrong? How did we come to a place where we wax eloquent about the Great Commission, storing up heavenly treasures, and servant leadership — but in reality send out so few? Why is it that we love the idea but resist the reality of becoming a "Giveaway Church"?

I think one reason is that we too often have a *truncated gospel*.

Now, I'm not talking about doctrine. I know the gospel. I can teach it well. But like many of you, I have often settled for a head knowledge that focuses on the facts instead of a heart knowledge that fully grasps the magnitude of Jesus' sacrifice and the scandalous improbability of a God who turns rebels like you and me into full-on sons and daughters of the king.

The simple fact is, anytime I can get my arms fully around what Jesus has done for me and all that lies ahead, it's hard to be stingy with the people, resources, and platforms I've been entrusted with.

A second reason is our long history of *clergy-centered ministry*. By lifting up those in vocational ministry (pastors, evangelists, and missionaries) as a special class of people who are uniquely "called" into ministry, we've unintentionally restricted and downsized our sending pipelines.

Every Christian is called into full-time ministry. Once we step over the line and begin to follow Jesus, everything we do is supposed to be done in his name, representing him, with the goal of advancing his kingdom.

But clergy-centered churches tend to downplay this. By seeking to identify and send out a few well-trained and fully funded missionaries, they inadvertently raise the entry bar to ministry so high that few can climb over it.

In contrast, "Giveaway Churches" lower the bar. They seek to identify and send out Jesus-following engineers, accountants, entrepreneurs, teachers, and truck drivers who are willing to ply their trade wherever they are needed to help the cause of the gospel. They understand that the frontlines of evangelism and ministry are most often found in the marketplace, not within the walls of our churches.

A third thing that makes "Giveaway Churches" so rare is our natural *spiritual myopia*. It's easy to confuse our castle with God's kingdom.

Now, I want to be clear. I am not against church growth or big churches. I pastor one of the larger churches in the nation. But when I stand before God, the ultimate measure of my ministry and stewardship will not be found in how many people we jammed into our campuses on a weekend. It will be measured by what those people did once they left the building.

I recently had dinner with a friend who is one of 66 pastors and church planters who have come out of a small church in Oregon. A number of them planted so-called megachurches, including a few that rank among the largest ones in the country. That's a "Giveaway Church." The pastor and congregation understand the exponential multiplying power of sending. They don't see it as a sacrifice. They see it as an investment.

While the church I pastor has been applauded and honored for its impressive growth and community impact, I have no doubt that when we both stand before Jesus, the unknown pastor of that little church in Oregon will receive a reward far greater than my own.

That's why I encourage you to read carefully and reflect deeply on the principles and practices spelled out in the following pages. You will find a roadmap that will guide you out of the swampland of a truncated gospel, clergy-centered ministry, and a myopic view of the kingdom. You will also find a game plan for becoming a "Giveaway Church," the kind of church that will one day hear, "Well done, my good and faithful servants."

—Larry Osborne
Author of *Sticky Church* and *Sticky Teams*
Pastor, North Coast Church, California

INTRODUCTION

Farmers in Oklahoma during the late 1930s faced an excruciating choice.

Throughout the 1920s, rain had been plentiful and the harvests abundant, and many city workers had left their factory jobs in the Northeast for a chance of a fortune in the great American Midwest. The stock market crash of 1929 motivated even more to take the journey west.

But in 1931, the rains stopped. To make matters worse, years of poor farming techniques had destroyed the grasses that preserved moisture during times of drought. The dry ground resulted in massive dust storms, which destroyed remaining fields. Fortunes were swept away in the clouds of terrifying, dull gray blizzards.

By the fall of 1939, thousands of farmers returned empty-handed to the East Coast. Some that remained faced an excruciating choice: they had just enough grain to feed themselves and their families for another year — but probably not much longer than that. If they planted these seeds and no rains came, their families would not survive the year. But if they held on to these seeds, grinding them into flour for bread, they forfeited any chance of receiving back a harvest.

Many planted, in faith — in hope — that rain would come.

In the fall of 1939, it did.[1]

Planting always involves risk. We release control of something we need in the hopes that it will come back to us in multiplied measure. But once we let go of it, we forfeit any ability to use it for ourselves. Seeds you plant you can no longer consume. Yet without the act of planting, there will never be a harvest.

Jesus turned to this principle of the harvest when he wanted to teach his followers how to extend his kingdom on earth:

> "Very truly I tell you, unless a kernel of wheat falls to the ground and dies, it remains only a single seed. But if it dies, it produces many seeds." (John 12:24)

I've always thought it was odd that Jesus described the seed going into the ground as "dying," because I don't think of a seed going into the ground as "dying." I think of it as just beginning to live.

But in one sense, a planted seed *is* dying. As its outer shell disintegrates, it ceases its self-contained existence as a seed. It has been given over to the earth.

In the same way, God grows his kingdom only as we take our hands off of what little portion he's given to us, "die" to our control of it, and plant it into the world. That feels just as scary to us as to those farmers planting their precious, remaining seed in the dusty plains of Oklahoma and praying for rain.

The Seed in Your Hands

In this book I want to press you to consider — whether you are a church leader or an "ordinary" Christian trying to figure out the best way to use your life — one, primary question: If you looked at every one of your blessings as "kingdom seeds," how many of them are you planting in the fields of God's kingdom, and how many are you keeping in storehouses to use as "food"?

If you are a pastor or church leader, I want you to ask this of the organization you lead. How many of the seeds God has blessed you with are you planting into kingdom fields — fields that have great potential but yet may contribute little to the "bottom line" of your organization?

Let's be honest: Too often, we church leaders measure the success of our ministries by one criteria and one criteria alone: *How large is it?* How large is the attendance? How big is the budget? And so we spend all our money on things that will increase our attendance, our budgets, and our capacity.

But if John 12:24 is true, then Jesus measures the success of our ministries not by how *large* we grow the storehouse, but by how widely we distribute its seeds. Jesus' measure of the church is not seating capacity, but sending capacity.

To church leaders and individuals alike, Jesus presents a very clear choice: *preserve* your seed and lose it; *plant* your seed for his sake, and keep it through eternity (John 12:25).

The Future of the Church

I believe that every church, every ministry, and every follower of Jesus Christ ought to be devoted to planting — giving away — what they have for God's kingdom. I am not against large churches — I pastor one. But as I will show you in this book, I believe that churches that give away both their people and their resources are the churches that will expand the kingdom of God into the future.

Throughout this book I will share stories of how God brought our church (and me, personally) to this conclusion. I warn you: The journey has not been easy — in fact, at times it has been downright painful. Like most young aspiring pastors, I graduated from seminary and had my sights set on acquiring a big, notable ministry — one with a big attendance and big budget and even bigger attention for the guy behind it. But early on, God confronted me with my idolatrous and self-centered approach to ministry. He showed me that quite often when I had prayed, "*Thy* kingdom come," what I really meant was "*My* kingdom come."

There are two basic questions about discipleship that we have to ask ourselves over and over, in every new season of life and in regards to whatever resources God has given us stewardship over:

— Whose kingdom are we actually building: ours, or God's?
— Do we really believe that Jesus grows his kingdom most as we "give away" what he's given to us?

Throughout this book I will introduce a number of ministry "plumb lines" — key phrases that we use at our church to keep our ministries and our lives centered on sending. I hope that they help you evaluate the shape of your ministry and consider its trajectories.

If you are a church leader, I hope this book helps you to see that your greatest kingdom potential lies not in your ability to gather and inspire your people at a weekly worship meeting, but in your capacity to equip them and send them out as seeds into the kingdom of God.

If you're not a church leader, I want you to understand the crucial role you play in the church's future. I believe that the future of Christianity lies in *your* hands, not in ours (that is, the hands of your church leaders). That's not pep-talk rhetoric. Jesus' promises about the greatness of the church are about ordinary people being filled with the Spirit, turning the world upside down. As leaders, our job is not to gather you, amaze you, and collect your funds; our job is to help you discover the power and potential of the Spirit in you.

As I will show you, *you* — the so-called "ordinary believer" — *you* are the tip of the gospel spear. The greatest gospel movements in history have been facilitated by ordinary people like *you*, not church leaders like me. And the Great Commission will be completed only when we church leaders get serious about sending you out to do what God has called you to do, and you get serious about doing it.

We Are Under Obligation

In Romans 1:14 Paul uses a strange word to encapsulate his life and calling, one with enormous implications for both church leaders and members alike. "I am under obligation," Paul says, to everyone who has not yet heard the gospel (see ESV). Many translations render "under obligation" as "debtor," because Paul is invoking language that describes a debtor's relationship to his creditor.

When you are severely in debt, your life no longer really belongs to you. It belongs to the creditor. You can't spend money however you would like anymore. If your boss gives you a $10,000 Christmas bonus, you won't be able to use it to take a vacation to Hawaii or to buy new furniture. The creditor has first and final say in how the money is spent. I once knew a church that was so severely in debt that representatives from the bank literally stood in the back of the lobby during the weekly offering, taking the money straight to the bank, where bank officials would decide how much the church could keep that week. The church was no longer free; it was "under obligation."

Paul thought of himself as a debtor to those who had not heard about Jesus. His future was not free. But why did he owe *them*? Because he knew he was no more deserving of the gospel than they were. He was not more righteous, nor had God seen more potential in him (see 1 Timothy 1:15). Paul saw God's grace toward him exactly for what it was — completely unmerited favor. Paul knew that placed him under severe obligation to the grace of God. Paul's future, bright as it may have been, having a great education and all the right connections, no longer belonged to him. Every spare resource — every ounce of energy, every moment of his time — belonged to his "creditor": the grace of God.

Every person who knows and understands the gospel is under this same debt of obligation. As David Platt says, "Every saved person this side of heaven owes the gospel to every unsaved person this side of hell." If you are saved, you are under obligation to leverage your life to bring salvation to the nations. Those of us called to be leaders in the church are under obligation to train you up and send you out.

We pastors are not free to build ministries that mainly make life more comfortable for us. Each of us is under obligation to do whatever we can to get the gospel to those all around the world who have never heard. And that means *releasing* — planting — the seeds we have been given. It means letting go and sending out our very best to bring a harvest in God's kingdom, even — especially — when it doesn't benefit our church directly.

The gospel is that Jesus Christ died as a substitute for sinners, offered now as a gift to all who will receive him in faith. Jesus has instituted a new kingdom, a kingdom that someday will bring final and ultimate healing to the earth through his resurrection, but one that begins now when sinners are reconciled to him through his death. God has given to us, the church, the mission of preaching his offer of reconciliation to all people everywhere — that Jesus lived the life we were supposed to live and then died the death that we were condemned to die so that we could be reconciled to God. We signify the message of that new kingdom through acts of healing and extravagant generosity, which depict for others the nature of the kingdom Jesus is establishing (2 Cor. 5:14–21). Everyone who has received the reconciliation is sent on that mission. Every believer is *sent*. You go from mission field to missionary.

Our God Is a Sending God

Our God is a **sending** God. He sent his best into the world to save us. Jesus is referred to as "sent" forty-four times in the New Testament. After his resurrection, Jesus passed on his identity to his disciples: "As the Father has sent me, I am sending you" (John 20:21).

To follow Jesus is to be sent.

Jesus' command to *every* disciple is to "go" (Matt. 28:19). We may not all go overseas, but we are all to be going. This means that if you are not going, you are not a disciple; and, church leader, if the people in our churches are not "going," we are not doing our jobs. A church leader can have a large church with thousands of people attending, but if people are not going from it "outside the camp" (Heb. 13:13), to pursue the mission and call of Christ, those leaders are delinquent in their duty.

Planting, investing, sending, and sacrificing are costly. It hurts. But the trajectory of discipleship is toward giving away, not taking in. As Dietrich Bonhoeffer famously said, "When Christ bids a man to follow, he bids him come and die."[2] Jesus did not say come and *grow*, but come and *die*. And he showed us what that means by his own example.

When Jesus laid down his life on that hill in Jerusalem, he had nothing left. Soldiers gambled for his last remaining possessions on earth. Everything he owned had been either given away or taken from him. But out of that death came our life. In giving everything away, he gained us. In Jesus' resurrection from death, God brought unimaginable life to the world — to you and to me. Jesus was the first of many seeds planted into the ground to die.

Why would it surprise us that the power of God spreads throughout the earth in the same manner? Life for the world comes only through the death of the church. Not always our physical, bodily death (though it includes that sometimes), but death in the giving away of our resources. Death in the forfeiture of our personal dreams. Death in our faithful proclamation of the gospel in an increasingly hostile world. Death in sending our precious resources, our best leaders, our best friends.

When Christ calls any of us to follow him — whether he is speaking to us as individuals, or to our churches and ministries — he bids us, "Come and die."

It is not through our *success* that God saves the world, but through our *sacrifice*. He calls us first to an altar, not a platform.[3]

His way of bringing life to the world is not by giving us numerical growth and gain that enriches our lives and exalts our name. His way is by bringing resurrection out of death.

We live by losing. We gain by giving away. What *we* achieve by building our personal platform will never be as great as what *God* achieves through what we give away in faith.

It's one thing to know these things, to believe they are true. It's another to implement them. That is what this book is about. What does it look like to live sent — in your personal life, in your ministry, or in the church that you lead?

I will warn you: It's relatively easy to nod our heads at this point and say, "Yes, like Jesus, we live by dying." But to go to the next step — to invest some of your most cherished resources, or say goodbye to those whom you love as they go to begin something new — that is hard, and it never gets easier. Yet it's how God's kingdom grows.

We gain by losing.

If you are ready to see what that looks like in practice, keep reading.

Part 1

Untapped Greatness

CHAPTER 1

Aircraft Carriers,
Cruise Liners,
and Battleships

Many people are bored in church. They are afflicted with a nagging sense that they ought to be doing something — that there is some meaningful mission they are supposed to be a part of. But they can't quite get their mind around what that is, and so, in the meantime, they sit in church, try to pay attention, give their tithes, behave as best they can, and wonder if when they get to heaven they are going to be rebuked for failing to do whatever it was God wanted them to do.

They remind me of a California man named Larry Walters, whose story I heard many years ago.[1] Larry went out to the Army-Navy surplus store, bought seventy-five used weather balloons, inflated them, and attached them to a lawn chair he had secured to the back of his pickup truck. With several friends watching, he climbed into the chair, settled in, and had a friend untie the rope.

"He was hoping," a friend later said, "to observe the neighborhood from a slightly different angle, and gain a new perspective on his life." He took nothing with him but a peanut butter sandwich, a six-pack of beer, and a fully loaded BB gun.

Two and a half hours later, the Los Angeles International Airport reported an "Unidentified Flying Object" in the skies above LAX at nearly 16,000 feet. "Lawnchair Larry," the reclining cosmonaut, was now three miles into the sky and a hundred miles from his original launch site. The pilot of the 737 who first spotted Larry said, "Well ... I see what looks like a perfectly still man sitting in a ... is it a lawn chair? And I think he is holding a rifle."

In a rescue stunt that would have made comedian Chuck Norris proud, SWAT teams lassoed Larry, who had passed out in the chair, and ferried him safely to the ground. (In case you are curious, his intention had been to lazily saunter up to the right altitude, then use his BB gun to pop the balloons to keep him there. However, when he untied himself from the pickup, friends said he shot up into the air as if he had been fired from a cannon. He panicked and did the only thing he knew how to do in a stressful situation: break open the six-pack. About 2,000 feet in the air, he passed out.)

On the ground, after being revived back to consciousness, Larry was promptly issued a $4,000 ticket by local police for "the obstruction of airport traffic." (He later got it reduced to $1,500.) A local journalist then asked him three questions:

Larry, were you scared? Larry said, "Yes." (Actually, he said more than that, but as this is a Christian book, we'll leave it at "yes.")

Larry, would you do it again? Larry said, "No." At least he's a quick learner.

Larry, why did you do it? Larry said, "I just got tired of always sitting around."

I find that a lot of Christians in churches feel the same way as Larry. They're tired of just sitting around. They feel like they are supposed to be doing something in the mission of God but don't quite know what it is.

They go to churches where they hear that Jesus is building his church and that the gates of hell will not prevail against them. But they don't see themselves, or their church, prevailing against the gates of hell. They seem to be just getting by. Many can't remember when a single adult convert — one truly brought out of darkness into light — came to Jesus in their church. And they certainly can't remember one whose story they were *personally* a part of.

Study after study shows that most Christians have never even shared their faith — most indicating that somewhere 90 percent of *evangelicals* have never shared their faith with *anyone* outside of their family. (Kind of makes you wonder how we get away with using the name "evangelical"!)

Most churches have a difficult time maintaining their ground, much less storming anything that belongs to Satan. Gates, after all, are defensive ramparts, not offensive weapons. "Prevailing against the gates of hell" does not mean keeping Satan out of our backyards, but plundering *his* kingdom. According to a recent Lifeway Research study, in the next seven years 55,000 churches in the United States will close their doors, and the number of those who attend a church on the weekend in the United States will drop from 17 percent to 14 percent. Only 20 percent of churches in the US are growing, and *only 1 percent are growing by reaching lost people.*[2] So 95 percent of the church growth we celebrate merely shuffles existing Christians around.

Don't you think these two problems — believers who don't know how effectively to disciple others, and a gradually shrinking church in the West — have to be related in some way? Yet very few pastors and church leaders see raising up disciple-making leaders as their primary objective. We measure success by size. In so doing, however, we neglect the one thing that can propel the church forward into the next generation ... and to the ends of the earth: Spirit-filled, disciple-making disciples.

Don't Miss the Boat

I believe we need a fundamental shift in *how we think* about the mission of the church. Let me illustrate, using three types of ships.

Some Christians see church as a *cruise liner,* offering Christian luxuries for the whole family, such as sports, entertainment, childcare services, and business networking. They show up at church asking only, "Can this church improve my religious quality of life? Does it have good family ministry facilities? Does the pastor preach funny, time-conscious messages that meet my felt needs? Do I like the music?"

If their church ever ceases to cater to their preferences ... well, there are plenty of other cruise ships in the harbor. In fact, often they get involved with three or four of them at once. After all, the music is great on Cruise Liner A, and the kids enjoy the youth program at Cruise Liner B, and we do most of our fellowship and Bible study with friends at Cruise Liner C, and we occasionally listen to the podcast of the angry young pastor down the road who tells the funny stories.

Other Christians believe their church is more like a *battleship*. The church is made for mission, and its success should be seen in how loudly and dramatically it fights the mission. This is certainly better than the "cruise liner"; however, it implies that it is the church institution that does most of the fighting. The role of church members is to pay the pastors to find the targets and fire the guns each week as they gather to watch. They see the programs, services, and ministries of the church as the primary instruments of mission.

I would like to suggest a third metaphor for the church: *aircraft carrier*. Like battleships, aircraft carriers engage in battle, but not in the same way. Aircraft carriers equip planes to carry the battle elsewhere. My grandfather served on the USS *Yorktown* during World War II, and he explained to me that the last place an aircraft carrier ever wanted to find itself engaged in battle was on its own deck. In fact, nowhere near it. We used to watch old World War II movies together — the kind where they intersperse actual battle video clips — and my grandpa once paused a John Wayne movie to show me where he was standing on the deck when a plane crashed on it and broke in half. When you are on an aircraft carrier, he said, the goal is to keep the battle as far away from you as possible. You load up the planes to carry the battle to the enemy.

Churches that want to "prevail against the gates of hell" must learn to see themselves like aircraft carriers, not like battleships and certainly not like cruise liners. Members need to learn to share the gospel, without the help of the pastor, *in the community*, and start ministries and Bible studies — even churches — in places without them. Churches must become discipleship factories, "sending" agencies that equip their members to take the battle to the enemy.

We Need a New Metric for Success

We need a new metric for success beyond size. To evaluate something's success, we first need to understand its function.

If you light a stick of dynamite and launch it 500 feet in the air and it explodes, was it successful? Well, in one sense, yes. The dynamite did exactly what it was designed to do. And it got a lot of people's attention. People for five miles around looked up into the sky to see what happened. Three minutes after it detonates, however, there is hardly any evidence that the explosion ever even occurred, other than a whiff of gunpowder and a few confused bystanders still staring blankly into the sky.

Take that same piece of dynamite, however, burrow it into the side of a rock face and light it, and you will have a different kind of "success." The bang will not be nearly as loud, but now you will have an opening where previously you had only a mountain.

Churches that want to penetrate their world with the gospel think less about the Sunday morning bang and more about equipping their members to blast a hole in the mountain of lostness.

Why the Future Belongs to Churches That Send

I want to suggest four reasons *why* the future of Christianity belongs to churches that send, and *why* those of us who want to see the world reached will be more committed to raising up and sending out than we are to gathering and counting. Those four reasons are:

1. Increasingly, in a "post-Christian" society, unbelievers will simply not make their way into our churches, no matter how "attractive" we make them.
2. Multiplication beats out addition, every time.
3. The presence of God accompanies those who send.
4. Jesus' promises of "greatness" in the church are always related to sending.

Let's consider these factors one by one.

1. Increasingly, in a "post-Christian" society, unbelievers will simply not make their way into our churches, no matter how "attractive" we make them.

For years, the Western church has enjoyed a common Christian language with the culture through which we could communicate the gospel. Not everyone went to church, of course, but the bedrock of the culture was Christian. Our primary focus has been calling "lapsed" or delinquent Christians back to the God of their fathers.

But our world in the West is changing. The number of people checking "none" for religious affiliation on censuses increases at an astounding rate each year.[3] "Nones," as they are called, do not casually make their way into churches — for any reason. We have to think of them as we would people of a completely different religion.

I lived in a Muslim country for several years, and I was friends with dozens of people who went to the mosque weekly. At no point did I consider going with them. I wouldn't have gone for a special holiday. I wouldn't have gone if I were facing hard times. I wouldn't have gone if the imam were doing a really helpful series on relationships or if he told really funny stories that helped me see how Allah was relevant to my life. I wouldn't have gone had they added percussion and a kickin' electric guitar to the prayer chants. Islam was a completely foreign world, and one in which I knew I clearly didn't belong. So I didn't go.

I take that back. I did visit the mosque one time, because a Muslim friend invited me, and I wanted to honor him by learning more about his life and faith. It was an unmitigated disaster. First, we had to sit in weird, uncomfortable positions for extended periods of time. And everyone but me seemed to know what to say at various points of the service. They would all suddenly stand up, in unison, leaving me clamoring to get to my feet, which was hard when you couldn't feel your legs anymore. They all dressed in the same outfit, and my Nike shirt and Levi jeans made me feel pretty out of place. At one point they sang out an "Amen." At that point I thought I knew the drill, hearkening back to my days in a country Baptist church. So I hit the harmony note. No one else deviated from the primary note. Everyone turned to stare at me. I felt like a side of bacon at a bar mitzvah.

It was an awful experience, and although my friend invited me back several times, I always managed to find a reason to not be able to go. The mosque was a portal to a completely different world, and I didn't have an Islamic faith that would compel me to put up with the discomfort required to learn the unfamiliar ways of that world.

This is a bit what it is like for people in the post-Christian West as they look into the Christian church. A British friend of mine, Steve Timmis cites a recent study in Great Britain in which 70 percent of Brits declare that they have no intention of ever attending a church service for any-son. Not at Easter. Not for marriages. Not for funerals or Christmas Eve services. For more than two-thirds of the people in Great Britain, nothing will carry them naturally into a church. In light of this, Steve comments:

> That means new styles of worship will not reach them. Fresh expressions of church will not reach them. Alpha and Christianity Explored courses will not reach them. Great first impressions will not reach them. Churches meeting in pubs will not reach them.... The vast majority of un-churched and de-churched people would not turn to the church, even if faced with difficult personal circumstances or in the event of national tragedies. It is not a question of "improving the product" of church meetings and evangelistic events. It means reaching people apart from meetings and events.[4]

Great Britain is a few years ahead of the United States in secularization, but judging by the rapidly increasing percentage of those reporting "none" for religious affiliation, I believe we will be there before too long.

This means that if we don't equip our people to carry the gospel outside of our meetings, our events, our gatherings and programs, we are going to lose all audience with them. A few flashier and flashier mega-churches will likely keep fighting for larger pieces of a shrinking pie.

There is another alternative: we can grow the pie. But that means teaching our people to engage people *outside* the church.

2. Multiplication beats out addition, every time.

The second reason that churches that care about the Great Commission will devote themselves to sending is a mathematical one.

Perhaps you can remember this math conundrum from middle school:

> If you have a choice between receiving $10,000 a day for 30 days, or getting $0.01 doubled each day, which would you choose?

Almost every middle school student chooses "$10,000 a day" — because ... think about what you could buy by the end of the week! Sure, $70,000 is enough to buy ten PS4s gaming stations with accompanying widescreen TVs ... and enough left over for a used BMW! And in thirty days, you'd have $300,000!

But your math teacher probably pointed out to you that choosing $10,000 a day instead of $0.01 doubled daily would leave about 10 million dollars on the table. Doubling your penny daily, however, would net you $10,737,418.23 in thirty days![5] In four months you'd have $13,292,2 79,957,849,158,729,038,070,602,803,364, compared to only $1.2 million if you had taken on the $10,000 a day.

Many churches still pursue success via the "$10,000 a day" model. Tell aspiring megachurch pastor Bob that you have a program by which he can add 1,000 people a month to his church for ten years straight, and he will likely faint with joy. Before the first year is done, he will be invited to speak at conferences all over the nation, and Christian magazines will have his face splashed across their front covers. Leaders would line up around the block to buy his books and have him sign their Bibles.

Yet if Pastor Bob trains up just one person each year to lead another to Christ, who in turn trains another person who leads another person, and they each do that for thirty years, by year 30 they will have won nearly a billion more people than he would have by adding 1,000 people every month.

But here's the rub: Netting $10,000 a day *feels* much more gratifying — at least at first — than getting $0.01 doubled during that first week. If you choose the doubled $0.01 route, after a week you would only have about $2, whereas your friend who chose $10,000 would be bouncing about town with $70,000 in his pocket. He'd be placing a down payment on a new beach house, and you'd still be living in your parents' basement.

In the same way, focusing on attendance growth — adding 1,000 people a year — *feels* much more gratifying to church leaders. The successes are immediate. You can brag about them. But this is not the road to long-term, kingdom growth.

Our church hit an important milestone this year. We grew by almost 1,000 people, which qualified us for *Outreach Magazine*'s one hundred fast-growing churches for the fifth year in a row. But that's *not* the milestone I'm talking about. This year the attendance at the churches we have planted grew by more than 1,100 people. In other words, our plants added more to the kingdom than our church did. Just five years in, we are already seeing the power of multiplication kicking in. From here on out, by God's grace, that gap will only widen. One day I'll stand up in front of the Summit Church and the attendance at the churches we've planted will be 100 times what we have at our church each weekend.

My point in sharing this is not to suggest that we have to choose between growing the attendance of our church and sending out disciples from the church. As I will point out in chapter 5, you can and should do both. Rather, I am trying to make clear that *if we take the long view of ministry, growing and sending out disciples will take priority.*

3. The presence of God accompanies those who send.

If we want our people really to know Jesus, we will teach them to live "sent." Our God is a sending God, and nearly every time he speaks to someone in Scripture he is sending them on a mission.

When God called Abraham to follow him, he made clear that the blessing he would bestow on Abraham was not only for him. Through him he would bless "all the families of the earth" (Gen. 12:1–3 ESV). The writer of Psalm 67, reflecting on that promise, prayed that God would bless Israel *so that* "your ways may be known on earth, your salvation among all nations" (v. 2 NKJV).

The Old Testament book of Jonah presents the sad picture of a nation running away from this commission, seeking only its own blessing. Jonah, who is a picture of the whole nation of Israel, is more concerned with his own creature comforts and personal vengeances than the message of mercy and blessing that God had given him to share with the nations.

Jesus came as the new Israel, the joyfully sent prophet that Jonah refused to become. Jesus is described as "sent" more than forty-four times in the gospel of John, and "you are sent" is his one-sentence commission for every disciple:

"As the Father has sent me, I am sending you." (John 20:21)

The church is now Jesus' vehicle for the completion of his mission. Jesus finished the purchase of our salvation, paying the full price for our sin on the cross and shattering the powers of death in the resurrection, but the mission of salvation is not yet complete. As Martin Luther said, it wouldn't matter if Jesus died a thousand times if no one heard about it. Through us

Jesus *continues* the work of salvation that he commenced in his death and resurrection (Col. 1:24; Acts 1:1). In that sense, his work is not "finished."

Christopher Wright says, "God's mission is what fills the gap between the scattering of the nations in Genesis 12 and the healing of the nations in Revelation 22."[6] God's worldwide mission, he says, defines every believer's primary responsibility until Jesus returns.

Thus, you can't really call yourself a follower of Jesus if you don't see yourself as sent. He sends each of us somewhere, to some group, to make disciples of those who do not know him.

We think of missionaries as God's "super servants," Jesus' Navy Seals. The word "missionary" is never used in the Bible, however, not even once. That's because *all* of God's people are sent; all of God's people are commanded to go. There is no "special class" of sent ones.

So the question is no longer *if* we are sent, only where and how. Many of us are waiting on a voice from heaven to tell us what God has already told us in a *verse*: "As the Father has sent me, I am sending you" (John 20:21). When you have the verse, you don't need to wait for the voice.

As Charles Spurgeon used to say, "Every Christian is either a missionary or an impostor."[7]

God, I've heard it said, is like a spiritual cyclone: If he pulls you in, soon he'll be hurling you back out.[8]

4. Jesus' promises of "greatness" in the church are always related to sending.

Jesus' promises of help to those devoted to sending are truly astounding. To be honest, they are so astounding that sometimes I have a hard time taking them seriously. In the gospel of John, Jesus told his disciples that they should be excited that he was leaving them, because that meant he would send them "another Helper" who would make them more effective than even he could make them. "It is to your advantage that I go away," he said, "because then you will get the Holy Spirit" (John 16:7 paraphrased).

Imagine how absurd that must have sounded to those disciples! It was to their *advantage* that Jesus leave? How awesome would it be to have Jesus as your personal pastor? Every sermon would be a "10," every mission strategy "heaven sent," and every decision "divine." If you had a theological question, he could just answer it. And if offerings were low one month, he could send out a deacon to catch a fish with a $1,000 in its mouth (see Matthew 17:27).

Even those benefits would be inferior, Jesus tells us, to a church of "ordinary Christians" empowered with the Holy Spirit.

In *Jesus Continued* . . . , I argued that this is a promise the church has yet to take seriously. We still think that the world will be won by a few hyper-anointed super-Christians who gather large crowds in big buildings. But Jesus said that a Spirit-filled church would be infinitely more effective than that, even if that one hyper-anointed individual was Jesus himself (see John 14:12).

The book of Acts is a witness to the truth that having twelve men operating in the power of the Spirit and teaching others to do so as well is greater than having Jesus himself stay to lead the mission personally.

Jesus was not against building large crowds. He preached to crowds of upwards of 15,000, and both he and his disciples rejoiced in the size of those crowds. But when he ascended to heaven, he left only 120 disciples. Onto those 120 he placed his Holy Spirit, however, and they turned the world upside down within two generations.

Leaving behind a church of 120 after a lifetime of ministry would probably not be celebrated as a huge ministry success today. But Jesus took the long view of ministry. He understood the power of exponential multiplication, so he didn't just gather a mega-audience; he built a sending community. He didn't leave a throng of 10,000 congregants awestruck at his sermons; he commissioned 120 believers equipped to carry the gospel into the world.

The apostle Paul also took the long view of ministry, seeing long-term leadership development as an essential component of his ministry. He told his young protégé, Timothy,

> The things you have heard me say in the presence of many witnesses entrust to reliable people who will be qualified to teach others. (2 Tim. 2:2)

In his letter to the Ephesians, Paul went so far as to say that God's primary purpose for "church leaders" was *developing other leaders* in the congregation (Eph. 4:11 – 12). Pastors are given, he says, for the equipping of the saints for the work of the ministry. The saints (in Paul's usage, ordinary Christians) are the primary ones to do the ministry. I often tell our congregation that based on Paul's explanation, when I became a pastor I left the ministry! My job now is to equip *them* to do it.

How we build our churches today turns this principle on its head. We are excited when large crowds throng to hear a talented teacher. That's simply not what Jesus was most excited about, and it's not how he built his own ministry.

The problem, of course, is not those large crowds of growing attendance. It's devoting most, if not all, of our energy into producing only that. Crowds won't last, even when you gather them by doing miracles, as Jesus did. Can any of us hope to have more interesting or memorable sermons than he gave? Yet, when he died, where were the 5,000 he had fed? Surely they had seen and heard enough to stick around. Even Jesus' preaching and miracles, by themselves, were not sufficient to produce enduring disciples.

Long-term movements are not built by swelling crowds, even when Jesus is the one doing the gathering. They come only as we take the time to replicate our faith in someone else's heart.

We need, like Jesus, the *discipline* to devote our energy into those things that will have the greatest, long-term impact on the world, even if it means having to wait years — maybe a lifetime — to experience return on our investment.

Many of the greatest gospel movements in history took this kind of time, and quite often the movement leaders never really got to experience the full measure of their success. For example, Adoniram Judson, America's first and perhaps most famous missionary, labored in Burma for seven years without a single convert, and then another six years before he had enough believers to form a church.[9] Yet, by his last year of ministry he could identify 7,000 believers in Burma — a place where hitherto no one had even heard the name of Jesus! A study done less than ten years after his death revealed 210,000 confessing believers in Burma. That's the multiplying power of God's Spirit at work, taking the seeds that Judson planted with his life and watered with his tears and turning them into a movement that impacted a nation.

Acclaimed historian Rodney Stark notes that the church has always grown this way. We often talk about the "rapid growth" of the early church in Acts, he says, but the best estimates indicate that by the end of the first century there were only about 50,000 believers. Most of these 50,000 were genuine disciples, however, and they were devoted to raising up a new generation of leaders after them. Soon the powers of kingdom multiplication kicked in, and by AD 400, 34 *million* people had professed faith in Christ. (Some estimates say over *half* of the Roman Empire had become believers!)[10]

Are *you* willing to take the "long view" of ministry and do those things that build long-term movements, even if they don't "feel" as gratifying or make you look as good in the short-term? *If so, you will devote yourself to building leaders, not inflating audiences.*

For me, this isn't just a ministry insight I'm trying to push in a book. It's intensely personal. In 1975, Lynn and Carol Greear moved to the city of Winston-Salem, North Carolina, so my dad could take a new job. They were cultural Christians, but not yet devoted followers of Jesus. Someone at my dad's workplace invited them to attend an exciting, growing church in town, one with an electrifying pastor who could preach the paint off the walls. My parents went, and there they were gripped by the gospel. They began to attend regularly, and soon God brought them to renewed faith in Christ.

This church was as devoted to discipleship as it was to growing its audience, however. The pastor took a personal interest in my dad and began to include him in times of prayer or when he went out on evangelistic visits. My dad said that none of Dr. E. C. Sheehan's sermons had as big an impact on him as simply observing him in those things. Dr. Sheehan taught my parents how to read the Bible and how to organize their new home around the gospel.

Because of that, I grew up in a home with two thriving spiritual giants. They, in turn, taught my sister and me to love the gospel. Now we are teaching our children to do the same.

I sometimes wonder what my life would be like had this church been focused only on swelling its weekend attendance. The church at that time may have had great attendance numbers to brag about at the annual convention, but my father's grandchildren would not be growing up to follow Jesus.

Discipleship multiplies the number of people engaged in the mission, and multiplication has exponential impact for years to come.

Ladies and Gentlemen, This Is a Church

As Pastor Pat Hood has said, it's time to go old-school Vince Lombardi on the body of Christ.[11] Vince Lombardi, renowned coach of the Green Bay Packers, held up a football in front of his team at the start of each season and said to them, "Gentlemen, this is a football." His professional coaching started with the basics.

We need a Vince Lombardi to stand up in front of us and say, *"Ladies and Gentlemen, this is a church."*

The church exists for mission. As Christopher Wright says, "Jesus did not give a mission to his church; he formed a church for his mission."[12] Without the mission, a church is not a church; it's just a group of disobedient Christians hanging out.

The church is a movement before it is an institution. And the number one characteristic of a movement is … movement. If something is not moving, it can't be called a movement. And people who are not moving are not part of the movement, even if they are members of the institution.

Are you moving in mission? Are you moving *outward* into the world with the gospel? Is your church moving that way? Or is it only drawing people inward, adding them to the rolls, providing religious services to "complete" their lives?

I can't think of anything more important for the church to recover than its missional essence. As I explained at the beginning of this chapter, the church, which Jesus said was unstoppable (Matt. 16:18), not only is failing to advance, but is *losing ground* in the West. So, it's time for us to take some drastic measures. And that means getting back to the basics.

We need to learn from our brothers and sisters in the African and Asian parts of the Global South, where the church is growing at exponential rates. There the church seems to understand it exists for mission. I once heard a pastor from a large church in Korea say that if one of their small groups went more than a year without adding a new convert, they were brought before the elders for questioning and possible church discipline!

In this book I would like to explore with you what it looks like to get serious about sending. I want you to understand how you are sent, personally, and then how you can foster a sending culture in your church or ministry.

But before we get there, I want to share with you how our church came to this conviction ourselves. It was pretty painful. And a little humiliating.

CHAPTER 2

Our (Painful) Journey Toward Sending

The church I pastor did not start out as a sending church. During my first years there, my focus was entirely on growing the church. I sincerely wanted to reach people for Jesus, but I was also pretty interested in making a big name for myself. (Did I just put that in print? Well, as they say, every young pastor's dream is a great, big church and a pretty, little wife — though typically he ends up with a pretty, little church and a [*Deleted by editor to protect the author*].)

So I wanted a great big church. And I was pretty sure God was into that, too, because it seemed like a win-win for both of us.

But throughout the Scriptures, before God built something great in the Spirit, he first tore down the efforts of the flesh. God let Abraham suffer in frustration with his natural sterility so that when God gave him a child, he would know where it came from. God has to take our eyes off our kingdom before he can build his. That's what he began to do in our church, and he started with me.

It's About the City, Stupid

During my second year as pastor I preached through the book of Acts, during which in Acts 8 I came to the story of Philip's revival in Samaria. As a result of Philip's ministry, Luke says, there was "great joy" in the city (Acts 8:8).

In the next chapter Luke tells the story of a disciple named Tabitha (who had the unfortunate nickname of "Dorcas"), a woman who made many coats for people in her community who did not have them. When she died, Luke says, they gathered at her bedside and wept (Acts 9:36–39). I asked our congregation if they thought there was "much joy" in our city as a result of our ministry or, if we were to "die," whether anyone from the community would gather at our bedside and weep. We felt the answer on both accounts was "no." If anything, our "death" would mean one less mail-out they had to throw away at Easter and the city's recovery of a tax-exempt piece of property. Our ministry did not seem to be having the effect on our communities that the early Christians had on theirs.

I had just gotten back from a short-term mission trip to Southeast Asia, where I had spent time in the small city in the Islamic country I lived in for two years as a church planter. As I passed through its city gates, all of these old emotions I had felt about that city during my time there flooded into my heart. That had been *my* city — I was the only church planter within a hundred miles, and I had felt like God had made me responsible for it. I had prayer-walked that city repeatedly; I felt that its schools were *my* schools; its problems, *my* problems; its lostness, *my* lostness. And then a question popped into my head:

Why don't you feel that way about your current city?

You see, I related to Raleigh-Durham (a part of North Carolina called "The Triangle"), where I pastored the Summit Church, the way a virus relates to its host culture. We were trying to draw people out from the city up into our organism, the church. Once they were in the system, we would utilize their energy, time, and money to make our institution great. Philip and Dorcas saw their communities differently. Their focus wasn't on building a big ministry; it was on blessing and winning the city.

God opened my eyes to see just how wrongheaded my focus had been. I told the church that I needed to repent. *No longer would our focus be on growing the church,* I said. *Instead, we would seek to reach and bless the city.*

Blessing the community might certainly include growing a big church, but it would also mean *giving away* some of our resources. It would mean serving populations in our community that would never make great "contributing members" in our church, and planting churches in the city that would "compete with" rather than contribute to the "bottom line" of the Summit Church. But the goal was to reach and serve the city; growing the church was only a means to that end. Up to this point I had had it reversed: growing a big church had been my goal, and reaching the city had been the means.

Our prayer, as a church, changed from "God, let us reach lots of people and grow huge" to "God, let us bless and bring joy to this city." The difference between those prayers may seem like a small, semantic shift to you, but for us it was profound. What's good for the kingdom of God in Raleigh-Durham is *not always* good for the Summit Church (at least in an institutional sense), and what is good for the Summit Church is not always good for the kingdom of God.

Thy Kingdom Come, or My Kingdom Come?

During this transition, God revealed that my focus on my kingdom went deeper than I'd realized. One afternoon I was praying for massive revival in our city — the kind that would change the shape of our city for the next two hundred years, the kind they would write about in history books. As I was praying, it seemed as if the Spirit of God suddenly asked, "And what if I answer this prayer ... and send a revival into Raleigh-Durham beyond all you've asked or imagined ... one that they will talk about for hundreds of years ... but I choose *another* church through which to do it? What if that church grows, and yours stays the same?"

In that moment I felt as if a disguise of religiosity had been ripped off of my selfish heart, and I was exposed. I only wanted to see *my* church succeed, *my* kingdom enlarged, *my* name magnified. Somehow "*thy* kingdom come" had become all jumbled up with "*my* kingdom come." Unlike John the Baptist, who prayed, "He [Jesus] must increase and I must decrease," my heart was "Jesus, I don't care if you increase, as long as I increase." Ministry, you see, is a great place for guys with the idol of success to hide, because we can mask our selfish ambition in the cloak of doing great things for God.

I realized that this was why I always got so jealous when other people's churches grew faster or got more attention than mine. I wanted the attention. How different was my attitude from John the Baptist's! You see, for a brief season John the Baptist was all the rage in Israel. He was everyone's favorite prophet, number one on the conference circuit. But then his cousin Jesus showed up, and the masses trickled away from

John to Jesus. Evidently John ended his ministry with substantially fewer people than he began with. His last days were spent penniless, in prison, with his reputation trashed. His response? "He must increase, but I must decrease" (John 3:30 ESV).

John compared his ministry to that of a best man at a wedding (John 3:28–29). The real man of honor in a wedding, of course, is the groom. The greatest moment in a modern wedding is when those big doors in the back open up ... and there she stands, prepared for him. I have performed many weddings, and I have yet to see a bride who did not look absolutely stunning in that moment. Everyone loves to look back and forth between the bride and groom, watching his reaction to her. That entire moment is about them.

Imagine, however, that as the bride walks down the aisle, the best man starts poking his head around the groom's, winking at her, and raising his eyebrows suggestively. You would ask, "What is he doing? Why is he trying to divert her attention away from the groom?" And you probably wouldn't be surprised when the groom turned around and punched him in the throat. Who is he to try and insert himself between the two of them in such a sacred moment?

Yet that's essentially what the pastor does who is concerned more about the size of his ministry than the kingdom of Jesus. It's an ugly thing. And if we could see it for what it really is, we'd be ashamed when we do it. The church is Jesus' bride. We leaders of the church are simply servants who escort the bride to the heavenly groom. It is never about us — it is only about him and them. When we are doing our best work, we are invisible — or, at least, no one is paying that much attention to us.

I needed to repent for my idolatry in ministry. By God's grace, I did, and my heart and approach toward ministry have never been the same. While I can't say that I've completely gotten over my idols of success and craving for the praise of others, that afternoon marked a turning point in which the eyes of my heart shifted from building my kingdom to building God's.

What did John the Baptist get out of all this? Well, for one, he got the praise of Jesus. Jesus called him the greatest prophet that ever lived (Luke 7:28). That's a better prize anyway.

A "sending" ministry always starts with a heart exam. Sending out people and giving away your resources, you see, will most often *compete with* your church's "bottom line," not benefit it. Sending means giving away some of your best leaders and letting go of needed resources. It means giving away opportunities in the kingdom, and watching others get credit for successes that you could easily have obtained for yourself.

The only way you'll be willing to do that is if you love Jesus' kingdom more than your own. If your heart prayer in ministry is really "my kingdom come," you will never be an effective sender. You won't really even want to try.

Mormons and Bacon, Egg, and Cheese Biscuits

A third defining moment in our transformation into a sending church came when college students "discovered" our church in 2003. Five college students visited our church one Sunday. They liked the service, and because college students travel in herds, the next week they brought back 300 of their friends. (I'm not kidding!) In a period of about three weeks our attendance doubled, and during that same time our weekly average giving increased by $13.48. College students bring a lot of great things to our church, but money is not one of them.

One Sunday morning an usher came into my green room with a bacon, egg, and cheese biscuit some college student had placed into the offering plate. It had a little note on it that read (quoting Acts 3:6 ad lib), "Silver and gold have I none, but such as I have, give I unto you."

We quickly realized that although this growing number of college students would probably never contribute much to the budget of our church, we would have plenty of potential missionaries. We began to challenge our graduating seniors to let ministry be the most shaping factor in determining where they pursue their careers. We tell them, *"You've got to get a job somewhere ... why not get it where you can be part of a strategic mission initiative?"*

We tell every graduating senior that unless they have heard from God audibly by the time they graduate, they should plan to spend their first two years involved in one of our church planting projects. (We call this our "Mormonization" strategy: "Give us your first two years for mission, and we'll change the world.") We meet with our seniors before they graduate and ask them if they will give us a "blank check," letting us tell them where their career could most greatly benefit the mission. Last year nearly a hundred of our graduating seniors accepted that challenge. We helped them relocate to cities in which we were planting a church and get a job in their career field there. Others raised support so that they could be more directly involved in ministry leadership at the new church.

Not every church has the benefit of having so many college students. So I share this with you, not to suggest that you emulate what we have done, but to challenge you to think about what unique resources you have been given and how you might steward them wisely in sending. Every church, every community, and every person has particular assets that can be leveraged for God's kingdom.

Ask yourself, "Are there mission fields in our backyards that could contribute to the global spread of the gospel that we have overlooked because they don't enhance the bottom line of our church? Are we evaluating ministry opportunities only by how they benefit us, or are we looking at the benefit they can bring to Jesus' kingdom even if there is nothing in them for ours?"

If you are a church leader, make it personal. What ministry opportunities are you personally involved with that are not enhancing you, your church, or your platform?

Getting Back to My Roots

God used these three moments and a handful of others to help take my eyes off myself and my kingdom and put them onto sending. As I said earlier: God is a spiritual cyclone. The way you know he's pulling you in is that you feel yourself being hurled back out. Going into that cyclone often *feels* destructive. But that's only God breaking open the shell of your "seed." Though painful, it's a good pain, because out of it comes gospel life.

Now, as I look back through my life, I realize that God has always been calling me toward sending. I had gone to college to pursue a degree in law when God gripped my heart with a vision of 2.2 billion people dying with no knowledge of the gospel. One Friday morning during my junior year, I was reading through the book of Romans when it finally made sense to me that faith in Jesus is the only way anyone can be saved, and that meant that millions were separated from him with no hope. I began to *feel* the weight of those 2.2 billion people on my soul.

That morning I asked God if he would allow me to go and tell them. Up until this time I had been waiting on God to tell me if he wanted to use me in his mission. But God had already made that clear. He had said, "Follow me, and I will make you fishers of men" (Matt. 4:19 ESV). The call to be involved in Jesus' mission is synonymous with the call to follow Jesus.

I had been asking God what his will was, telling others I was trying to "find God's will for my life." That has to be one of the dumbest phrases Christians use: "finding God's will." We don't have to "find" God's will, because it's not lost. "The Lord ... is not willing that any should perish, but that all should come to repentance" (2 Peter 3:9 NKJV). His will is that we be involved in that mission.

That semester my prayer changed from "God, if you command me to go, I'll go," to "God, show me *where* and *how* you want me to go." The question, you see, is not *if* we're called to pour our lives out for the mission, only *where* and *how*.

My first assignment was to go and live among a Muslim unreached people group. Before I left there, I had a conversation that has shaped the rest of my life. One of my Muslim friends, with whom I had shared the gospel dozens of times, came over, literally minutes before I was to leave for the airport, to tell me about a dream he had had. "In my dream, I was standing on earth, when suddenly, open before my feet, was the 'straight and narrow way' leading to heaven. As I looked up along this pathway to heaven, I couldn't believe it... I saw *you*! You were walking up the road to heaven!" (He seemed so surprised by this, I felt a little offended!)

"I called to you, but you did not hear me. I saw you arrive at heaven's gates, these huge, brass doors.... I thought, 'Surely his journey ends there. He will never be able to get through those gates.' But then, as I watched, I heard someone inside call your name. The doors swung open wide for you, and you went in ... and my heart broke, because I really wanted to go with you. And as I sat there despairing, the doors opened again, and you came back out.... You walked all the way back down to where I stood, stretched your hand out to me, and pulled me up into heaven with you."

He then looked at me and said, "What do you think my dream means?"

Now, please understand that I was raised in a traditional Baptist home. Dreams and visions were not a part of our standard spiritual repertoire. But in that moment, I knew instinctively what to say: "Brother, you are so in luck. Dream interpretation is my spiritual gift!"

I explained the gospel to him (again) for over an hour, but sadly, it was still too much for him, at that point, to believe. Yet what he said next I will never, ever forget: "J.D., I know what my dream means. God sent *you* here to help me find the way of salvation. But, my friend, you are going home, and you are the only Christian I have ever known. Who will show me the way of salvation?"

My friend, Ahmed, is never far from my mind when we commission members to leave and plant churches. Each time we do this I'm reminded why God saved me and called me into the ministry: he blessed me to be a blessing.

⁝⁝⁝

With the gospel comes responsibility. As I said in the introduction, receiving the gospel immediately makes us "debtors" to those who have yet to hear about it. No longer can we live as people "free" to do whatever we want; our resources, our talents, and our futures are all "under obligation" to the Ahmeds of the world.

As I look back from this vantage point, I can see that my call to the pastorate began as a call to the mission field. Jesus has never rescinded that call to the nations; he fulfills it through my work as a pastor.

The details of your calling will not be the same, but the substance is. Jesus calls every follower to be involved in his mission to the nations. The assignments are different; the trajectory is the same.

The question is no longer if we are called, only where and how.

How would your life change if you *assumed* that you were already called and now needed to know only where and how?

A Longer Story I Had No Part In

A few years ago I learned that just as God had written sending into the DNA of my calling, he had written it into the foundations of our church.

Our church was planted by a man named Sam James in 1962. God called Sam and his wife, Rachel, to be missionaries to Vietnam, but their departure was slowed by a medical problem with their oldest son. Sam was frustrated by the delay, but he used the time to help get a new church started in northern Durham, North Carolina. After working with them for eight months, they officially launched "the Homestead Heights Baptist Mission" on March 4, 1962.

The sermon Sam preached to launch the church was from William Carey's famous missionary text, Isaiah 54:2 – 3:

> Enlarge the place of your tent, stretch your tent curtains wide, do not hold back; lengthen your cords, strengthen your stakes. For you will spread out to the right and to the left; your descendants will dispossess nations and settle in their desolate cities.

Carey had used that text more than 300 years ago to remind churches in England that with the blessing of the gospel came the responsibility to take it to others. Sam told that new congregation the same thing, and then he and Rachel left that very afternoon for Vietnam.

I met Sam for the first time in 2009. He told me, "William Carey's dream for the English-speaking world has always been my dream for this church. And they started well, but after a few years the church seemed to have lost its way, getting mired in the maintenance of the status quo. Yet I knew God had given this church a special commission to reach the nations."

In 2012, Sam joined us for our ten-year anniversary celebrating the 2002 "re-launching" of Homestead Heights Baptist Church as the Summit Church. Most people in our church had never heard of its founder, Sam James. He stood on our stage with tears in his eyes, and with a tremor in his voice, he said, "Honestly, I thought the vision God had given me of starting a church that sent missionaries to the nations had failed. But seeing you here today, and hearing about how God is now using you among the nations, is enough to make an old man's dream come true."

That weekend our church realized a profound truth: God founded our community with sending in mind.

Even if you don't have a story like that, God had that in mind when he saved you, too. He blessed you to be a blessing. When he began his work in you, he had in mind your family, your friends, your community, and even other nations, too. He has no interest in making you a gospel reservoir. He wants to make you a gospel river.

Maybe your church has an even cooler story than ours. Maybe it doesn't. Either way, every church is founded for the same purpose: to finish the Great Commission. Jesus birthed the church on a promise from the Father: "Ask me, and I will make the nations your inheritance" (Ps. 2:8). If a church is not pursuing the Great Commission, it really has no point in existing.

The apostles planted their first churches in the soil of those promises, and every church since then has inherited them.

Do You *Really* Want the Presence of God?

Perhaps the most common petition uttered in churches goes something like this: "Lord, just let your presence be with us today." Every church wants the presence of God. But have you ever noticed how so many of Jesus' promises about his abiding presence, however, are connected to our involvement in the global spread of the gospel?

"Therefore go and make disciples of all nations, . . . and surely I am with you always." (Matt. 28:19–20)

"Whoever serves me must follow me; and where I am, my servant also will be." (John 12:26)

Let us, then, go to him outside the camp, bearing the disgrace he bore. (Heb. 13:13)

In other words, if we want to "be with" Jesus, we must go where he is going. When we ask for the Lord's presence, it is as if he issues an invitation in return: "Do you want to be with me? Come to where I am. Leave your comfortable camp and follow me into the nations."

Sending is already in the DNA of any Jesus-following church. *How* and *where* you are sent will be revealed by God's Spirit, but *that* you are sent has been declared once and for all in God's Word.

The closer you walk with Jesus and the more you understand what he did to save you, the more natural sending will become. Sending, like all spiritual fruits, grows out of a healthy gospel culture.

So how do you develop that culture — whether in your church, your ministry, or even in your own heart? That's where we turn next.

Part 2

The Ten Sending Plumb Lines

I am terrible at woodworking. I have never attempted to build a tree house for my kids because … well, to be honest, my wife won't let me. She loves our kids too much. She knows that the things I build with my hands tend to fall apart, and she would prefer not to have our kids in them when they do.

I think one of the reasons why I'm bad at building things is that I lack patience. Getting angles right, taking careful measurements — these are details I tend to ignore. Getting the details right is essential, however, when you are building a structure that lasts.

To get angles right, builders use something they call a "plumb line" — usually just a weight suspended from a string that shows the straight line of gravity's pull. Plumb lines help builders line up corners and make sure wall measurements are even. You want the walls, the floors, the ceiling all to be *plumb*. Only then will the structure stand the test of time.

At the Summit Church we have developed a number of "plumb lines" that serve as directional markers for building our ministries.[1] Think of them as "North Stars" that point ministries in the same destination, keeping them aligned in converging trajectories.

In the chapters that follow I want to share ten of those plumb lines. Each is a short, memorable statement we repeat often around our church. And when I say, "often," I mean *ad nauseum*, so much so that several staff members have told me that their spouses have complained about them muttering them in their sleep. You think I'm joking. I would challenge you to go to one of our staff members' homes at 4 a.m., shake them violently out of their sleep, and see if they don't wake up muttering one of these statements.

These plumb lines aren't familiar only to our staff members. People who have been around our church for any length of time know them, too. I tell our staff that when I am sick of saying one of them, it usually means that they (the staff) have probably *just* heard it. And when they, the staff, are sick of hearing it, our congregation has probably just heard it for the first time.

These statements shape our ministries, keeping them plumb with the Great Commission.

CHAPTER 3

Swimming in the Gospel

PLUMB LINE:

"The Gospel Is Not Just the Diving Board, It Is the Pool."

When my oldest daughter was a toddler, she loved helium balloons. So for her third birthday party I blew up about fifty balloons — with my breath. It was not an easy feat. Do you think she appreciated it? She walked into the party, picked one up, and said, "Daddy, what's wrong with your balloons? They don't float like the ones at the fair." I tried to explain to her that my balloons were superior to helium ones, because we could play games like "see who can keep the balloon off the floor the longest." She wasn't buying it. She thought my balloons were lame. She wanted balloons that floated.

If a balloon is filled with your breath, the only way to keep it afloat is by smacking it upward every few seconds. The moment you stop, however, it will sag back down to the ground. For many people, this is similar to how their pastor keeps them engaged in the mission. Each week he yells something at them like, "Be generous!" So that week they put their lunch money in the offering. The next week: "Witness to your friends!" And they spend the week awkwardly trying to find a way to work the four spiritual laws into a conversation. "Volunteer at the church!" And so they sign up for the nursery. Each time he smacks them, they hover for a few seconds in the air of obedience, only to sag back down into the lethargy of convenience. Next week they keep their money, and their service at the nursery lasts only until the first blowout diaper.

Fill a balloon with helium, however, and it soars on its own. No smacking required.

Fill a heart with passion for the lost, and it develops the skill of sending. No shouting required. What keeps us from proficiency in sending, you see, is not a lack of competency, but a lack of conviction; not a scarcity of skill, but a paucity of passion.

Don't get me wrong: we need to rethink our strategies and structures. (That's in large part why I wrote this book!) But as business yoda Peter Drucker famously said, "Culture eats strategy for breakfast." What your organization *does* best grows out of what it *loves* most. To send effectively, we must love the glory of God and the lost more than we love anything else. Then sending comes naturally.

A culture that values sending will naturally give rise to structures necessary to facilitate that sending. The French poet Antoine de Saint-Exupéry explained,

> If you want to convince men to build ships, don't pass out shipbuilding manuals. Don't organize them into labor groups and hand out wood. Teach them to yearn for the vast and endless sea.[1]

When a man yearns for the sea, his lack of know-how will not keep him land-bound for long. He'll figure out the skills necessary to sail. Our problem is *not* that we haven't found the right program that enables us to reach the world. Our problem is that we don't *yearn* to see God's glory spread over the earth enough to build whatever ships are required to reach people for Christ and see his glory awakened in their hearts.

We can't change heart problems through external programs either. If we try, we will end up imposing superficial structures that not only fail to deliver results, but lead to resistance and resentment among our people. Most people won't sacrifice for the mission because they don't feel, deep within their souls, that the mission is really worth sacrificing for.

The apostle Paul said he worked harder than any other Christian leader. Why? Because every day he felt anguish over the fate of his lost Jewish brothers. He said, "I could wish that I myself were cursed and cut off from Christ" if it would mean the salvation of his fellow Jews (Rom. 9:3). That passion for souls drove him to effectiveness. He figured out how to open doors that were closed, how to train others to carry on his work, and how to pen letters from prison that would still bless and edify us two thousand years later. His "will to save" found a way to thrive in mission.

Before we attempt to emulate Paul's technique, we must embody his spirit.

So how can we develop that kind of spirit, both in ourselves and in those whom we lead?

Paul explains the genius of our own passion: "We have concluded this: that one has died for all...; and those who live [should] no longer live for themselves but for him who for their sake died and was raised" (2 Cor 5:14–15 ESV). Motivation for mission grows out of deep, personal experience with the gospel. When we are amazed at the grace God showed in saving us, going to great lengths to save others seems an insignificant thing. We yearn to see the glory of our saving God spread throughout the earth and others find in Christ what we have found.

The cross of Christ provided Paul with the *motive* for sacrifice (love of Christ), a *measure* for his sacrifice (Christ's death on the cross), and a *mission* in his sacrifice (seeing people reconciled to God; see 2 Cor. 5:14–21). Paul wanted to see others reconciled to God as he had been reconciled.

Paul sacrificed so much for the mission people thought he was a madman (2 Cor. 5:13). *When is the last time your sacrifices for the mission made someone question your sanity?* When the gospel has really gripped your soul, it produces such levels of sacrifice that people simply *have to* ask you why you live as you do. You seem to them like a freak who has lost his mind (2 Peter 3:15).

This intensity to do comes only from a deep awareness of what God has done for you. As a friend of mine says, "The fire to do comes from being soaked in the fuel of what has been done."[2] The gospel is the helium that fills the heart with passion and propels us to soar in mission.

Everything in the Christian life grows out of the gospel. Thus, the deeper you and your people go in the gospel, the higher you will soar in the mission.

The Gospel Is Not Just the Diving Board

Around our church we say it this way: "The gospel is not just the diving board; it is the pool." The gospel is not just the beginning point of Christianity; not just a prayer we pray that commences our journey with God. The gospel is the whole experience.

Most Christian people think of the gospel as the "A-B-Cs" of Christianity — an entry rite you go through and from which you move on to "meatier" things (eschatology, Greek word studies, Old Testament history, tithing, etc.). That's how I learned it, literally. A-B-Cs: You "Admit" your need of Christ's gift of forgiveness, "Believe" in his willingness to give it to you, and then "Call" on him to do it. After that, you get into the D–Z of Christianity, which came from reading books, going on mission trips, and listening to sermons about the rapture. But as Tim Keller says, the gospel is not just the A-B-Cs of Christianity; it is the A through Z. Every virtue of the Christian life grows out of a deeper experience in the gospel.[3] Spiritual growth happens not by going beyond the gospel, but by going deeper into it.

Paul told the Corinthians that the more they beheld God's glory in his gift in Christ, the more "glorious" they would themselves become (2 Cor. 3:18; 4:4). He told the Romans that they would accomplish God's will as they "renewed their minds" in God's extravagant mercies toward them (Rom. 12:1–2).

We don't become better disciples by mastering "10 steps to becoming more like Jesus." We become passionate followers of God when our hearts are gripped with awe and wonder at the 10 billion steps he took toward us when he came to rescue us in Christ.[4]

From Selfishness to Generosity

So when Paul aims to cultivate generosity of spirit in us, he points us toward the generosity of Christ *for us.* For many years, my favorite tool for compelling generosity was *guilt.*

> "How can you live in such abundance when so many languish in squalor? Do you realize how many orphans you could feed for the price of that Frappuccino? Are you ready to face Jesus, having lived on so much when so many have so little?"

And certainly we *ought* to feel guilty if we turn a deaf ear to the poor. (See Amos 5:21, 24 or Isaiah 58:6–7 as an example!)

But this kind of motivation never lasts. Guilt produces a dramatic, knee-jerk reaction, but the human spirit has mechanisms for getting beyond guilt. We assuage it by comparing ourselves positively with others. We rationalize our indulgences. We numb ourselves to others' pain. "Smacking" us with guilt never produces sustained generosity.

Other pastors turn to *greed* as their weapon of choice for generating generosity. I once heard a TV preacher say:

> Do you want God to bless you? Call the number on your screen right now and give to this ministry. God blesses those who pour themselves out for others. Are you tired of driving that old beat-up car and want God to bless you with a new one? Give a minimum $1,000 gift to this ministry. Are you in credit card debt and want God to take care of it? Fill up any space left on your credit card with a gift to this ministry, and watch God get rid of this debt.

Oh, I wish I were making that up.

It is certainly true that God blesses and enriches those who give. (See, for example Proverbs 3:9–10; 2 Corinthians 9:6–15).[5] But when Paul wanted to motivate generosity among the Corinthians, he didn't *start* with promises of how God would bless them in return. Instead of guilt or greed, Paul turned to *grace* to compel generosity:

> For you know the grace of the Lord Jesus Christ, that though he was rich, yet for your sake he became poor, so that you through his poverty might become rich. (2 Cor. 8:9)

It is neither guilt over what you are not doing nor excitement over how God might bless you that produces a truly generous heart. It is deep gratitude for what Christ has already done for you at the cross. Remembering the grace of the Lord Jesus Christ does more to compel generosity than a hundred sermons that pummel you with guilt or inspire you with promises.

One of my favorite stories illustrating this is Jesus' story about the man forgiven 10,000 talents.[6] In those days, 10,000 talents was *a lot* of money. In case you don't have a "talent converter" app handy, a talent was about twenty years' wages.[7] And since 10,000 was the highest number they counted to in Greek, saying "10,000" was like saying "infinity." In other words, this man owed an infinite amount of money to his lender, an amount so steep he would literally have to work in eternity to pay it off.

The day came when the debt was due, and the man was called in to pay. If he couldn't pay, he would be sent to "debtor's prison," where he would labor, along with his family, until the entire debt was paid off.

The debt-ridden man, penniless and hopeless, threw himself on the ground before his lender and began to plead for mercy: "More time!" he cried out. "Just a little more time to pay off the debt. Please don't take my kids to prison!" More time? It was an eternal debt. I imagine everyone watching this pathetic scene began to feel uncomfortable. Loan officers don't give out "more time" for large debts. (They are not called "loan bunnies" or "loan puppies," after all; they are called "loan sharks." If you don't pay, someone named Bruno shows up at your house to break your kneecaps.)

Yet, Jesus' story takes an unexpected turn. The lender feels an emotion toward the groveling man that Jesus calls *splagma*, a Greek word meaning "gut-level compassion." Compassion that springs from the depths of one's soul. A tear filled the man's eye. His bottom lip began to quiver. The lender said to the man, "Your request for more time is denied ... because I absolve your debt entirely. You are free to go."

No one in the room could believe what has just happened, least of all the forgiven man. He begins to stand, getting up off his knees, only to fall on them again to thank his lender for giving him back his life. Walking out of the courtroom, he is hit with the surreal realization that a whole new life has just opened up for him and his family. For the first time in as long as he can remember, he is *free*.

But then, as he walks out of the courthouse, he sees a friend who owes him $1.50 walking down the street. He shouts out, "You owe me $1.50!" His friend responds: "I'm sorry, bro. I've had a bad week. I don't have any cash. I get paid next week. I'll pay you then." "No!" the man shrieks, grabbing him by the neck. "If you can't pay now, I'm throwing you in prison."

How do you think the crowd listening to Jesus tell this story would have reacted to this turn of events? I suspect they might have rolled their eyes and said, "Come on, now! *Nobody* forgiven of millions of dollars would throw someone else in prison over $1.50." At which point Jesus probably said, "Exactly! No one forgiven of that much could be unforgiving and ungracious toward others." Which means, Jesus continued, that if you are not a generous person toward others, you must not ever have experienced God's forgiveness toward you. You must not realize, at a heart level, the eternity of debt you have been forgiven.

It is impossible to truly believe the gospel and not become like the gospel. Experiencing grace transforms us into people willing to make great sacrifices to bless others.

If we want to grow in our generosity of spirit, we need to feel more deeply the great sacrifice Jesus has made for us. The gospel is the root; eagerness to sacrifice is the fruit.

Believe the Gospel, Become Like the Gospel

Recently we commissioned twenty-two individuals to join one of our "Dwell" teams, where members relocate from one neighborhood in our city to another to live out the gospel there. We had never been very effective reaching these parts of the city through our yearly forays of "Vacation Bible Schools" or our Easter promotional mailouts. To really win people in those neighborhoods, we had to dwell with them, living out the gospel day-in and day-out in front of them.

So far, we have had more than a hundred people join one of our Dwell initiatives, including young professionals, families with kids, and retired couples. They have moved into refugee neighborhoods, apartment complexes filled with international students, and lower-rent districts. Sometimes they continue to come to our church, sometimes they help get a new church started there, and a couple of times we have encouraged the team to transfer their membership to a church better suited to reaching the people in that community.

The results have been amazing. We have seen scores of people baptized who would have otherwise never even stepped foot in our church.

Recently one man, explaining his family's decision to join a Dwell team, said to our church,

> Jesus left everything for the sake of the mission ... shouldn't we, also? If we have to leave jobs, family, friends, familiarity, our first culture, even the Summit Church — our home church that we love — to reach them, isn't that still far less than he left for us?

THE DISAPPEARANCE OF CLARA

A few years ago, our church received news that "Clara," a single girl in her twenties who had joined up with one of our church planting teams in Asia, had been kidnapped by Islamic fundamentalists. No trail, no ransom notes. She just disappeared. To this day, she has never been found. Every indication is that she was executed.

Our team leader on location in the country tells the story:

⋮⋮⋮

Clara was taken early one morning on her way to work. For several days we heard nothing, and then we got word through a local source that she was being held captive in the mountains. I and a few others from the team ended up negotiating with the hostage takers for five months. During that time, we received news that she was being moved around to keep her hidden. The US military tried several rescue attempts. Twice they got very close. One of those times, we found out later, she had been moved to a neighboring house as the troops arrived. Another time she was hidden in the basement of the house, and the rescue team just missed her. You can only imagine the frustration Clara must have felt to hear her rescuers just feet away — and then realize that the attempt had failed.

I wish I could share with you that this story ends happily. But this story has no real ending. We do not know exactly what happened to Clara. She kept being moved from village to village, handed off from one group of rogue men to another. The last we heard, she was handed over to a nomadic group of arms smugglers that wandered through the "Desert of Death" in southeastern Afghanistan. And then she disappeared. They had threatened to kill her because they had found Christian literature on her computer, but we have no proof, no body. She has not been heard from in over seven years. She simply disappeared.

Is she an extraordinary hero of faith? Well, in a sense she was. When news of Clara's kidnapping got out, local women from this fundamentalist Islamic community were outraged. For the first and only time in the history of that oppressed place, 300 women marched to the governor's mansion to demand that he do something to free her. These women had benefited from her kindness. They had seen Christ in her.

But, honestly, it's hard for me to think of her in the "hero" category. If I sit and remember her as she was, she was a regular young woman from the United States. A smiling friend. A person who struggled along with the rest of us when the weather was hot, and who loved to go on vacation. A regular American girl who decided to step out in faith and obey a calling from the Lord to go.

The only reason she was here in Central Asia is because of the gospel. It was her understanding of what Christ had done for her on the cross, and how he "made himself nothing, taking the form of a servant," that led her to leave her life in the suburban American Southeast to move to one of the most forsaken places on earth, a place where dust storms were a daily occurrence, where windows had to have blast film because of the risk of explosions at any time, a place where there was no electricity to run a fan in the 100-degree heat in the summer, where she would have only sporadic Internet access to write emails or get news from home, a place where an armed Islamic group that is hostile to the gospel operates with impunity. She did this because she understood that Christ had come to earth to face even greater dangers, even more separation from his Father, even more discomfort for our sake.

Just one week before she was kidnapped she had shared with a group of women on our team a verse that the Lord had impressed on her: "For it has been granted to you that for the sake of Christ you should not only believe in him but also suffer for his sake" (Phil. 1:29 ESV).

Where, people ask, did she get the motivation to serve in a place where she knew this might happen? Her answer was simple: "Where would I be had Jesus not come for me? The same place that millions of people in this country are without me. They can't call on Jesus' name if they haven't heard of him, and they can't hear about him unless we live here to tell them about him."

︙

Believing the gospel leads to becoming like the gospel. Those who go the farthest and give the most are those who are most aware of how far Jesus went and how much he gave up to reach them.

Missional heroes like Clara, you see, are not superheroes with extraordinary skills. They are normal people who take seriously the good news of the gospel and think soberly about its implications.

Do you want to become someone joyfully willing to go to great lengths to reach others? Do you want to lead your people to become enthusiastic servants of the mission? Study the gospel — not like a seminarian studies doctrine to prepare for an exam, but the way you would study a sunset that has left you speechless, or the way a soldier longing for his fiancée studies her picture. Amazement at the grace of Jesus and excitement for his return will produce a passion to go to the ends of the earth that can never be extinguished.

Do you want to develop a sending culture at your church? Teach your people to delight in the glorious riches of what Christ has done on their behalf. Marvel in it every week. Ask God to open the eyes of their hearts to see how high, how wide, how deep, and how long the love of God is for them. Ask God to let them *feel* that love. Let it simmer in them until it sets their hearts on fire. And then, I promise you, they will figure out a way to reach their world. They will soar in mission — without any need for you to smack them into action.

Let me say it as plainly as I can: *Apart from genuine, gospel-rooted heart change, sending will never take root in our churches.* With it, we won't be able to stop it. Without heart change, we may succeed in working up a little excitement for a season, but those balloons will sag to the ground when they encounter the slightest bit of difficulty. The sacrifices will just not seem worth it.

The gospel alone produces the passion that sustains the mission. Programs and institutions can be useful servants of passion, but never its sustenance. The gospel is its sustenance.

So abide in the gospel, and teach your people to abide in it as well. Sending fruit will grow naturally from deep gospel roots.

As Jesus said, "If you remain in me and I in you, you will bear much fruit" (John 15:5).

CHAPTER 4

The Myth of Calling

PLUMB LINE:

"Everyone Is Called."

James, a successful businessman, a wonderful father, and prominent lay-leader in his church, wondered why God hadn't called him into ministry. God had radically saved him during his mid-twenties, and by that point he already had a well-established career in industrial engineering. But James loved Jesus and genuinely wanted others to know him. He knew nothing was more important than the spread of the gospel. He loved to teach the Bible and had led several of his work colleagues to Christ. He was good at his job, but he wondered why God hadn't called him to play on the "varsity squad" of full-time ministers.

There is a widespread myth in the church that "calling into ministry" is a secondary experience that happens to only a few, privileged Christians. We believe that God takes the spiritual elite and entrusts them with the ministry, and for everyone else, their duty is to show up faithfully at the events planned by the ministers and foot the bills.

Few lies cripple the mission more than that one.

According to the book of Acts, men like James are not the B-squad in God's strategy; they are God's plan-A for reaching the world.

One of the achievements of the Protestant Reformation was the removal of the wall of distinction between "clergy" (vocational ministers) and "laity" (regular Christians). Martin Luther explained that through faith in Christ we are all on equal footing: we are all priests; we are all prophets; we are all ambassadors for Christ (1 Peter 2:9–11; Eph. 4:11–13).

In many Protestant denominations, the wall never really came down, and in those that did, leaders have been gradually re-erecting it over the years. Not doctrinally, but functionally. We say that all believers are priests, but we look to vocational, seminary-trained Christian workers to shoulder the work of ministry. Jesus entrusted the ministry to the entire church, however. To every disciple he says: "Follow me, and I will make you fishers of men" (Matt. 4:19 ESV). The saints, Paul says, are responsible for ministry — pastors and full-time workers are merely equippers (Eph. 4:13).

Each believer is called to leverage his or her life for the spread of the gospel. As we said earlier, the question is no longer *whether* we are called, only *where* and *how*.

Pour Out Your Life for Jesus' Kingdom

Jesus taught this once at a party he attended thrown by a wealthy businessman in the community. The host had stocked the party with the best foods and wines and a guest list that included all the "who's who" of Jerusalem. (Jesus wasn't himself rich, but when you can walk on water and raise the dead, the bouncer typically lets you through.)

As the party got started, Jesus was called on to make some remarks. Never the crowd-pleaser, he said,

> "When you give a dinner or a banquet, do not invite your friends or your brothers or your relatives or rich neighbors, lest they also invite you in return and you be repaid. But when you give a feast, invite the poor, the crippled, the lame, the blind, and you will be blessed, because they cannot repay you. For you will be repaid at the resurrection of the just." (Luke 14:12–14 ESV)

Talk about an awkward moment! Jesus looked around and says to those gathered, "When you have a party, don't invite *these* people. Everybody knows you're just inviting them so that they'll invite you back to their parties."

What Jesus counseled here was not just a little awkward; it would have been economic suicide. Parties like these were as much business functions as they were social engagements. Rich people would invite rich friends to their parties, with the hope that these new friends would, in turn, return the favor, allowing each to expand their networks. The rule was simple: be generous to those who could be generous to you in return. Think of relationships as investments and steward them wisely.

Jesus told them instead to invite people who would never be able to return the favor. People who have no perks to offer or no "friends" whom you want to meet. Then, and only then, Jesus said, will you be "repaid in the resurrection."

I don't believe Jesus' primary purpose is regulating whom we invite to our birthday parties. He's asking us a bigger question about the entire trajectory of our lives (and ministries): If you thought of your life as a party, for whom would you be throwing it? Are you investing your talents and resources primarily into those who can "pay you back"? Or are your eyes on a reward not found in this world?

Perhaps this story provides the clearest illustration of what it means to follow Jesus. It proves that missional living applies to *everyone*. Jesus' audience is not a group of mission-field-bound seminarians, but *businesspeople*. Every follower of Jesus, in whatever career field, is called to throw the party of his life for the spread of the gospel.

If you are in business, ask yourself: *Why* did God make me good at this business? Surely it was not just to fill up your earthly kingdom with creature comforts or allow you to save enough so that you could spend the last third of your life on vacation. He gave you these talents as a means of blessing others and as a platform to spread the gospel.

We have a man in our church who, because of his entrepreneurial skill, made enough money in his thirties to retire for life. Yet now, in his fifties, he is busier than ever. He is neck-deep in a ministry that spreads the gospel among the deaf. He provides consulting for a Christian school and mentors young entrepreneurs seeking to use their business skills in the kingdom. And he is crazy generous. He lives simply and gives extravagantly. He may not be called to (so-called) full-time, paid, vocational ministry as I am, but his calling is every bit as missional as mine. I am a professional Christian, which means I get paid to be good. He is good for nothing. Wait, that didn't come out right! But you get the point: *He is throwing the party of his life for Jesus' kingdom*, not his own.

If you are a stay-at-home mom, you need to ask yourself: What role do I play in the advance of the mission? My wife views the rearing of our four children as serious, spiritual, missionary work. Ask her what she does, and she'll say she is a missionary to the unreached people group known as "the Greear children." Or, to borrow the words of another Christian mother:

> I am socializing four Homosapiens into the dominant values of the Judeo-Christian tradition in order that they might be instruments for the transformation of the social order into the kind of eschatological utopia that God willed from the beginning of creation.... And ... what do you do?[1]

My wife explains that Psalm 127 tells her that children are like "arrows" that God places into the hands of a warrior, and her role is to draw back those arrows on the bowstring of faith and launch them deep into the heart of the Enemy. Right now, that's her primary role in the mission. And, of course, being in this stage provides her some unique opportunities to share Christ with and disciple other mothers in the same stage.

The same principle applies if you are a public school teacher, a police officer, or a federal court judge. God didn't make you all to be vocational pastors, but he put you all on the front lines of the mission.

And when I say that, I don't mean that you simply exploit your platform to force awkward evangelism encounters or give your business a cheesy Christian name. God has a purpose for the vocation itself; your witness grows out of the excellence with which you carry out your vocation. Your vocation is God's means of blessing the world, and doing it excellently gives you a chance to tell others about the God who cares for them body and soul.

Let's explore that just a touch deeper, because it is essential to understanding how every believer is to "live sent."

God Has Given to Each a Specific *Vocation*

Our "secular" vocations, Martin Luther said, are like "masks" God wears in caring for the world. "When we pray the Lord's Prayer," he said, "we ask God to 'give us this day our daily bread.' And how does God answer that prayer?" He does so, Luther said, "by means of the farmer who planted and harvested the grain, the baker who made the flour into bread, the person who prepared our meal. All these are in play when God answers our prayer for daily bread."[2]

Our English word "vocation" comes from the Latin word *voca*, meaning "to call." The Reformers saw our vocations, whether "secular" or "sacred," as callings by God to assist in his care for the earth.

God created the world, you see, in an imperfect state, with things left to do to "perfect" it. Repeatedly in Genesis 1 he declared his creation to be *good*. "Good" is good, but good is not *perfect*. Perfect means "cannot be improved upon." Good means that the raw material is good even if there are improvements that can be done. Whenever I am with my wife out in public, I think she looks perfect. Her dress, her makeup, her hair — she literally cannot be improved upon. When she first wakes up in the morning, however, she's good. (Big smile. And my wife did not approve of this paragraph.) God put man into a good creation, not a perfect one, with the responsibility to cultivate the creation into all that it could be.

He made Adam a gardener, not a park ranger. A park ranger preserves the natural habitat; a gardener, however, *develops* it. As a gardener, Adam took the raw material of soil and seed and cultivated it to produce humanity-blessing beauty and food.

Furthermore, the opening narratives of Genesis establish that God made man "in his image." What does that mean, exactly? Well, twelve times in Genesis 1 – 2 God *creates*. Thus, if you defined "the image of God" using only Genesis 1, you would have to conclude that being in God's image means being a creator. We "co-create" the world with God. We develop the raw materials of the earth for his glory and the benefit of others.

Martin Luther, reflecting on the words in Psalm 147:13 – 14,

> He [God] strengthens the bars of your gates and blesses your people within you. He grants peace to your borders and satisfies you with the finest of wheat.

asked, "How exactly does God do those things?"

— How does he strengthen the bars of the city? By city planners and architects and politicians who pass good laws to protect the city.

— How does he bless our children within our midst? Through the work of teachers and pediatricians.

— How does he make peace in our borders? By means of good lawyers and police officers.

— How does he fill us with the finest of wheat? By farmers and factory workers and restaurant owners.

Luther believed that every believer must discover how he or she is gifted by God to develop his world, because this is in large part how followers of Christ fulfill their callings. Thus, if God has given you "secular" skills — in business, banking, painting, landscaping, medicine, art, law, or the like — understand that there is nothing second-class about them. God uses your vocation to care for his world through you. As you work, you are being used by God in his original mission.

I believe this is one of the least understood concepts in the evangelical church. The first time I preached on this subject, I got more response than I did for any other message I preached that year — including the ones on sex!

When you say to the average Christian, "Serve Jesus in business," most assume you mean opening a hair salon called "A Cut Above," a coffee shop called "He Brews" or "St. Arbucks," or a restaurant called "The Garden of Eat-In'." Or perhaps forcing awkward moments into sales calls: "Now that I have gotten you set up with life insurance, have you thought about life-after-death insurance?"

Perhaps you have heard about the 2004 incident of an American Airlines pilot who, in his pre-flight announcements, asked Christians on board the plane to raise their hands. He then suggested that during the flight the other passengers talk to those people with their hands raised about their faith, and he said he would also be happy to talk to anyone who had questions.[3] Understandably, it freaked a lot of people out: the pilot of your airplane talking to you about whether you are ready to meet Jesus? While they might admire the brother's zeal, many Christian businesspeople think, "I just don't think I could do that and keep my job." And they are probably right.

Serving Jesus at work is about doing your work for the glory of God and the benefit of his creation and leveraging appropriate opportunities to make disciples through those relationships as you go through life.

The Calling to Make Disciples

Every Christian, you see, has at least two major callings: (A) The call to use your vocation for the glory of God and the blessing of others; and (B) the call to make disciples. Thus, every believer should ask these two questions about their lives:

1. *What skill has God given me by which I can bless the world?* What did God make you "good" at? What is your passion? Or, to say it in business terms, "What is your money maker?" Do you recognize this skill was given to you by God as a means through which he can bless his world? He gave you that teaching ability so you can help children learn the beauties of his world; or that artistic ability to bring out beauty for others to enjoy; or that passion to work with your hands so that you can build structures for others to dwell in.

2. *Where and how can I do it most strategically to advance the mission of God?* Rather than asking only, "How can I use this to make the most money?" we should also ask, "Where might my skill be of greatest service to others, particularly as a bridge over which I can share the gospel?" Ask yourself this: How do you decide where to pursue your career? Is it simply a "what's best for my finances" decision? (There's nothing wrong with that being *a* factor; but should it be the *only*, or even primary, factor?) Why not make where you can be useful in the kingdom of God the primary factor? Jesus tells us to seek *first* his kingdom in all we do, and all the rest will be added to us (Matt. 6:33).

At our church, we simplify these two questions into a single statement:

Whatever you're good at, do it well for the glory of God, and do it somewhere strategic for the mission of God.

This is where you must begin in order to understand how you are to live sent.

Why Christianity Spread So Fast in the First Century

When "normal" Christians embrace this idea of calling, the gospel spreads like a prairie grassfire. Luke, the writer of Acts, goes out of his way in Acts to show us that the gospel travels faster around the world in the mouths of regular Christians than it does through full-time, vocational Christian workers. Luke notes, for example, that the first time the gospel left Jerusalem, it was not in the mouths of the apostles. Regular people "went everywhere preaching the word," while the apostles stayed in Jerusalem (Acts 8:1–4). The first time the gospel actually went out into the world, *not a single apostle* was involved.

The first "international mission trip" was taken later in that same chapter by Philip, another layman. The Spirit carried him to a desert road where he met an Ethiopian government official, and Philip led him to Christ. The church at Antioch, which served as the hub for missionary activity for the last half of the book of Acts, was not planted by an apostle, but simply "some brothers," whose names Luke did not even bother to record — presumably because no one would have known whom he was talking about. Apollos, a layman, first carried the gospel into Ephesus, and unnamed brothers first established the church at Rome. These Christians didn't travel to Rome on a formal mission trip, but were carried there through the normal relocations that come with business and life. As they went, they made disciples in every place (Acts 8:5–8; 18:24–19:1; 28:15).

Steven Neill notes in his classic *History of Christian Missions* that

> ... nothing is more notable than the anonymity of these early missionaries.... Luke does not turn aside to mention the name of a single one of those pioneers who laid the foundation. Few, if any, of the great Churches were really founded by apostles. Peter and Paul may have organized the Church in Rome. They certainly did not found it.[4]

This pattern continued down through Christian history. Today, the greatest opportunities for mission advancement still lie with Christians in the business community. Consider this: If you overlay a map of world poverty with a map of world evangelization, you will find that the areas most in need of business development are also the most unevangelized.

Many of the most unreached places in the world, most closed to Christian missionaries, have arms wide open to any kind of businessmen. Patrick Lai observes of the Muslim world,

> Twenty percent of the world's population lives in Muslim countries, yet only 4% of world trade comes from these countries.... We are living at a point in world history of unprecedented opportunities for the expansion of the Christian faith. No country is closed to business. In no country is it illegal to love people. There are huge doors of opportunity wide open before us, if we are willing to equip ourselves adequately and walk through them. Countries considered "closed" to missionaries welcome Christians who come as [businesspeople].[5]

Missiologists frequently refer to a "10/40 window" in which the most unevangelized, unengaged peoples live (lying between the 10 and 40 degree latitude lines). But here's the thing: Enough Christians *already* live in the 10/40 window to sextuple the mission force there — that is, if those Christians were effective disciple-makers. If you add up all the Christian missionaries from all denominations and missions agencies in the 10/40 window, there are about 40,000 "missionaries." The number of Americans working in secular employment in the 10/40 window is 2 million.[6] Assuming that the faith of Americans working overseas resembles that of Americans living at home, about 35 percent of them identify as born-again with some semblance of engagement in the faith, such as church attendance. If even one-third of that number were effective disciple-makers, that would increase the number of Christian evangelists on the front lines from 40,000 to 240,000, all without costing mission agencies another dime. For business leaders, the 10/40 window is not a *window* at all; it's a wide-open door.

The next wave of missions will be carried forward, I believe, on the wings of business. I saw this happen with my dad: He worked for thirty-five years for a large, American-based textile corporation. In his last few years before retirement, he volunteered to oversee the construction of some new plants in East Asia. There he was able to rub shoulders with businessmen I would *never* have been able to get close to had I gone as a missionary and set up an "English corner" there. My dad led one of the businessmen to Christ. His "mission trip" did not cost the church a dime. In fact, he got paid to do it.

About six times a year my friend Nick goes to Japan, where he engages with top business officials in one of the least evangelized countries in the world. Another man, Jerome, chose to use his prestigious law degree to get a job working in the Middle East, where he engages with legal officials in a country completely closed to foreign missionary work. Erica works as a guard at a female prison facility, where she treats the prisoners with dignity and respect and prays for them to find true freedom in Christ.

We need to help "ordinary believers" in our churches recover the understanding that they are called to the mission and shaped by God for a specific role in that mission. I'll say it again: The question is no longer *if* we are called to leverage our lives for the Great Commission, only where and how. Each disciple of Jesus must do an assessment of his or her life and ask how it can most profitably be used for the Great Commission. Again:

> Whatever you do, do it *well* for the glory of God, and do it *somewhere strategic* for the mission of God.

Think about what could happen if people in our churches really began to think this way! What if every believer saw their profession as a divinely appointed platform for the spread of the gospel and executed their work with that in mind? Wouldn't that provide them with an incredible sense of purpose in their vocations and a motivation to pursue them with excellence?

King Solomon promises:

> Do you see someone skilled in their work? They will serve before kings. (Prov. 22:29)

The man or woman who does their work well might gain the opportunity to stand before the lost kings of the earth and testify to the gospel.

That is an exciting thing to live for.

Specific Callings and General Obedience

All believers are called to leverage their skills and lives for the Great Commission. We shouldn't be waiting for voices when we already have verses. "But wait," you say, "are there not times in Scripture where we see someone, like Paul or Barnabas, directed by the Spirit into a specific, full-time ministry capacity?" Certainly! I experienced a very *specific* calling to teach the Bible and lead others onto the mission field. God verbally told Paul to take the gospel to the Gentiles (Acts 9:15), and he specifically directed the Antioch church to set apart Barnabas and Saul "for the work to which I have called them" (Acts 13:2).

But there are just as many (if not more) biblical examples of people in the mission who did not have such a dramatic, specific calling by the Spirit. Timothy joined Paul on his missionary journeys simply because "Paul wanted Timothy to accompany him" (Acts 16:3 ESV). Priscilla and Aquila worked alongside Paul, leveraging their tent-making business to travel with him to Ephesus to be a help to him and continue his work after he left (Acts 18:2–3, 18–26). Scripture records no special vision or warm fuzzy moment preceding these decisions. It just seemed like a profitable thing to do, and they assumed the Spirit of God was in it.

In Acts 8:26 the Spirit revealed specifically to Philip that he should travel to a special spot on a dusty road to share the gospel. But at the beginning of that chapter, the Spirit scattered thousands of believers into other new places to preach the gospel. No Spirit-voice seems to have accompanied that scattering. But we are left to assume that this scattering was the work of the Spirit of God.

So don't wait around for warm-fuzzies to ask where you should get involved in mission. Use wise judgment and the counsel of others to help you determine where your gifts and presence could be most strategically used in the kingdom. And then get to work. God will guide you from there.

We ask our college graduates in a senior-year interview if they will give us a "blank check" about where they pursue their career. "You have to get a job somewhere," we say. "Why not let us point you to a place where God is doing something strategic?" Many of them go with our church planting teams to form the core group of the new launch. Some of those have had an "Abraham/Paul" experience in which God gave them specific instructions, but most simply see a strategic opportunity to pursue their careers in a place that makes good sense for the kingdom.

Multiple factors go into where you pursue your career: how much money you are paid, potential for advancement, proximity of family, etc. So why not make ministry potential the primary factor? Why should earning potential be what we most think about when choosing a location for our careers? I often repeat to our students a statement I saw John Piper make on Twitter: "Lot moved to Sodom not for ministry, but for money (Genesis 13:9–13). It did not turn out well for Lot. How do you choose where to live?"

A Mandate for All; Not a Calling for Some

The Great Commission is not a calling for some; it is a mandate for all. Therefore, to become a disciple of Jesus means evaluating your passions and talents in terms of how they can best be used in God's kingdom. The call we are waiting for has already been issued: "Go and make disciples of all nations" (Matt. 28:19). So, again, when it comes to calling, we don't need a voice; we have a verse. It is now our responsibility, under the direction of the Holy Spirit, to evaluate how we are best suited to fulfill that call. The Spirit might reveal that to us through a special act of guidance, but more often than not he will give to us and our church leaders the wisdom to make that decision.[7]

When the church begins to operate with the assumption that *everyone is called*, our approach to mobilization will shift dramatically. We won't limit our mission engagement to a bulletin board in the lobby with images of people serving in New Guinea that church members should pray for, as important as that is. We will see every member of our church as a potential missionary to be equipped and mobilized. Our goal is not to send *some*, or even our best, but to send *all* into the mission — to our city, across the country, or to the other side of the world. As my friend Bob Roberts often says, "The church doesn't send missionaries, it *is* the missionary."

When we grasp this, we will begin to cast that vision to our children and students from the earliest stages of their discipleship. We will push them to consider, "What role has God given me to play in the expansion of the kingdom?" (Why should their school provide their primary guidance counselors? Shouldn't we be playing the role of "kingdom advisers?")

As we saw in chapter 1, the church is best understood as an aircraft carrier, not a cruise ship dispensing religious luxuries. Every believer is a fighter plane. When church members understand that, they will move from being spectators of the production to owners of the vision and ambassadors of the mission.[8] Pastors will move from gathering audiences to empowering armies. When *that* happens, the gates of hell will not be able to withstand the advance of the church.

CHAPTER 5

Missional or Attractional? Yes.

PLUMB LINE:

"The Week Is As Important As the Weekend."

I was sitting with nearly 200 church leaders listening to a very charismatic, giga-church pastor explain that at least once a week he has to remind one of his staff members, "It's the weekend, stupid." He wanted his staff to understand that the primary factor in determining whether someone attends their church is the quality of the weekend experience. Period. Thus, most of their energy, money, and creativity should be spent crafting that weekend experience. A church can have the most incredible programs running throughout the week — they can excel at caring for members, small groups, counseling, outreach, and youth programs — but if their weekend experience stinks, the church will not grow.

What he said made sense. And I cannot deny that the quality of the weekend experience is often the reason people begin attending a church, at least in certain parts of the United States.

But is building an *audience* the same thing as growing a church? Is "attendance increased" the same things as "mission accomplished"?

Not hardly. Our mission, according to Jesus, is not to gather audiences, but to grow *disciples*.

Pundits criticized President George W. Bush for declaring "Mission Accomplished" from the deck of USS *Abraham Lincoln* on May 1, 2003, after US forces had obliterated Iraq's defenses and captured

Saddam Hussein. Crippling Iraq's defenses through a "shock and awe" campaign, the analysts said, is not the same thing as establishing a stable regime. In their view, President Bush had accomplished only the first — and easier — part of the mission, premature for celebrating a mission accomplished.

Do churches that proclaim "success" when they gather large audiences make the same mistake? Do they confuse a milestone *en route* to the mission with the end *goal* of that mission?

To be clear, I'm not against celebrating large weekend numbers. New Testament writers do that regularly. They often tell us when Jesus or the apostles gathered large crowds and sometimes exactly how many people were in those crowds. Twice Luke celebrates the specific number of baptisms the church performed on a given day. Jesus' "good shepherd" in Luke 15 was so in touch with the number of his flock that he knew immediately when just one lamb had gone missing! And, of course, there's a whole book in the Old Testament called … well … *Numbers*.

God is into numbers, because they represent people. Think about it: We know, to a penny, how much offering was collected the week before. Why would we not know then, to a soul, how many people were at church? Are pennies of more value than souls?

I believe, however, that we should be counting and celebrating the *right* numbers. Weekend attenders aren't the primary number to celebrate. The number of disciples is. Unfortunately, what gets you on our lists of "fastest growing" or "largest churches in America" doesn't necessarily correspond with the rolls in heaven. And if that's the case, the week is every bit as important, if not more so, than the weekend.

The Weekend Is Only the Beginning

What happens during the week establishes the difference between a disciple and an attender. And in our post-Christian age, the weekend is becoming less effective for reaching truly unchurched people. Fewer and fewer lost people are moseying their way into our weekend services. Thus, equipping disciples to reproduce *outside* the church, during the week, is becoming vastly more important than having a great weekend show. As our society becomes more and more "post-Christian," training members to "go" will be far more effective than inviting the community to "come."

We see our weekend gathering of the church like a huddle, where instructions are given for how the players can run the "mission" play throughout the week. The evangelistic "play" will need to be carried out by our members in the community throughout the week. A large part of my responsibility on the weekend is to get them ready to do that.

That being said, we recognize that the weekend gathering still plays an important role in the evangelism process. Paul certainly thought that way about his church services — giving strong admonitions and detailed instructions to the Corinthians about how to make their weekend services intelligible and attractive to unbelievers (1 Cor. 14 — more on this in a moment).

For nearly half a century now, church leaders have debated the question of which approach is more effective: attractional or missional. (Just for clarity, by *attractional* I mean ministries designed so that unbelievers will be drawn into them to hear the gospel; and by *missional* I mean equipping Christians to carry the gospel (and its good works) to unbelievers outside the church.)

Let's start with understanding the historical context of the debate and then take a look at the biblical basis for both. Then we'll discuss how each might be applied.

The History of Missional

The word *missional* originates from a mid-twentieth-century missionary named Lesslie Newbigin. Serving among the Indian people in South Asia, Newbigin was frustrated with his converts, because most of them assumed that it was *his* job to spread the gospel, not theirs. Newbigin was bothered on two accounts: first, he believed Indian believers were developing an unhealthy dependence on foreigners; second, he believed Indian nationals could spread the gospel more effectively than foreigners. He saw in the book of Acts that "regular" Christians were at the forefront of gospel expansion, and he was convinced that empowerment of "ordinary" Indian believers was the key to expansion of the gospel in India, too.

After Newbigin retired and returned to England, he saw that his native English churches worked in the same unhealthy way. Western Christians viewed their paid professional clergy as the ones responsible for mission advancement. Newbigin argued that the key to gospel advance in any society lies in the hands of the laity, for the church, in its very essence, is "missional." Every believer, he said, is an ordained, Spirit-anointed missionary.[1]

Toward the end of the last century, leaders such as Alan Hirsch and Ed Stetzer began to popularize Newbigin's ideas, coining the terms *attractional* and *missional* to distinguish between an evangelism model that seeks to draw people to church events and one that seeks to equip ordinary members to carry the gospel outside the church in the power of the Spirit.[2]

As I hope you can tell, I am thoroughly convinced the missional mindset is the way forward for the church. But in our zeal to pursue this, we should not overlook the numerous ways the Bible prescribes attractional evangelism, too. So let's take a moment to examine its biblical basis.

Attractional: "Come and See"

A great deal of the evangelism we see in the Bible could very easily be called "attractional." God told Israel they were to be like a "city set on a hill," a shining light the Gentiles would *come* toward (Ex. 19:5–6). As Gentile nations saw God's glory radiating from his people, they would be attracted to Jerusalem to worship (Isa. 2:2).

Perhaps the best Old Testament example of this is the Queen of Sheba. During the reign of Solomon, she came to behold the glory of God in Israel's midst because she had heard so much about it. After traveling for many miles, according to 1 Kings 10:5, "she was overwhelmed." She exclaimed,

> "The report I heard in my own country about your achievements and your wisdom is true. But I did not believe these things until I came and saw with my own eyes. Indeed, not even half was told me; in wisdom and wealth you have far exceeded the report I heard. How happy your people must be! How happy your officials, who continually stand before you and hear your wisdom! Praise be to the LORD your God, who has delighted in you and placed you on the throne of Israel. Because of the LORD's eternal love for Israel...." (1 Kings 10:6–9)

We shouldn't assume that she was the only one to whom this ever happened. God had commanded the Jews, after all, to construct an outer court for the Gentiles in their temple, so that Gentiles (like the Queen of Sheba) could come and observe the Israelites in worship, learn about their covenant with God, and *call out to God for themselves*. God had said that the Jewish temple should be known as "a house of prayer for all nations" (Isa. 56:7).

In the New Testament the emphasis shifts to "go and tell," but the concept of "come and see" is still decidedly present.[3] For example, New Testament writers apply to the gathered church the metaphors God had used of Israel's attractive power:

- Jesus told his followers they should be like a "city set on a hill," doing their good works in public, and that others will see and glorify the Father in heaven (Matt. 5:14–16). The church is to conduct itself with such dignity and charity that our presence in any community is like a glorious light on a dark night, drawing those wandering in darkness. As they come close and observe its good works, they will "glorify your Father in heaven."
- Peter, quoting from the book of Exodus, told his churches they are to be a holy nation, a kingdom of priests, and a light in the midst of a dark world, living in such a way that others *come* to them and ask a reason for the hope within them (1 Peter 2:9–11; 3:15).

As in the days of Solomon, the "Queens of Sheba" today should hear about the work God is doing among his people, be drawn into our midst, and fall down to worship God for themselves. In 1 Corinthians 14:25, Paul talks about unbelievers doing this very thing: they come into a church service, "the secrets of their hearts are laid bare," and they "fall down and worship God." Doesn't this sound almost exactly like what happened to the Queen of Sheba?

Lesslie Newbigin himself — chief among missional advocates — said that evangelism in Acts is essentially a group of people gathering to ask the believers, "Can you explain what is going on among you Christians?" and then someone standing to answer that question.[4] However you spin it, that's *attractional*. People see, wonder, attend, and inquire.

At every turn we see Jesus and the apostles *attracting* large crowds because of the way they lived out the gospel in front of the community, the signs they performed, the persuasiveness of their teaching, and how they worshiped God in Spirit and truth when they gathered (Acts 2:42–47). As the believers were teaching, unbelievers exclaimed things like, "Never man spoke as this man spoke" and they marveled at the authority with which both Jesus and his followers taught. In other words, it wasn't only the way believers lived in the community that attracted unbelievers; it was how they conducted their worship services, too. Amazement led to attraction; attraction led to observation; observation led to conversion.

Recently, several small groups in our church got involved with a struggling local school. Over an entire summer they renovated teachers' lounges, stocked the library, and collected supplies. Their project culminated in a morning breakfast for the teachers the day before school started. At the breakfast, one of the teachers stood up and said, "I've always known you Christians said you should love one another, but I've never really known what you meant by that until now."

Several members of that school's faculty have begun attending our church, and over the past few years I have baptized dozens of teachers. One said, "I wanted to know what made you all tick. And I didn't understand the half of what I was missing."

De-Cluttering the Court of the Gentiles

Not only should we live and worship in ways that draw people in, but we also should do everything we can to make our worship and message *intelligible* to them. Think about it: If God commanded Israel to create a "court for the Gentiles" so that Gentiles could easily observe the Israelites in worship, would he not also want us to do whatever we can to help unbelievers understand what is going on in our worship services?

In the Gospels, Jesus appears to get the most angry when he observes Jewish leaders cluttering up of the Court of the Gentiles with conveniences for the saved. Just before his death, he went to the temple and saw that the court had been overrun by peddlers selling sacrifices to be used in temple worship. Not only was Jesus angry over the sheer attempt to profiteer from the ministry; he was also angry that they had consumed the only space Gentiles had to encounter the God of Israel. Angrily, and with the backing of a whip, Jesus exclaimed, "My house was intended to be house of prayer for all nations, but you have turned it into a den of thieves" (Mark 11:17 my paraphrase).

Typically, when I hear pastors preach on Jesus' words there, I hear them focus on the last part only — how angry Jesus was at those who were using the temple to make money. But don't miss the first part of his statement: "My house was designated to be a house of prayer for the nations." Jesus was angry not only at what they were doing, but also at what they were *obscuring*.[5] They had transformed the only open-access point for the Gentiles into a catalogue of comforts and conveniences for the already saved. Having a place to change money and buy and sell sacrifices so close to the altar was very convenient for believers and served their needs well, but it kept outsiders from being able to see what was going on.

I'm sure some of the Jews objected to Jesus' emphasis on the importance of the court: "But Jesus, this temple is not primarily for the Gentiles. The temple exists for already believing Jews to worship." And technically, they were correct. The temple was *primarily* for the "already saved" to offer sacrifices. But God had also commanded them, as a part of their worship, to provide the lost Gentiles access to the beauties of worship, and when they didn't, he became furious. They had transformed a portal for the outsider into a butler for the insider.

Why would we not assume Jesus feels the same way about a church today that makes no accommodations to make the gospel accessible to outsiders — in their preaching, music, language, practice of traditions, children's programs, and even things like parking and signage? (I've been in many churches where, if you hadn't grown up there, you could hardly find your way into the worship center. The obscurity even made me — a seasoned believer — feel uncomfortable! I'm sure unbelievers — already nervous about being in a church — do even more so!) By not thinking of the "observing outsiders" whom God is drawing to himself during our worship, are we not creating the same roadblocks for "Gentiles" as the Jews did in Jesus' day?

So how must Jesus feel when a church refuses even to *consider* what it needs to change to reach the community and the next generation? It seems to me that a lot of churches never even consider change because they care more about their own preferences than they do making the gospel accessible to the outside world. They care more about holding on to their traditions than they do reaching their own grandchildren.

Dare we defend someone's refusal to change with the excuse, "Well, church services are primarily for the saved to worship God, not to reach unbelievers"? Based on Jesus' response to the Jewish moneychangers, I wouldn't suggest it.

One evidence of God's Spirit at work in a church is when seasoned members begin to put their preferences aside to reach the next generation. About a month after I became pastor at the Summit Church, we found a set of handbells in a storage closet. We thought that if we sold them, we could have some money to buy some newer musical equipment — specifically, we wanted to get a couple of electric guitars.

A few weeks later a sweet lady — who had been a member at our church since the 1960s — approached me, telling me she had heard about our plans and asking what we would do with the money. We hadn't told anyone what our plans were, and when she asked me that, my heart stopped. This lady loved worship, but she was more of the "organs, bells, and horns" persuasion than the "drums, guitars, and rhythm loop" one.

I stuttered out, "We plan to buy electric guitars." She said, "My mother, who died a few years ago, donated the money to purchase those handbells [which I had not known]. Why was no one going to check with me about this?"

Silence. Somewhere in the distance a dog barked. I made vows and promises to God.

After a couple of long, awkward seconds, I said to her, "Well, don't you think your mom in heaven would be glad to see us using instruments that would help us reach this next generation — including her grandkids and their friends?"

She thought about that for a second, and then said, "Well, yes ... I suppose my mom would be happy with that." She requested that we not sell the handbells but donate them to another church, which we gladly did. Yet she did not resist seeing them go, and she did not leave our church when we shifted our worship style to a more contemporary one. Today, over 2,000 college students attend our church each weekend. Because of the selflessness of this woman and many others, our church is reaching a whole new generation.

Any gospel-loving believer should long to see the Court of the Gentiles overflowing with seekers, and Scripture promises us that a Spirit-filled ministry will capture the attention of them for miles around! I feel that we can safely say that both the Old and New Testaments heartily commend a type of *attractional* ministry, and we would be foolish to neglect it.

Please understand that when I say that, I am not advocating that laser light shows and loud music become the centerpieces of our worship. *That's* not what attracted people to Jesus and the apostles' ministries in the first century. Paul said that the power that is able to convert sinners comes not from wise and persuasive words (or laser shows and zip line tricks), but from a presentation of Christ and him crucified (1 Cor. 2:2–4). What Christ preached clearly on the cross is the greatest attractional power available to the church.

The world may be entertained by our musical, theatrical, or oratorical skills, but they will never be converted by them. The only power that amazes the soul, the only wonder that silences the skeptic, the only vision that drives out our idols is the glory of the Christ revealed through preaching. When *he* is lifted up, he said, and only then, *will he draw* all men to himself (John 12:32).

Many churches today, lacking confidence in God's promise, substitute the gathering power of entertainment for the transforming power of the cross. As Vance Havner used to say, "The deader your gospel, the flashier your package." Smoke and subwoofers can never do what one glimpse of Christ crucified can do.

As we seek to draw people to our churches, we should be very cautious not to develop a strategy dependent on "wise and persuasive words," funny stories, or great music. There is nothing wrong with these things in themselves, and employing them can be good stewardship. Our trust, however, must remain in the power of Christ crucified and that alone. Worship need not always be spectacular, but it must be supernatural. If not, it is worthless. And if we are not careful, our lust for the sensational can keep us from reliance on the supernatural.

Furthermore, don't mistake audience participation in the entertainment for spiritual transformation. Entertainment can engage a crowd; only the power of the Spirit can transform them. And when the buzz of entertainment wears off, believers transformed by the gospel will still be turning the world upside down.

Having said that, we make no apologies for doing everything we can to attract unbelievers to our services and make the gospel accessible to them. I try very hard to be interesting, writing every sermon with unbelievers in mind, choosing words and examples that make sense to them. I address unbelievers directly multiple times in every sermon. I try to be engaging. Our worship teams choose music styles that engage our culture; they are really talented.

We pay a lot of attention to guest services and try to eliminate anything that might unnecessarily confuse or alienate outsiders, including outdated furniture. We constantly try to walk through our facilities with "fresh eyes," asking what things might confuse those unfamiliar with our church or the faith. We think this is part of becoming "all things to all people so that by all possible means possible I might save some" (1 Cor. 9:22) and one of the ways we can keep our "Court of the Gentiles" clear.

Furthermore, we capitalize on those times of year when unbelievers are more willing to go to church, such as Easter, Christmas Eve, weddings, and funerals, and we preach the gospel in especially simple, culturally compelling terms on those occasions.

I devour books written by pastors and church leaders who understand how unbelievers think, even when I disagree with some of their applications. "Eat the fish and spit out the bones," I often tell our staff.[6] We want to learn anything and everything from anyone that will help us reach unbelievers. We evaluate everything by Scripture, of course — but the Son of Man came to seek and save the lost, and that's what we want to be about, too. If you can help us do that, we're all ears.

Missional: "Go and Tell"

I'm going to spend less time building a case for a missional approach to ministry, primarily because the majority of this book is about that. But let's at least examine a couple of places in the Bible where we see a missional approach expressly advocated.

Even in the Old Testament (where God's strategy is "come and see"), we see numerous examples of God *sending* his people outside its borders to preach salvation among the Gentiles. Several of the Old Testament prophetic books had sections written to Gentiles (and sometimes, as with Obadiah and Nahum, that preaching makes up the whole book!). And most of us are familiar with the story of that bitter prophet, Jonah, who did everything he could to circumvent God's command to *go* and preach mercy to the Gentile nation of Nineveh.

When the children of Israel were sent into exile because of their disobedience, prophets such as Daniel and Jeremiah perceived a redemptive purpose in their exile — that God wanted to use the scattered Israelites to testify to the Gentiles about the grace of God. Thus, the prophet Jeremiah tells his generation of exiles to "seek the peace and prosperity of the city [of Babylon]" and "pray to the LORD for it" (Jer. 29:7). Daniel uses his position in the Babylonian government to testify to Nebuchadnezzar that God, and God alone, can save (Dan. 2:28; 3:14–17). The writer of 2 Kings tells us how a young Israelite slave girl persuaded the mighty Assyrian general Naaman that God alone has power to heal and cleanse (2 Kings 5:1–4).

The apostle Peter takes this idea of believers living in exile and presents it as the *primary* identity of the church today. We live here as exiles, he says, commissioned to "declare the praises of him who called [us] out of darkness into his wonderful light." He urges us, therefore, to "be prepared to give an answer to everyone who asks you to give the reason for the hope that you have" (1 Peter 2:9; 3:15). We are to pray for and bless our cities. In Peter's epistle you see the "go and tell" and "come and see" approaches unite — as we *go into* the world, living out the gospel, unbelievers are *drawn into* our community to ask us a reason for why we live as we do.

And, of course, we have the Great Commission, where Jesus says as plainly as possible that believers are to "go into all the world" and to be his witnesses. We are to do what Jonah initially refused to do — to go and live among hostile people and declare God's salvation to them with gladness.

For Peter, this command to go was not a special assignment for a handful of specialized missionaries, either. Peter explains that all of God's people are ambassadors, prophets anointed with the Spirit of God. In his inaugural sermon, Peter made the astounding declaration that the Spirit had been poured out on *all* flesh and that even our "sons and daughters" would prophesy (Acts 2:17). To a Jewish audience, that was a staggering promise — "prophet," to them, meant someone like "Ezekiel," who got a book of the Bible named after him. With the coming of the Spirit, however, that kind of anointing is now available to all believers. What had been reserved for Jewish heroes in the Old Testament was now standard fare for all believers. This does not mean, of course, that we write Scripture the way some of the Old Testament prophets did, but that we preach with the same power and authority that they did.

Jesus would go so far as to say that the least believer in the New Testament is greater than the greatest Old Testament prophet because they know the truth about the resurrection and have the Holy Spirit permanently fused to their souls, ready to speak through them whenever they yield themselves to be his mouthpiece (Matt. 11:11). The "least" believer reading these words right now has access to greater power than even John the Baptist had!

In the New Testament, the balance of ministry shifts away decidedly from specialized leaders to ordinary people. Paul, in fact, said that God's primary purpose for church leaders is equipping of the saints for the work of ministry. The *saints*, he said, do the work of the ministry; pastors and leaders are only there to equip! As I said earlier, I tell our church, tongue only slightly in cheek, that according to Paul, when I became a pastor I *left* the ministry. That means I should not be the first one from whom their neighbors hear the gospel, nor should I be the first one to visit one of our members during a time of suffering. The congregation's job is not merely to invite unbelievers to hear me preach, but to be the primary means by which God testifies to their friends.

Get this: Of the 40 miracles recorded in Acts, 39 happen *outside* the church walls. That's 97.5 percent! You can safely conclude from this that the main place God wants to manifest his power is outside the church. Think about how foreign this is to most church members' thinking! Ask most church-going Christians to describe a time when they saw or felt the power of God, and they will point to a moment in the sermon or the musical crescendo during the choir special. (And we should be thankful for Spirit-filled church services!) But most of what God wants to do in our society happens outside the church, facilitated by the hands of ordinary people. The one place you seem to be unable to find the apostles much in Acts is ... well ... in church! Like Jesus, his disciples went "outside the camp," taking the power of the gospel into the lost wilderness of the world (Heb. 13:12–13). To know Jesus is to be sent.

Physician Thomas Hale, commenting on the work of Lesslie Newbigin, captures the essence of the missional approach:

> No one can say: "Since I'm not called to be a missionary, I do not have to evangelize my friends and neighbors." There is no difference, in spiritual terms, between a missionary witnessing in his hometown and a missionary witnessing in Katmandu, Nepal. We are all called to go — even if it is only to the next room, or the next block.[7]

You are either a missionary or a mission field. There is no third option.

Run the Play!

Imagine watching an American football game on TV where after the quarterback calls the play in the huddle, the team applauds him, pats him on the back, and then runs back to the bench to have Gatorade and snacks. After a few minutes, they hustle back out onto the field, huddle back up, and tell the quarterback to call another play. This time a few tell him he's the best play-caller they've ever heard and that they plan to bring their friends back to hear him call the next play. Then back to the bench for more snacks. A few podcast his play and listen to it again while they munch on energy bars. A few minutes later, back out to listen to another play. This happens for the duration of the first quarter. At some point you yell in exasperation, "Fellas!... The point is not listening to the quarterback call the play; the point is to *run* the play."

As the pastor, my role at our weekend gathering is to call "the play" for the church. I love it when our congregation takes notes on the play, when they re-podcast the play later in the week, and when they share that play with their friends and bring them back to hear me call another one next week. But my real joy comes when they *run* the play. The only point of me calling the play is for them to run it.

No matter how good pastors get at calling the plays, if we don't get people to start running the plays, we're going to forfeit the game. As I noted at the beginning, with each succeeding generation in the West our "Sunday services" become less and less effective at bringing in the lost. If believers do not learn to carry the gospel outside the church, *no one is going to hear us.* We might as well be screaming in a closet. To return to my British friend, Steve Timmis:

> We can no longer assume that if people want to find God or discover meaning or cope with a personal crisis, they will go to church. They may attend any number of religious bodies or sects. Or they may go to a therapist. Or read a self-help book. Merely opening our doors each Sunday is no longer sufficient. Offering a good product is not enough.... What is clear is that great swathes of America will not be reached through Sunday morning services.[8]

For those of us in the Western church, I think we are at a crucial decision point. I love seeing big audiences gathered to hear the gospel, but if we want to reach the next generation, we are going to have to equip our people to reach them *outside* the church.

Balancing Depth and Width

Most leaders, when you press them, will acknowledge that evangelism has both attractional *and* missional dimensions. The rub comes in determining how much time and attention you devote to either. Resources are limited, so the dollars you spend developing the weekend experience are likely dollars you can't spend on developing discipleship and equipping ministries, and vice versa.

So what's the right allocation of time and resources? Unfortunately, I can't give you a percentage. What I can do is warn you that it's easy to veer toward extremes and neglect one or the other. It's easy then to label yourself and villainize those who balance it differently. For example, you can start to pride yourself on your weekend attendance, using that as your sole metric of success and devote little to no attention to ministries that don't directly result in more rears in seats, more coin in the offering, or more bodies in the baptismal.

On the other hand, you can self-righteously eschew the attractional approach and condescendingly criticize all the large ministries in your city, saying things like, "Well, of course that big church draws in a lot of people. But people never stay there. Eventually they make their way back to us." You then feel justified in putting little to no effort and energy into guest services, weekend environments, or accessibility of the message, because largeness equals a sell-out.

Both those who neglect the missional and those who neglect the attractional are unfaithful to God. God intended both for his church, and what he has joined together, we must not separate.

Charles Spurgeon said,

> It will be seen that those who never exhort sinners are seldom winners of souls to any great extent, but they maintain their churches by converts from other systems. I have even heard them say, 'Oh, yes, the Methodists and Revivalists [or, in our day, "the megachurch, church-growth" guys] are beating the hedges, but we shall catch many of the birds.' If I harboured such a mean thought I would be ashamed to express it. A system which cannot touch the outside world, but must leave arousing and converting work to others (whom it judges to be unsound) writes its own condemnation.... *I would sooner bring one sinner to Jesus Christ than unpack all the mysteries of the divine Word, for salvation is the thing we are to live for.*"[9]

Faithful churches, in other words, seek to grow deep *and* wide. Pursuing width without depth creates audiences instead of churches; but pursuing depth without width fails to take the urgency of the Great Commission seriously. In fact, churches that only seek to grow wide, and not deep, are probably not nearly as wide as they think, because heaven counts disciples, not congregants or confessions of faith. And churches that attempt to grow deep with no concern for growing wide are probably not as deep as they think, either, because depth in the gospel always leads to a yearning for, and usually an effectiveness in, evangelism.

It sounds so spiritual to say something like, "We should only worry about the depth of our ministries, and let God worry about the width." But disregarding the width of your ministry is blatantly unfaithful to the Great Commission. Wasn't Jesus so concerned about the "width" of his flock that he left the ninety-nine to go after one more? Do we think he is no longer concerned with that today? How can we not care about how widely God extends the gospel through us?

Again, Spurgeon — a man not known for shallow, seeker-sensitive preaching — said,

> It is true that a fisherman may fish and never catch any fish, but, if so, he is not much of a fisherman. And so, if there were no souls saved when I preached, perhaps I might find some way of satisfying my conscience, but I don't know what it is yet.
>
> If my hearers are not converted, I feel like I have wasted my time; I have lost the exercise of brain and heart. I feel as if I lost my hope and lost my life, unless I find for my Lord some of his blood-bought ones.[10]

Faithful pastors, if they are not seeing people saved in their ministries, look to heaven and ask God why he is not giving the harvest that he promised. There certainly can be seasons when we see little to no tangible fruit through our ministries (I've had a number of them — including a two-year stint where I only saw two people come to Christ), but those seasons are not normal, and we should never be okay with them.

Faithful churches seek to reach as many people as possible, as fast as possible, because that's what good fishermen and compassionate shepherds care about. If we are not concerned about this, can we really call ourselves disciples of the One who said, "Follow me, and I will make you fishers of men" (Matt. 4:19 ESV)?

Furthermore, it seems to me that a lot of missional ministry advocates have overstated the case against attractional ministry. I agree with them that our culture has changed and that people don't flock to citywide revival services the way they did in the 1950s. But dare we underestimate the drawing, converting power of a Spirit-filled preacher of the gospel? When a preacher of God's Word "lifts up" the beauties of Christ, should we really be surprised when the community throngs to hear him? Missional advocates love to emphasize the church *going* (as they should), but they overlook the fact that Jesus and the apostles had a whole lot of people *coming* to them as well.

I know several gospel preachers thriving in some very difficult places — some of the most unchurched, de-churched, post-Christian places in the Western world. Old Testament Nineveh was a foreign, "unchurched" culture hostile to God when Jonah went in, *preaching*, and the whole city came out to hear him. The land of Ireland was entirely pagan when Patrick went in, preaching, in the fifth century, and throngs of people flocked to hear him. In the revivals in Buddhist Korea of the early twentieth century — in which 50,000 people came to Christ during the first year, including 90 percent of the student body of a local college — preaching to large groups featured prominently.

Dare we assume such preaching has lost its power? Jesus' promise that he would draw people to himself when he was lifted up did not come with an expiration date. And when God starts drawing sinners to your church, you will likely need to find a large venue in which to gather them. That might feel attractional, but it's also biblical.

The bottom line? Faithful ministries pursue both width and depth, because neither is *really* possible without the other. Depth in the gospel leads to width in the mission.

CHAPTER 6

How to Transform
an Audience into an Army

PLUMB LINE:

"A Church Is Not a Group of People Gathered Around a Leader,

But a Leadership Factory."

Mark was moving quickly up the corporate ladder in his biotech company in the Research Triangle Park. A former Division 1 football wide receiver, he was good-looking, charismatic, and smart. The business world was wide open before him. He had nowhere to go but up.

But Mark was beginning to feel uneasy. He wanted to accomplish something more with his life than topping an organization chart. Over long lunches and Bible studies, he told me that pursuing a seven-figure salary no longer cast the spell over him that it once had. Although he was well on his way up the ladder of success, he had already figured out it was leaning against the wrong building.

Mark shocked his CEO — and almost everyone he knew — when he resigned his role as vice-president and moved overseas to pioneer an investment portfolio focused on raising capital for kingdom-oriented, for-profit companies working in the 10/40 window (the least-evangelized part of the world). Today Mark lives with his wife and three children in one of the most unreached cities in Southeast Asia, where he creates platforms for kingdom-minded work and shares Christ with high-powered Asian businessmen.

— Total formal seminary training: 0 hours
— Ordination status: unordained
— Clear, Damascus Road-type calling experience: yet to happen
— Total cost to the church: $0

Mark upgraded from "paying consumer" to "enlisted soldier," and as a result the gospel is spreading through a part of the business community in Southeast Asia that I, as a pastor, could likely never penetrate by moving there on a tourist visa and opening an "English corner."

I believe the future success of the spread of the gospel in unreached places lies, in large part, in the hands of businesspeople like Mark. And I believe his potential lies largely untapped. In this chapter I want to suggest some practical ways we can raise up more men and women like him.

The Promise Behind the Power in Acts

As we discussed in chapter 4, the gospel's most powerful advances in the book of Acts come via the hands of regular people. Those first disciples experienced the fulfillment of the promise Jesus gave in John 14:12:

> "Truly, truly, I say to you, whoever believes in me will also do the works that I do; and greater works than these will he do, because I am going to the Father." (ESV)

Greater works than Jesus did? Did they really do *greater* works than Jesus? Have you? Ever walked on water, raised the dead, or multiplied loaves and fishes? Preached with greater power or prayed with greater insight?

Yet Jesus said their — and our — works would be greater than his, and they are in at least two ways: First, our preaching and testifying to Jesus' finished work lead lost people to the salvation that his miracles only foreshadowed. Jesus' miracles were signs pointing to the greatest of all miracles: salvation of the world from the curse of sin. Jesus opened physically blind eyes to illustrate how our preaching opens spiritually blind eyes. Jesus multiplied bread loaves to feed hungry bellies to illustrate how our preaching feeds the bread of life to hungry souls.

Think about it: Which is truly greater — the healing of a temporary limb, or the saving of an eternal life? Jesus made clear it is the latter, and he did the former only to illustrate his power to do the latter (Mark 2:1–12).

Second, our works are greater because *they* reach farther than his did. Now that his Spirit dwells upon every believer, Jesus can work in more places than when he was bound to a body of flesh.

In another place, Jesus told his disciples it would be to their advantage for him to go away, because then he could send the Spirit to them:

> "But very truly I tell you, it is for your good that I am going away. Unless I go away, the Advocate will not come to you; but if I go, I will send him to you." (John 16:7)

Think about how absurd that statement must have sounded to those first disciples. They had enjoyed his personal company for three years, and now he is telling them it would be to their advantage for him to leave?

How awesome would it be to walk around with Jesus for three years?

— Have a hard theological question? BAM. Jesus answers it.
— You're throwing a church fellowship and you run out of Chex Mix: BAM. Jesus multiplies the remaining crumbs so you have enough for each guest plus twelve more bowls.
— Your dog gets run over. BAM. Jesus resurrects your dog back to life.
— Your cat gets run over.... Jesus digs a hole to help you bury it.

Okay, so maybe that's not exactly what it would be like. But how great would it be to have Jesus on your ministry team? Imagine your pastor announces that the youth pastor your kids love is transferring to a new church. You feel sad, but then your pastor tells you, "Good news, Jesus Christ has turned in his resume. He is going to be our new youth pastor." I'm assuming you would be pretty excited.

Yet Jesus said that if we really understood what is being offered to us in the Spirit of God, if we had to choose between that and a church in which every believer has the Spirit of God inside them, we would take the latter. The ministry potential of the Spirit of God in ordinary people is *greater* than if he himself stayed on earth to lead the mission. Doesn't the fact that we are not as excited about the Spirit *inside* us as we would be about Jesus as our youth pastor show how far removed we are from Jesus' promise?

The first church took this promise seriously. They didn't see themselves as building the church for Jesus as much as him building the church *through* them. The same divine power that fed the 5,000 was at work through them. Luke opens up the book of Acts (the follow-up book to his gospel), with the words:

> In my former book … I wrote about all that Jesus began to do and to teach until the day he was taken up to heaven. (Acts 1:1)

What Jesus did for his thirty-three years on earth was only what he *began* to do and teach. The book of Acts is about what he *continued* to do and teach — no longer through his incarnated body, but through his Spirit in the church.

In his Gospel and the book of Acts, Luke draws a parallel between the works Jesus did in his earthly body and the works the church did by the power of the Spirit. In fact, Luke seems to go out of his way to point out that Jesus accomplished this by the same power of the Spirit the church had received. He says that Jesus healed by the power of the Spirit (Luke 5:18) and preached in the power of the Spirit (Luke 4:16–19).

I remember that when I first read Luke 5:18, my thought was, "Of course the power was present to heal — Jesus was there." But Luke is referring to the power of the Spirit, not Jesus' inherent power. Evidently Jesus did his miracles not through his own power, but the power of the Spirit. Luke wanted us to see that the same power Jesus used we have access to as well. This means that ordinary people — people with problems and faults and stubborn habits and personal weaknesses — can be used *mightily* in the mission of God, because it's not about their abilities to do things *for* God, but about his ability to work *through* them.

As we saw in the last chapter, Jesus made another staggering promise in Matthew 12 when he told his disciples that the "least" believer in his kingdom was greater than John the Baptist. That man was the greatest of the prophets, Jesus said, yet the "least" in his kingdom was greater than him (Luke 7:28). How? Because even the "least" believer in the church knows the truth about the resurrection and has the Spirit of God permanently fused to his soul.

Think about that for a minute. Right now, someone, somewhere, in the kingdom of God is the "least" gifted of all Christians alive. Mathematically, that has to be true. Right? Who knows … maybe that person is right now reading this book. You are sitting there saying, "Hey, I think it might be me!" And God is up in heaven nodding his head saying, "Yep. It's you. You're at the bottom of the pile."

Yet, even if that is true, Jesus says you have more potential for the kingdom of God than John the Baptist! Have you grasped that? Does your boldness in ministry demonstrate your belief in that promise? If you are a church leader, do you see your people that way?

As I noted in chapter 1, how we have built our churches turns this principle on its head. We gather throngs of people to bask in the Spirit's anointing on a few megastars and call that "mission accomplished." That's great, but it's not what got Jesus most excited. His vision for the future was a multitude of ordinary, Spirit-filled believers turning the world upside down with his power, not their talent.

Now, perhaps you're saying, "I realize that things in Acts were crazy. But surely things have calmed down a bit today. We're in a different stage." When exactly did the "stage" of Acts end? Scholars point out that Acts has no real ending. Luke concludes the book in a cliffhanger, with Paul in prison. Meanwhile, people in Rome are getting saved by the dozens ... and ... *What happens? Will Paul die, or start a revival in Rome?* What about Paul's desire to take Christ to places where he's never been named — like the edges of Europe, or China, or the Southeast Asian isles? Luke doesn't tell us. The book just trails off in a series of ellipses ...

When I was a kid, I liked to watch a TV show called *The Dukes of Hazzard.* It always seemed to end with the two main characters, Bo and Luke Duke, suspended in midair, jumping between two cars. Would they make it, or was this the end? You had to tune in the next week to find out. Acts ends the same way. We see the movement hovering in midair, suspended between death and success. What will happen?

Perhaps Luke doesn't tell us because he wants us to realize that the story continues through us. We're not continuing to write the Bible — that is complete — but what Jesus "began" to do in his three-year earthly ministry and "continued" through his church in Acts he continues through us today. We are the next episode. We're still in the same season, and the finale is still to come. Every believer now has a part of the story to write.

The Church Is a Leadership Factory

The church ought therefore to see itself as a leadership factory that stirs up the gifts of God in people, not an auditorium that gathers people behind a leader. Jesus did not build his church by recruiting the twelve brightest from the rabbi's list of "up and coming stars" and platforming them in large stadiums around the world. His disciples were mostly blue-collar workers with little to no formal theological training.

Nor were they men of outstanding character — at least not at first. These future church leaders bumble their way through the Gospels arguing about who will be the greatest, calling down judgment on people they don't like, turning little kids away, and staring at Jesus like a calf at a new gate. Had there been puppies running around, they probably would have kicked them. They were just not the spiciest Doritos in the bag.

Yet through his Spirit, Jesus uses this ragtag group of misfits to turn the world upside down. Peter, the disciple with a foot-shaped mouth who wilted before a teenage girl, became the church's most courageous leader and premiere preacher (John 18:15 – 18). When Jesus chose Peter, he was not a star. He was a man in desperate need of development. Jesus made him into a star.

If developing leaders is what Jesus got most excited about in the church, isn't that what we should be most excited about, too?

Let me suggest four important implications for how we should approach ministry.

1. WE MUST *CHALLENGE* OUR PEOPLE TO BE LEADERS.

We need to put forward a new vision for the church. We should not allow people to see the church as a weekly service they attend to make God happy. The gathering of the church is preparation for heavenly battle. We "huddle together" for a few minutes each week to worship God together and build each other up so that each of us can more effectively run the "missional play" throughout the week.

The church I grew up in had large signs over the exits that read, "You are now entering the mission field," to remind us that we were leaving the "holy huddle" to carry the gospel to the mission fields all around us. Today we end every service with the benediction, "Summit Church, you are sent."

Furthermore, we must turn both the authority *for* and responsibility *of* ministry back over to our people. Too many church members feel that it's the pastor's job to win the lost, pray for the sick, and counsel the broken-hearted. Pastors need to put before their people the vision of Acts: 39 out of every 40 miracles that God wants to do in the world he wants to do through them, in the community.

We need to celebrate, as often as we can, what God is doing through our people. What you celebrate, you replicate. Several times throughout the year the Summit Church features testimonies of members leading out in various projects in our city. When someone in our church leads a friend or family member to Christ, we ask them to stand in the baptismal pool with us, helping us baptize them. We want it to be clear who is on the front lines of ministry.

We frequently commission "missionaries" at the end of our services, sometimes to go to foreign lands, other times to engage in missional activities right in our own community. A couple of times I have had every believer in our congregation who works a "secular" job stand so that we could commission them to bless the city in the power of the Spirit through their work and their witness.

2. WE MUST *EMPOWER* OUR PEOPLE TO BE LEADERS.

Jesus' promises in John 14:12 (about our work being greater than his) and John 16:7 (about the Spirit in us being an advantage over Jesus beside us) tell me that the greatest ideas for ministry are likely in the minds of *congregation* members, not my mind. Jesus' vision for the church was not a few mega-geniuses with thousands of foot soldiers at their behest, but millions of believers filled with the Spirit, following his lead directly. Furthermore, if the majority of what Jesus wants to do he wants to do in the community, it shouldn't surprise us that he puts his best vision into *the* hearts of the people who live and work there for the majority of their hours each week.

Thus, one of our primary responsibilities as church leaders is to help

God's people uncover these ideas and to encourage them, as Paul did with Timothy, "to fan into flame the gift of God," which he has put within them (2 Tim. 1:6). I love Paul's imagery there: Each week the congregation gathers, and it's like I get in the pulpit and take a great big sheet and fan into flame the smoldering spiritual gift fires the Spirit has started within them. (While it reinforces the idea that I am full of hot air, I still like it.)

We should expect God's Spirit to be leading our people the same way he led Philip, Apollos, Barnabas, and Silas — all "laypeople" — in the book of Acts. Luke says that when Paul was waiting in Athens, God's Spirit provoked him to do something about the idolatry he saw. Shouldn't we expect the Spirit to put those same provocations in the hearts of our people in their contexts? Just as God did not put his Spirit into only a few ordained leaders, he does not put the Spirit's ideas into only a few heads.

Business guru Jim Collins says that the greatest leaders in the business world are those who surround themselves with people smarter than they are and empower them. He says that merely "good leaders" function as "geniuses with 1000 helpers." The leader sees himself as the one with the great ideas and recruits others to help him execute his vision. *Great* leaders, by contrast, are those who surround themselves with leaders with as much vision and ability as themselves.[1] Great leaders see themselves as the servants who empower the ideas of those around them. Collins uses Jack Welch, legendary CEO of General Electric, as an example: Welch's greatness came from his ability to surround himself with the most capable leaders in the industry. His "genius" was in his ability to marshal and empower the ideas of others. In an interview with Piers Morgan, Welch said:

> I was never the smartest guy in the room. If you're a leader and you're the smartest guy in the room, you've got real problems.[2]

Shouldn't leaders in the body of Christ be even *more* committed to this approach? Aren't "great" pastors those who empower and serve the leaders in their congregations, not those who merely recruit volunteers to execute their own ideas? Shouldn't pastors see themselves as servants of the movement rather than celebrities of the moment?

I am not saying that pastors are not themselves leaders with great vision of their own, just that the primary function of their leadership ought to be helping their people discover and unleash the ministry potential God has placed inside of them. Congregants are not to be merely gathered, counted, organized, and assigned volunteer positions as cogs in our ministry machines. They are to be empowered into *their own ministries.*

Training leaders is different from recruiting volunteers. "Volunteers" primarily serve as cogs in the machine that a leader has built. Leaders generate their own ideas, and usually want to build their own machines. I'm not downplaying the need for volunteers: our church has more than 1,200 faithful volunteers who execute our services each weekend. I'm saying that great churches will do more than simply recruit volunteers — they will multiply leaders.

Having an organization filled with leaders means that some do things differently from how I would have done them. That bothers the perfectionist in me, but it is a necessary cost of empowering leaders. (Of course, in saying that, I don't mean we take a totally "hands-off" approach to ministry. God has appointed pastors as stewards and guides of the church. We have to guard against heresy or unhealthy ministry practices. And, of course, we can't endorse every idea that someone in our congregation comes up with. Just because Sister Suzie thinks that it would be a blessing to take her "Gospel Riverdance Clogging Extravaganza" to every middle school in Raleigh doesn't mean I need to get behind it or to put our church's name on it.)

Furthermore, what independent leaders accomplish in the community often does not fit neatly into the bottom line of our church's annual report. Both these things — seeing leaders pursue ministry in ways different from how we might have done it, and seeing them devote their resources and energies into things that don't contribute to the bottom line of our church's "success" — can be difficult to swallow. Multiplying leaders, however, means letting go of both the ownership and honor of ministry, both tough for type-A pastors. But it is totally worth it.

Amy had a desire to develop a mobile pregnancy clinic that would provide ultrasounds for girls considering abortion in parts of our cities where they would likely never make it to a clinic. When a girl sees her baby in a 4D-ultrasound, the likelihood of pursuing abortion drops dramatically. Many, however, have no exposure to the clinics. "If they can't get to these clinics to see the ultrasound," Amy thought, "why not bring the clinic to them?" She met with us and explained her vision, and we supplied her with some start-up funds and helped her enlist other people in the church to help. Today her "mobile clinic" ministers to thousands of women around the Raleigh-Durham Triangle, and her teams have saved the lives of hundreds — if not thousands — of children.

As a leader, which comes more naturally to you — recruiting volunteers or raising up leaders?

At the Summit Church we have developed three classifications for ministries that help us balance our ministry approach:

— **Ministries we OWN:** These are ministries that we, as a pastoral team, conceive, fund, and execute. Congregation members serve in and support these ministries, but the primary ownership, leadership, and responsibility lies with us. Things like the development of small groups, elder and ministry leadership training, and weekend worship all go in this category.

— **Ministries we BLESS:** Ministries we "bless" are on the other end of the spectrum. These are ministries that we do not own at all; we function more as cheerleaders and prayer support for members of our congregation. Brother Billy tells me after the service one Sunday that he wants to provide every teacher in Raleigh with a #2 pencil that has "Jesus Loves You" engraved on the side and plays "What Can Wash Away My Sin?" whenever you erase something. I say, "Billy, that's interesting. Let's have a word of prayer about that, and then you come back in a couple of years to tell me how that worked out," and that's about the extent of our involvement. We just don't have the bandwidth to get behind everything, and there are some things we would be wise to hesitate putting our name on. That said, some of the best ministries happening in our church have started this way.

— **Ministries we CATALYZE:** Between "own" and "bless" are ministries we "catalyze." A congregation member has an idea, brings it to us, and we feel that it lines up enough with our church objectives that we bring the resources of the church behind the idea to help make it even more successful. ("Resources" can mean financial support, networking potential, our name, and more.) Though we are invested in it, we don't take responsibility for it. We leave the ownership in the hands of the member and empower them so *they* can accomplish it.

We believe the greatest potential for ministry multiplication lies in this last category, and each staff member is responsible to facilitate this where they can. We have as a goal the catalyzation of at least one hundred community-blessing ministries out of our church. We might be instrumental in getting them started, but we want them quickly to become 501 C–3s with budgets and leadership boards of their own.

DO YOU HAVE A PROCESS?

If you are a ministry leader, ask yourself this question: *Do you have a clear process for identifying and training up new leaders in your church, and for helping ordinary congregation members generate good ideas?* In *The Leadership Baton*, Bruce Miller points out that while most leaders acknowledge an urgent need to raise up leaders in the church, they "have no apparent strategy for developing [those] leaders."[3] Without a clear process it is unlikely to happen.

We once offered ten $1,000 grants to the small groups that could come up with the best "community blessing" ideas. As for any other grant, they submitted proposals that we judged, and then we awarded the top ten ideas so the groups could pursue them. It was the best $10,000 we ever spent on community ministry, launching ministry that goes on to this day! But even greater was the effect this exercise had on the psychology of our church members: It challenged them to see their community through the eyes of the Spirit and empowered them to pursue what the Spirit put into their hearts.

If you want to be a "sending" church, you have to develop a process for producing leaders.[4] Without a process, it is unlikely you will move the leadership needle much in your church. As the old saying goes, insanity is doing the same things over and over again and expecting different results. To produce leaders, you have to think and act differently.

Have you taken up your responsibility as ministry multiplier? Real leaders are not those who simply get the job done. Leaders empower others to get the job done. "Doing something well" does not a leader make. "Empowering others to do it well" does.

3. WE MUST HAVE THE COURAGE TO SEND OUT OUR PEOPLE AS LEADERS.

Churches that take Jesus' promises and the Great Commission seriously are committed to sending out some of their best leaders into the mission. Honestly, this is one of the hardest things for me to do: finding someone with great potential, developing them, and then watching them leave to establish a ministry somewhere else. Down in your heart you know you ought to be happy about this — but still, they are no longer there benefiting *your* church.

Every year we employ four "church planting residents" on our staff for nine months, giving them few responsibilities other than preparing for their church plant and recruiting other Summit members to go with them. This past year we planted a church on the North Carolina coast, and Ethan, the planter, took 55 of our best people on his core team. Seeing them line the stage the weekend we commissioned them was at the same time both painful and joyful.

But here's a principle we have learned that sustains us when our courage flags. This principle is of such crucial importance it needs its own paragraph:

Sending out leaders creates more leaders. What you send out inevitably comes back to you in multiplied form.

I think this is true for two reasons — one natural and the other supernatural.

The "natural" reason: *Leaders are attracted to places where they can grow to their potential, and sending out when the time is right is part of* *that process.* If leaders see that you are primarily seeking cogs for your machine, they will likely stay away ... or, if they do come to your church, stay safely disengaged on the sidelines.

I remember reading how at one point some absurd number of upper management of Fortune 500 companies had grown up underneath Jack Welch's leadership at General Electric. It wasn't that Welch couldn't keep talent — quite the opposite. Leaders knew that if you worked for Jack Welch and had the capacity to become a Fortune 500-level leader, he would develop you and "send" you out — assuming he did not have a position at GE that suited your talent. Even though that was not always in the immediate short-term interests of GE, Welch was committed to it. It turns out, however, that this *was* in the best interests of GE, because that reputation *drew* new talent to GE. For every one they sent out, three more got in line.[5]

Business analyst Liz Wiseman calls this the "cycle of attraction." She says,

> The cycle of attraction begins with a leader possessing the confidence and magnetism to surround him or herself with "A players" — sheer raw talent and the right mix of intelligence needed for the challenge. Under the leadership of the Talent Magnet, the genius of these players gets discovered and utilized to the fullest. Having been stretched, these players become smarter and more capable. A players become A+ players. These people are positioned in the spotlight and get kudos and recognition for their work. They attract attention and their value increases in the talent marketplace, internally or externally. These A+ players get offered even bigger opportunities and seize them with the full support of the Talent Manager.
>
> And then the cycle kicks into hyperdrive. As this pattern of utilization, growth, and opportunity occurs across multiple people, others in the organization notice and the leader and the organization get a reputation. They build a reputation as 'the place to grow.' This reputation spreads and more A players flock to work in the Talent Magnet's organization, so there is a steady flow of talent in the door, replacing talent growing out of the organization.[6]

The supernatural reason: Just as God promises to multiply our money when we are generous with it, he does the same with the leadership talent we give away for his kingdom. Read these verses that we typically apply to financial generosity through the lens of giving away leadership talent:

— One person gives freely, yet gains even more; another withholds unduly, but comes to poverty. (Prov. 11:24)

— A generous person will prosper; whoever refreshes others will be refreshed. (Prov. 11:25)

— "Bring the whole tithe into the storehouse.... Test me in this," says the LORD Almighty, "and see if I will not throw open the floodgates of heaven and pour out so much blessing that there will not be room enough to store it." (Mal. 3:10)

The little boy who bravely gave his five loaves and two fish to Jesus not only got to see Jesus use it to feed the multitude, but also got to take home twelve more baskets full of leftovers (John 6:13). You can't outgive God. Not with money, not with leadership talent, not with anything.

That doesn't mean giving away leadership talent is not scary. Sacrificial giving of *any kind* always is. You give up control of something you feel like you need, or at least something you know you would love to keep, and sow it into the fields of God's harvest.

It is painfully costly, especially in the short run. According to some business studies, sending out an employee equates to a loss of two years' investment of salary and training.[7] God promises, however, to multiply your provisions when you are generous. He promises to "multiply our seed for sowing" and "enrich us in every way" so that we can become even *more* generous (see 2 Cor. 9:10–11 ESV). As we give away our leaders, he multiplies the numbers of leaders we have to give away.

Pastors know how to teach the principle of the harvest as it relates to their people's money. Why would we not abide by the same principle when it comes to our leaders? (Pastors, maybe our people don't really believe in this principle because they can see we don't actually believe it, either! If we did, we would have an open hand with *all* of our resources, including our leaders!) Faith-based generosity, you see, is about more than having an open hand with money; it's about having an open hand with *every* good thing God has put in your life. As you give away precious seed, he multiplies it.

I have seen this principle play itself out time and time again at our church. It seems that for every one leader we send out, several more seem to pop up in their place.

A couple of years ago we sent out Andrew, a good friend and one of our most capable pastors. I would have loved to have had Andrew on our team at the Summit Church for the rest of his life! But we knew he could serve the kingdom better as a church planter, leading a congregation on his own. I told him not only that he could go with my blessing, but also that he could take anyone he wanted. Almost anyone.

I wondered how in the world we would replace Andrew. To be honest, I was tempted to raise his salary significantly to seduce him not to go. (But I knew that one day I would have to write this book, and manipulating him with money to stay would not make for a very good story.) Andrew recruited about 40 of our best people to go with him, and for a year he stayed on our staff, building that team. Each recruit began to tithe to this new church plant rather than us. At the end of that year, we gave him $100,000 and sent him out.

Now, two years later, Andrew is leading one of the fastest-growing new churches in North Carolina.

And what has happened to us? Not only do we have the joy of watching this great church in Greensboro grow like crazy, but also God has increased our budget and our attendance and has given us Todd, Chuck, and Bowe (just to name a few) — three pastors of equal caliber and similar giftings — to take Andrew's place. Our seed for sowing was multiplied, and we were enriched in every way.

A PATTERN JESUS AND THE APOSTLES ESTABLISHED

God sent his best to the world (John 1:14), and through his sacrifice we live. Everything else in the kingdom grows in the same way. As we discussed in the introduction, the harvest comes only as seeds are planted and die (John 12:24). Life in the world comes only through the death of the church.

The apostle Paul regularly left his best with the congregations he planted. Often these leaders were his most trusted friends and loyal colleagues: Paul called Timothy and Titus, whom he sent out to establish new congregations, his "true sons" in the faith. Both possessed considerable leadership giftings and were personally beneficial to Paul (1 Tim. 1:2; 3:15; 4:11 – 12; 2 Tim. 1:6; Titus 1:4 – 5). Yet he sent them away, like seeds into the harvest.

Should we not also be sending our best? Can we really expect to extend the kingdom if we do not? Do we expect that God builds his kingdom differently in our day than he did in Jesus' and Paul's day? Blessing comes only through sacrifice.

God calls his leaders, not to a platform to build a great ministry *for* themselves, but to an altar where they die *unto* themselves. This means sending out our best with abandon.

4. WE NEED A NEW METRIC FOR SUCCESS.

Finally, as we have discussed throughout this book, we need a new metric to determine success. As I have noted: Sending and planting is rarely good — in the short run — for *our* church's attendance or budget bottom line. Of the twenty-five domestic and ninety international churches we have planted, not one has ever contacted us and said, "We had such a surplus budget this year we wanted to give some back to you!" Church plants are like teenagers — they only want your money and affirmation and then for you to stay out of their way. (Smile.)

Sending is costly and painful, but the harvest is a thousand times worth it. When I was able to share with our church this past Easter that the churches we have planted in the last five years had a greater collective growth in attendance that year than we had, it gave us a joy we could never have experienced in only our own growth. I'm a dad, and there is a joy I experience in my children's successes that goes beyond what I feel for my own. The same is true for the "children" of our church. Just as sending multiplies the kingdom, it multiplies our joy as well.

Release the Army

The church is not an audience to be entertained; it is an army to be empowered. The large crowd will not change the world; the mobilized force of Spirit-filled believers will.

Jack Welch says,

The future belongs to passionate, driven leaders — people who not only have enormous amounts of energy but who can energize those whom they lead. One of the jobs of a leader is to pump confidence into your people. And when you've got somebody who's raring to go and you can smell it and feel it, give 'em that shot.[8]

John Calvin concurs:

The more anxious a person is to devote himself to upbuilding, the more highly [he is] to be regarded.[9]

If Jack Welch and John Calvin agree on something, surely it is settled in heaven.

CHAPTER 7

Painting the Invisible Man

PLUMB LINE:

"The Church Makes Visible the Invisible Christ."

As a boy, I loved superheroes. Truth be told, I still do, but I no longer dress up and run around the neighborhood masquerading as the Dark Knight, the caped crusader, or your friendly neighborhood Spider-man. It creeps the neighbors out.

The one superhero whose disguise I could never quite master as a kid, however, was the Invisible Man. The closest I could come was going into my sister's room when she was away, messing her stuff up, and telling her the Invisible Man had done it.

On the *Invisible Man* television show, when someone wanted to make him visible, they would pour paint on him. Then you could see his shape and track his movements. I suggest that the local church is the paint that makes the invisible Christ visible to our community. In its fellowship, its holiness of life, its multicultural diversity, its selfless acts of love, and its forgiveness and boldness, it reveals the contours of the eternal, heavenly Christ that dwells within them. When local churches equip their people to embody the gospel in the streets, they make the movements of an otherwise invisible Christ visible to their community.[1]

A Church That Needed to Repent

In chapter 2 of this book I explained how returning in 2004 to my city in Southeast Asia made me realize I did not have the right attitude toward my current city, Raleigh-Durham. Our church had the wrong focus: we were trying to use the city to build a big church; instead, we should be trying to reach and bless our city and if we built a big church in the process, so be it. The goal should not be the size of our church; it should be the salvation and blessing of our city. In addition to our planting other churches in the city, that meant discovering where our city was hurting and applying Christ's healing in those places.

So we began to ask ourselves: "Where can we bring 'great joy' (Acts 8:8) to our city as a demonstration of the gospel?" I met with the mayor and asked him to list the five most underserved parts of our city so we could get involved there.

Shortly thereafter, God brought to our attention an underperforming public elementary school in the inner city of Durham. It was the worst-ranked school in our county and scheduled to be shut down within two years. We approached them about getting involved. Schools in our area were generally leery of church involvement because they assumed that meant zealous, smiling Christians passing out tracts, blaring positive, encouraging Christian music and giving away hot dogs at the annual school fair with John 3:16 stenciled in mustard across the top.

Toward the end of 2004, however, an unbelieving teacher from this school, neighbor of one of our pastors, told him that a family in the school had fallen on hard times and that if we were looking for a place to help, this might be a place to start. We helped that family find temporary housing, and one of our church members, about to get married, asked his guests to redirect any wedding presents to this family to stock their house.

Taking care of this family led to an invitation to care for a few others. At the end of that year, the principal, Starr Sampson, came to us and said, "If this school is going to survive, we really need to do well on our 'end of grade' [EOG] exams. Could some of your people come and pray over our students while they take them?"

And so several Summit people wandered the halls of this school during exams, praying over students and classrooms. It probably looked weird, but it worked. Their test scores were the best they had been in years. Mrs. Sampson says that those EOG scores marked the beginning of a turnaround in the school's performance.

That summer we renovated the school, painting classrooms and scrubbing floors. When school started, we brought breakfast to the teachers. Small groups adopted classrooms and teachers and met the physical needs of families in the schools. We provided dental clinics and tutoring after school.

By the fourth year of our involvement, the school ranked near the top for end-of-year exams passed, and the principal was awarded "Principal of the Year." In a newspaper interview that year she said, "Of course I want to thank the teachers for the hard work … but I have to give credit where credit is due. God gets the glory, and he worked specifically through the people of the Summit Church."[2]

A couple of years later I was invited to speak at our city's annual Martin Luther King Jr. rally. Durham is 40 percent African American, so this event is a big deal. Local news televises it, and all of the city and county government officials attend.

Not being the typical candidate to keynote an MLK rally, I asked the lady who extended the invitation what exactly they wanted me to speak on. She said, "Well, you'll have twenty minutes to say whatever you want, to explain why you love our city like you do. All we ask is that you not be controversial."

I said, "Can I talk about Jesus?"

She said, "Sure. He won't be controversial."

I was tempted to reply, "I'm not sure you know him that well."

I do enough public speaking that I rarely get nervous in front of crowds anymore, but backstage before the event, I was a nervous wreck. I mean, really nervous — like "Joel Osteen about to address The Gospel Coalition" kind of nervous. The county manager, sensing my anxiety, said, "J.D., do you know why you were asked to speak today?"

"No sir," I said.

"It's because of how your church has blessed our city." Another city official shared with me later that afternoon, "It seems that everywhere in our city we find a need, we also find people from the Summit Church meeting that need. And we couldn't think of anyone to better embody the spirit of brotherly love we want to honor on this day than you all at the Summit Church."

For eighteen of my twenty minutes I explained how the grace of our Lord Jesus Christ transforms self-absorbed people into those who love and pour themselves out for others. We love because we have been first loved. When I was finished, the entire city council, the mayor, and all his staff gave us an extended standing ovation.

We are still learning what it means to serve our community. But as I stood on the stage that day, an idea that had been growing inside me crystalized: *the church is God's demonstration community.* Our works don't replace the verbal preaching of the gospel, but in them we demonstrate, tangibly, the love and grace that we proclaim with our mouths. Effective gospel preaching is explaining with our words what we demonstrate with our lives. In our service, we make visible the invisible Christ. God has called us to bring joy to our city the way Philip brought joy to Samaria (Acts 8:4–8), by preaching the gospel of peace to the city and demonstrating its power to heal and bless through acts of extravagant generosity.

The Church Is God's Demonstration Community

Let me be clear: The church's *primary* objective is to preach the gospel, not to beautify the city, care for the poor, or renovate the ghettos. That's because the gospel testifies to what God has done to save the world, not what we can do to patch it up. The gospel is an announcement about Christ's *finished* work.

The Greek word for "gospel" was not originally a religious word — it referred to any announcement of good news. For example, if a Greek general won a battle, he would send back a "gospel" about his victory: "No longer need you live in fear. I have won the battle. You are free." The Christian gospel is an *announcement* about the victory Christ has accomplished.

Thus, our ministry begins with, and focuses on, testifying to what Christ has *done*. Any "service" to our community that does not make that message clear *disserves* them. Acts of kindness apart from the gospel only make people more comfortable on their way to hell.

Maybe you've heard the old adage attributed to Francis of Assisi: "Preach the gospel; if necessary use words." Quaint and tweetable, but very wrong. You *cannot* preach the gospel without words. The gospel *is* an explanation about an act that occurred in history once and for all. We testify through words that Jesus did for us what we could never do for ourselves by living the life we should have lived and dying the death we should have died, in our place, so that others can believe that message and trust in it. Saying, "Preach the gospel; if necessary use words," is like me saying, "Tell me your phone number; if necessary, use digits." Apart from digits, there is no phone number. Apart from words, there is no gospel.

Whenever the gospel of words was preached in the New Testament, however, its messengers substantiated those words with *signs*. Jesus' miracles were not just cool magic tricks he did to convince listeners he had crazy power. He never said, "Now, for my next trick, I'll make Peter disappear." Or "write down a number between one and a billion, and I'll guess it correctly on the first try." Rather, he did things that demonstrated salvation. He healed bodies to show that the gospel can restore what sin has destroyed. He multiplied bread to show that those who feast on him will never be hungry. He walked on water to show that God reigns over chaos and walks on top of judgment for us. He raised the dead to show that he makes all things new.

Tim Keller says, "Jesus' miracles did not merely show off the naked fact of Jesus' power; they revealed the redemptive purpose of his power."[3] As people saw Jesus' signs, they understood his message, and they believed it.

In Acts, we see the apostles signify the gospel through miraculous works such as like healing the sick and casting out demons. But we also see the church in Acts signifying the gospel in less "miraculous" ways, as when Tabitha made coats for her community (Acts 9:36–42). Stephen's care for widows signified the gospel to antagonistic Jewish priests , and it won their hearts (Acts 6:1–7). The unity between races in the church, Paul said, demonstrated to the world the reality of the power of God (Eph. 3:7–11).

In his first epistle, Peter told his church they were to live with such love and grace that the government, their employers, and their spouses would be compelled to ask "Why?" (1 Peter 2:12–3:17). In so doing, he said, they would be a sign of the coming age. The church was to be the one place in a broken and fractured world where the seeds of renewal and hope flourished. Encountering the church, it has been said, should be like walking through a city block that has been leveled by an earthquake and finding a flower sprouting out through the rubble. The beautiful flower shows you that there is hope in the chaos, life pressing up through death.

A church's demonstration of the coming reign of God might look like renovating schools, helping alcoholics, healing marriages, providing job training, offering medical care, or blessing teachers. Which signs are most effective in your community will be based on your context. In cities where spiritism was common, the apostles cast out demons (see Acts 16:16–18; 19:11–12). Where cruelty and sorrow overshadowed the city, the apostles lived with generosity and joy (Acts 16:19–34). In a place where the poor were oppressed, they stuck up for the needy. Where races could not get along, they demonstrated the unity of the gospel.

These "signs" do not replace the preaching of the gospel; they help prove it. Contrary to the popular bumper sticker "Perform random acts of kindness," our kindness is to be neither random nor senseless. Ours is intentional and logical. We demonstrate by our actions the kingdom that we declare is coming with our lips. As N. T. Wright says, we "sketch out with pencil what Jesus will one day paint in indelible ink."[4]

In saying that our primary focus in all that we do is persuading our neighbors to believe the gospel, I do not mean that we serve people only to convert them, as if our acts of love are conditioned on their acceptance of our message. We serve them whether or not they ever show any interest in the gospel, because that's how Jesus served us. The good we do for them is a good, God-pleasing end in itself. Just as God makes his sun to shine "on the evil and the just," the light of our kindness should shine upon all, indiscriminately. As I've heard said: We don't serve to convert; we serve because we're converted.

But if what we believe about the gospel is true, we can never be satisfied to put food in people's bellies or education in their minds when their souls are in jeopardy. I'm glad we can put "Tom's Shoes" on people's feet, but I'm also concerned about Tom's soul. Shoes can't fix that; only Jesus can.

At the Summit Church we say, *People, not projects, are our mission* (another of our plumb lines). Our acts of generosity and healing demonstrate to the world that God so loved us that he gave his only Son so that we could be reconciled to him.

Love on Display Is Our Most Powerful Apologetic

Francis Schaeffer once said that the final apologetic Jesus gives is the observable love of Christians for one another.[5] We certainly see this borne out in Acts, particularly in Luke's account of the gospel's spread in the Roman colony of Philippi.

In Acts 16 Luke tells the stories of three different people in Philippi who came to faith on Paul's first missionary journey there. They all came to faith in completely different ways. The first was Lydia, a rich, put-together religious businesswoman who came to Christ through one of Paul's "seeker" Bible studies (vv. 13–15). The second was on the opposite end of the spectrum: a slave girl, poor and demon-possessed. She came to Christ when Paul cast a demon out of her, freeing her from her physical and economic bondage (vv. 16–18).

The third was the Philippian jailer. Roman jailers were typically retired soldiers who were given a jail to run by Caesar as a reward for their service. They were battle-hardened, older, and typically cynical. This jailer came to Christ by observing Paul and Silas's joy in the midst of suffering (Acts 16:19–34). Paul and Silas sang psalms of joy that night after being beaten, which the jailer couldn't understand. And then, when God sent an earthquake, instead of running away Paul went back to the jailer to keep him from killing himself. The jailer, shaken not by the earthquake but by Paul's kindness, fell to his knees and said, "Sirs, what must I do to be saved?"

These three individuals can serve as examples of three very different kinds of people in our cities and the different ways we should go about reaching them:

- **"Lydias"** are spiritually interested people who will be reached through our evangelistic events (such as discovery Bible studies or Easter services).

- **"Slave girls"** are physical, economic, or spiritual captives who will likely never come to our seeker Bible studies or Easter services, no matter how good they are. And this girl couldn't have come to Paul's seeker Bible study even if she had wanted to! Paul had to go to her, delivering her from bondage.
- **"Philippian jailers"** are cynics who comprise the ruling, educated, or artistic elite in our society. This jailer was won by seeing Paul's generosity and joy on display in the midst of persecution.

Furthermore, these four very different people, (counting Paul) would never have shared community in the ancient world. According to the *Siddur*, the first-century Jewish prayer book, Jewish men would thank God each morning that they were not "a woman, a slave, or a Gentile." Of the many people saved in Philippi, why does Luke record these three? He is demonstrating that the first church in Philippi consisted of three people sitting down together in love and fellowship who would never have done so in any other context! This unity in and of itself was a sign to the Philippians of the power and truth of the gospel.[6]

Schaeffer, who spent a lifetime developing compelling intellectual arguments for the Christian faith, recognized that Spirit-fueled, gospel-love on display has a power to change the human heart in ways intellectual arguments cannot. The Roman emperor Julian, one of the fiercest second-century persecutors of early Christians (whom the early church aptly referred to as "Julian the Apostate"), admitted in disgust to a friend that he couldn't stop the church from growing no matter how many he jailed or killed because "these infernal Galileans feed our poor in addition to their own."[7] Historian Eberhard Arnold notes,

> Most astounding to the outside observer was the extent to which poverty was overcome in the vicinity of the communities.... Christians spent more money in the streets than the followers of other religions spent in their temples.[8]

Recently I met with a very well-known cultural and academic leader in Durham who had been very antagonistic, publicly, toward our church. She had accused us of bigotry, insensitivity toward the marginalized, and discrimination toward women. As we met together for coffee that afternoon, she told me, however, that her neighbor, a single mother, had fallen on hard times and some people from our church had really come to her aid. She said, "I think I'm going to have tone down some of my rhetoric about you." Demonstrating the gospel in tangible ways can soften even the most ardent critics.

A Church Empowered to Demonstrate the Message

Earlier I noted that of the 40 miracles in Acts, 39 take place outside of a church gathering. As a pastor, my job is to help our people expect and seek these outpourings in our community. Being a "sending church" means equipping our members to demonstrate the gospel every day in their workplaces, neighborhoods, and schools and to then be prepared to give an answer to those in our community who ask us to "give the reason for the hope that you have" (1 Peter 3:15).

Recently we got this note from a local high school administrator:

Dear Summit Church:

Words cannot begin to express the gratitude with which I compose this message. The students and staff of Cary High have been tremendously blessed by your efforts last week during your "Serve RDU." Not only have you nourished our bodies by providing food to our staff on multiple occasions, you have truly nourished our hearts and souls by loving our students, wholeheartedly and unconditionally. You have served as mentors to them, becoming role models and actively listening to them.... Specifically over the Christmas season, your congregation has deeply touched at least three different families with a variety of gifts. As we have a growing homeless population and a multitude of needy families in our school, this alone has been awe-inspiring to students, their families, and our staff members.

Your love, your faith, your generosity, and your prayers really have impacted us. I am so thankful for all that you have done for our school. Thank you, thank you, thank you!

I have to tell you, I will never get tired of receiving letters like that. We get our share of hate mail, too, so when we also get a letter like this telling us that God has used us as "the fragrance of life," I know that we are being the conundrum to our community that Jesus commissioned us to be — the fragrance of life to some and the fragrance of death to others (2 Cor. 2:16). During Jesus' final week on earth, some shouted, "Hosanna!" because of how he had blessed and healed them; others cried out for his execution. The religious and political leaders plotted his death while a former prostitute washed his feet with her tears in gratitude. A gospel-saturated church on mission generates both responses.

That conundrum becomes our greatest evangelistic witness. Gospel ministry is truth wrapped in grace. Truth without grace is fundamentalism; grace without truth is only sentimentality. When truth and grace are divorced, we impede the progress of the gospel. When we unite them, we multiply it.

Some guys in one of our small groups got to know a young man at a gym they frequented. "Mike" was very friendly, but also quite antagonistic toward religion. He told them that he thought their belief system was basically a fairy tale made up by people who couldn't otherwise cope with life. Still, they befriended Mike, prayed for him, and invited him to church, which for several months he politely declined. A few months later, however, Mike developed a rather serious condition and was admitted to the hospital. Although his condition was treatable, the treatment was quite expensive, and Mike did not have health insurance. So the men in this small group raised over $2,000 to cover Mike's hospital stay.

Mike, who didn't have much family to speak of, was overwhelmed by their generosity. "Why are you doing this?" he asked. They answered, "Because we serve a Savior who gave up everything for us when we didn't care anything about him."

About three months later, we baptized Mike.

Love on display is our most convincing apologetic.

Where to Start

How do you know where to begin in loving your city? Does "adopting a school" sound intimidating for your church? Or maybe you are a father reading this trying to figure out how to engage your family in the mission. When we started, seeking to bless our city, we didn't have much of what you might call "a strategy." We picked up whatever service projects were available to us. We renovated playgrounds, pulled weeds out of flower-beds, and trimmed bushes. Just start with wherever you see a need.

Over time, we have seen our focus shift from projects to people. This past year, we put thousands of our people on the streets in nineteen different city-blessing ministry projects run (primarily) by people in our church who maintain them year-round. It all started with an awkward conversation with a mayor and a relationship with one elementary school principal in which we offered to serve in whatever way we could.

Last year, we had seventeen families and young professionals move out of wealthier neighborhoods into an under-resourced one so they could incarnate the gospel there together. Sometimes I look out from the pulpit and see these families sitting together, usually with people they have brought from that neighborhood. At other places in the auditorium I see small groups sitting together with rehabilitating prisoners they have incorporated into their lives. I see a family that brings half a dozen unwed mothers from a pregnancy support ministry they run. I know that this is beginning to approach what Jesus said a church should look like.

A couple of months ago, one of our pastors received a call from the central office of the public schools about "a potential ministry opportunity." When he arrived at the school official's office, he was escorted into a conference room in which a large county map had been spread across the table. The representative asked our pastor, "Does the Summit have plans to launch a campus in *this* part of the county?" Our pastor said, "Uhh ... I'm not sure ... why?"

The representative replied, "There is a school in the eastern part of our county where 70 percent of the students receive free or reduced lunch. The school is failing, and nothing we've done has been able to help. We were hoping that the Summit Church could plant a campus nearby and adopt this school."

Ten years ago they would hardly let us onto a school campus. Now they are rolling out maps in front of us and asking us to help them.

Some of our most exciting stories of redemption come out of these community-engaging ministries. A couple of years ago a few folks at our church got involved in a prison ministry. It started out small — just a couple of our church members leading a Bible study in the prison. While doing it, they learned that the prison has a program in which inmates, for the months leading up to their release, can get out of prison for a few hours once a week with a "sponsor" family. Several of these prisoners opt to come to our church during those few hours with families from our church.

I have baptized many of those prisoners. A few of them have started Summit small groups in their cellblock, and this past year we launched our first campus in the Wake County correctional prison. Earlier this year I baptized the imam of the Islamic community from that prison, who had been brought to Christ by the faithful love, prayer, and outreach of our brothers there in the prison. He now helps facilitate a Summit campus in that prison.

Some of the prisoners have begun to ask how God might use them in the mission after they are released. One recently testified to our church:

> I always viewed God as somewhere "out there." ... I knew that he was real, but I didn't really take him seriously. Now, since experiencing Christ at the Summit Church, I feel like my purpose isn't just to stay here after I am released. I love The Summit, but I think God wants to send me overseas.

Another told me how friendship with a family from our church had changed his life — "They showed me for the first time in my life that I mattered to someone — at least to God and his people." He told me that the first thing he was going to do when he got out of prison was get his family to join the church, and his plan is to have them adopt a prisoner so that he could show someone else that they mattered, too.

From prisoner to missionary. From "taking from" society to seeking to bless it. "So there was much joy in that city" (Acts 8:8 ESV).

The gospel creates a culture in which people leave their comfort to demonstrate the beauty and power of the gospel "outside the camp" (Heb. 13:13 ESV). As they do, people you would never expect to step foot in a church, like the Philippian jailer, begin to ask the reason for the hope and generosity at work within us (see 1 Peter 3:15). Soon enough, by God's grace, they will be asking, "Sirs, what must I do to be saved?" (Acts 16:30).

Jesus truly is beautiful. When he is lifted up, he draws people to himself. Jesus always had crowds of thieves, prostitutes, tax collectors, and down-and-outs gathered around him, even before they had reformed their lives. Sinners far from God will still gather around the Jesus of grace and truth today, and they will throng to our churches to hear more about him as they experience his healing touch through our people.

Are you painting the invisible Christ for the homeless, the orphan, the international student, the Muslim cleric, the prisoner, the unwed mother, and the at-risk teen? Are you painting his love for the gay and lesbian community in your city?

Do you expect these groups to walk into your church and want to hear the message just because of your engaging style and great music? Likely, the only way to reach these kinds of people will be through radical demonstrations of love, grace, relationship, and Spirit power in the community.

If you are a leader, give your people "permission" to listen for what the Spirit of God wants to do in and through them about the needs they encounter every day in their community. Teach them to yearn for those 39 of 40 miracles that God wants to do through them, to see their city through the lens of the gospel, and to yearn for the "vast and endless sea" of gospel-expanse in their community.

Encourage them to begin ministries — ministries that they, not their pastors, will own.

Give them vision, and then stay out of their way.

Our journey toward that vision started with one simple question: *Where can we bring "much joy" to our city as a demonstration of the gospel?*

Ask it, and then sit back and watch what happens.

CHAPTER 8

Without This, You Fail

PLUMB LINE:

"The Point in Everything Is to Make Disciples."

On paper, President Abraham Lincoln couldn't have hoped for a better general than George B. McClellan. Referred to flatteringly as the "Young Napoleon," McClellan was a phenomenon. At the age of fifteen, he had been the youngest member ever to be accepted at West Point. He graduated second in his class, only because he couldn't draw maps well. He served in the Mexican-American War and then in the Crimean War, both with distinction.

Perhaps McClellan's greatest gifts, however, were his ability to recruit and organize. When Lincoln appointed him to head up the new Army of the Potomac formed in July 1861, McClellan immediately expanded its ranks from 50,000 to 168,000, all the while bringing a level of organization and precision to the troops that stunned McClellan's superiors.

Furthermore, his troops loved him. Even amidst the grueling conditions of the Civil War, he kept their morale high, inspiring them to give more and do more because the cause was worth it. And that's all the more amazing, considering they had been decimated at Bull Run just prior to his commission. Under McClellan, they started to believe again.

No one was surprised when, in October 1861, President Lincoln made McClellan his General-In-Chief. McClellan had the resume. He had the experience. Now, he had a powerhouse army behind him, outnumbering his enemy more than two to one. There was just one problem.

The man wouldn't fight.

For weeks General McClellan readied his position, organized, and strategized, while Lee's army lay dangerously exposed just a few miles away. Lincoln urged McClellan to put his numerical and tactical advantage to use and crush the rebellion with one, swift attack. McClellan understood the strategy. He knew his favorable odds. But he wouldn't pull the trigger.

After an excruciating year of inactivity, Lincoln removed the greatest military mind of his time and eventually replaced him with a man with only half his tactical talent, but a man who would have picked a fight with a beehive buck naked: Ulysses S. Grant.

The greatest asset of a military man is his ability to fight. Without that, all other assets are useless.

Many skills make for an effective minister, but there is one without which everything else we do is useless: make disciples. Apart from that, all the money we raise, buildings we build, ministries we organize, sermons we preach and songs we write won't move the mission forward. Without that one thing, we fail.

Everything else we do is ultimately in support of that one thing. Disciple-making was the central component of the Great Commission (Matt. 28:19), and it ought to be the standard by which we should judge *every* ministry in the church. In his classic book *The Master Plan of Evangelism*, Robert Coleman said,

> The great commission is not merely to go to the ends of the earth preaching the gospel, nor to baptize a lot of converts into the Name of the Triune God, nor to teach them the precepts of Christ, but to "make disciples" — to build men like themselves who were so constrained by the commission of Christ that they not only followed Jesus themselves, but led others to follow him, too.
>
> *The* criteria upon which any church should measure its success is not how many new names are added to the roll nor how much the budget is increased, but rather how many Christians are actively winning souls and training them to win the multitudes.[1]

Are We Raising Up Our *Own* Leaders?

Kevin Ezell, president of the North American Mission Board (the domestic church planting arm of the Southern Baptist Convention), said that the greatest obstacle to planting churches today is not a lack of funds, but a lack of qualified planters. Southern Baptists claim 16 million adherents in 42,000 churches, and we have a problem finding 500 qualified planters? Only 1 of every 320,000 Southern Baptists — 1 planter out of every 840 churches — needs to become a church planter in order to have more planters than we can support. How are we *not* producing that many?

Other evangelical tribes do not seem to fare much better. I once heard the leader of a large North American church planting network explain that they were looking for creative ways to attract qualified planters from outside their network to plant churches through their network. Why would a successful church planting network need to look *outside* of its own churches for prospective church planters? Shouldn't they be raising them up from within their churches? If everyone is doing the importing and no one is doing the exporting, how can the economy survive? And if our *church plants* are not effective at making new disciples, who is?

Many of the fastest growing churches in America are not growing by winning and discipling new believers, but by importing them from other places. Maybe you've seen this happen in your city. Some new, hot church with great music comes into town, and everyone flocks there. That church boasts "New Testament–level" growth, but the total number of people in church in the city on any given weekend has not increased. Reshuffling members is not advancing on the gates of hell; it is merely reassigning the soldiers into new platoons. At some point, somebody has to engage the enemy, or we forfeit the war.

I have been inspired by our college ministry, which does this extremely well. Each year they launch about fifty students into ministry, most of whom come from non-Christian backgrounds. A couple of years ago they sent a full-time church planting team to Southeast Asia that consisted of eight college graduates, seven of whom became Christians at our church during college. The next year they supplied us with fourteen interns to help reach more students in the area, all fourteen of whom had become Christians during their time in college.

The difference? This college ministry puts extraordinary emphasis on discipleship. Disciples don't just get counted on the balance sheet once; they multiply into more disciples.

To reach more people, we don't need better gathering techniques; we need better discipleship. Larger audiences and more "decisions for Christ" are just not cutting it. If we are going to move the mission needle in America, we have to turn unbelievers into church leaders, atheists into missionaries. We have to get good at making disciples.

Ironically, numerical growth can *deceive* us into thinking we are advancing the kingdom, when we really are not. For many years we rarely thought about how well we were making disciples because we didn't feel the need to — lots of people were coming to our church! But when our growth curve leveled a little (as inevitably it does), we noticed that our existing members were not bringing that many new people to Christ. And we had a huge back door. A lot of people came for the excitement, but we hadn't done a good job of turning them into life-long disciples. Some weren't even winning their own kids to Christ!

The Most Basic Component of Our Calling

J. D. Payne points out that there is not a single passage in the Bible commanding us to plant churches.[2] What we do find, he says, are commands to make disciples. He sees church planting as the prescribed *means* for doing so — properly discipled believers come together in churches — but disciple-making is the goal. Payne says:

> The mission of God is not about a church-planting movement, but rather a disciple-making movement that leads to the multiplication of new churches across a people group or population segment, resulting in the transformation of societies.... We must not only ask questions such as "How many churches were planted last year?" but we must also ask, "How many disciples were made in the planting of those churches, and are now obeying all that Christ commanded?"[3]

Is it possible we might be sending out guys to plant churches who know how to pull off events, gather crowds, and build organizations — but don't know how to make disciples?

Whenever we consider a planter we ask, "Are they making disciples effectively now?" Why would we send out a guy to do somewhere else what he is not even doing here? When you have the title of "church planter," an angel doesn't come along and sprinkle you with magical "evangelistic effectiveness dust." Nor do you become an effective evangelist by moving overseas. "There is no transformation by aviation."

We have noticed that the most effective planters are those who grow and multiply small groups here in our church long before they ever draw a salary for it. Essentially, we send them to go and do in another city what they are already doing well here.

Dawson Trotman, founder of The Navigators, used to ask prospective missionary candidates, "How many persons do you know by name today who were won to Christ by you and are living for him now?" He said,

> The majority had to admit that they were ready to cross an ocean and learn a foreign language, but they had not won their first soul who was going on with Jesus Christ. A number of them said that they got many people to go to church, others said they had persuaded some to go forward when the invitation was given. I asked, "Are they living for Christ now?" Their eyes dropped. I then continued, "How do you expect that by crossing an ocean and speaking in a foreign language with people who are suspicious of you, whose way of life is unfamiliar, you will be able to do there what you have not yet done here?"[4]

Are you personally making disciples? Can you point to others serving in the mission now who were not believers when you met them? Are you reproducing yourself?

Is your *church* making disciples? Can you look around your church and point to people leading ministries who, ten years ago, were not even believers?

The good news is that making disciples is fairly easy. You simply bring people along in your spiritual journey. Making disciples is more about intentionality than technique: Discipleship means teaching others to read the Bible the way you read it, pray the way you pray, and tell people about Jesus the way you do. If you have Christian habits in your life worth imitating, you can be a disciple-maker. It doesn't require years of training. You just teach others to follow Christ as you follow him.

I asked one of the most effective disciplers I know to share with me his discipleship "system." I was expecting a fancy curriculum with a silver bullet. Instead, he sent me a scanned list of verse references he had typed out by hand on a word processer from the 1980s. He explained that he gives this list to the person he's trying to bring to faith and asks them to read the verses and then write out on a sheet of paper what they think each verse means and what God might be saying to them through it. He then meets with them the next week to discuss their answers. After that, he said, he asks them if they want to read a book of Bible together and do the same thing.

That was it. No secret sauce, no electrifying jolt of discipleship genius. Yet just about every time we do a baptism, that discipler has somebody represented in the lineup — either from him directly or through someone he's led to Christ who is now bringing someone else to Christ. I think he is at least a spiritual great-great-great-grandfather.

Coleman makes this observation about the ministry of Jesus:

> Whether he was addressing the multitudes that pressed upon him, arguing with the Pharisees who sought to ensnare him, or speaking to some lonely beggar along the road, the disciples were close at hand to observe and to listen.... Through this manner of personal demonstration, every aspect of Jesus' personal discipline of life was bequeathed to his disciples.... One living sermon is worth a hundred explanations.[5]

Earlier in this book I mentioned the impact my parents' first pastor had on them. They had been drawn to the church by the quality of his preaching, but his real impact on them came when he opened up his life to them. Recently my dad and I traveled to Georgia for his funeral, and en route my dad said again to me, "You know, I'm not sure I remember a single sermon Dr. Sheehan preached in those early years. It wasn't his sermons that changed me. It was hearing him pray and listening to him as he told others about Jesus that taught me how to walk with God."

Effective discipleship is not about a curriculum; it's about one person learning from another person what it looks like to follow Jesus. Our college pastor says, "About 75 percent of discipleship is informal."

If you know how to love and walk with Jesus, you can disciple someone else. Even if your life is far from perfect. Any sincere believer can teach another how to seek God, repent, read the Bible, pray, and share with others.

If a Ministry Doesn't Make Disciples, Why Does It Exist?

Making more and better disciples ought to be the goal of — and justification for the existence of — every ministry.

A well-run program doesn't mean we are accomplishing the mission, though it is easy to confuse those two. Peter Drucker says that the worst kind of failure in business is success in the things that don't matter. Maybe the worst failure for a church is success in things that aren't producing reproducing disciples.

At our church, we periodically force ourselves to ask about every one of our ministries: *Is it making disciples?*

- **Are our kids and student ministries teaching parents to make disciples of their kids?** Are we raising up kids who will go out as gospel leaders into the world?
- **Are our small group ministries raising up new leaders to plant new groups?** Are they bringing in new people from the outside — people who have yet to attend a weekend service?
- **Is our community outreach making disciples or simply completing projects?** The *ultimate* mission is not to paint a fence, feed a prisoner, or tutor a child, but to make a disciple. We prioritize projects that help us engage in long-term relationships. We encourage our members to bring unbelievers with them to these acts of service because serving together is one of the best forums in which to share the gospel.
- **Is my preaching making disciples or merely communicating knowledge?** What I now do each week with thousands of people is really just an extension of what I did in college with the five people I was discipling. Preaching to thousands, you see, is not something fundamentally different from discipling five; only the size of the audience has changed.

Let me expound a little bit on this last one. Some preachers delight in filling their people's heads with Bible knowledge. Others seem to aim for an emotional response or an outburst of applause. Some simply hope to entertain the people enough that they'll come back the next week. But every pastor is first and foremost a disciple-maker, and that ought to be the focus in every sermon. The criteria to answer, "Am I an effective preacher?" is not, "Do other pastors admire my skill with the text?" or "How many people shouted while I preach?" or "How much did we grow during the past year?" but "Am I moving my hearers to grow in Christlikness?"

Personally, my favorite preachers are those whom I can tell are focused on moving the congregation to maturity as they preach. I hear a lot of great expositors that don't seem to be focused on that goal — their goal, rather, seems to be interpreting a text thoroughly and accurately. That's a good thing, of course, and I'm not trying to say these two things are ever at odds, just that the shape and tone of your sermons change based on which is your *primary* goal. If I am discipling a new believer who has just been saved out of a life of crime, I don't tell them, "Meet with me for the next ten years and I'll walk you through every verse of the Pentateuch line by line, showing you the hidden jewels buried in the Hebrew language." Instead, I ask, "What areas do you most need to grow in, and how can we study the Bible together so that you can resist sin and live victoriously?"

I get agitated when I hear preachers who seem more focused on their subject than on their people. While their knowledge and insight of the text might interest me, what good is preaching if it is not increasing my love for Jesus or moving me forward in the mission?

In college, I had a professor who loved to talk about the inner workings of Civil War battles. His knowledge was impressive — in fact, I am pretty sure he knew more about them than many of the people fighting at the time! But somehow I think Robert E. Lee and Ulysses S. Grant approached those battles differently than my professor would have. Grant and Lee weren't trying to understand the nature of warfare; they were trying to stay alive and win. Their quest to master the details of warfare was subservient to their desire to win the battle.

Yes, I want to know the beauties and complexities of the Bible. I think preaching should have as its subject matter the Bible, and the best preaching works its ways through books of the Bible so that we don't leave out anything God wants us to know. But the Great Commission is a mission, so every sermon should have as its focus inviting people to salvation and launching them out into that mission. Christianity is a movement, and movements, by definition, move. Thus, if your preaching is not moving people into action, it is not true gospel preaching.

David Platt, president of the International Mission Board, uses a great example to illustrate this. Once during a sermon he had a bunch of people come onto the stage to act out the various roles on a fire truck. One person was assigned to drive the truck; another the navigation; one controlled the siren; another honked the horn; one took charge of the hose; another turned that strange little steering wheel in the back.

After getting them all in place and having them commence their activities, he asked each of them, "Now, what was your job, again?" Each answered by telling him their specific roles. After they had all answered, he said, "You're all wrong. Your job — every one of you — is to *put out fires!*"

Every spiritual gift serves the larger purpose of making disciples. The gifts are varied, but the mission is the same.

Success = Disciples Who Reproduce

Any ministry's success should be judged, not by its size, but by how well it raises up disciples who raise up more disciples. If I ask you, "How's your family?" And you say simply, "Well, there are five of us now!" you haven't told me how your family is actually doing. If I want to know how your family is doing, I also want to know, "Are your kids healthy? Are they maturing into responsible adults?"

When I look at Ginger, I see a snapshot of what I want our church to be. I met Ginger at a cell phone store. One of her coworkers went to our church, and together that coworker and I invited her to start coming to church with us. She was not a church-going person, but she agreed to give it a try. We didn't know this at the time, but Ginger was a practicing lesbian and struggling with severe depression. A few months after coming to our church she intended to commit suicide by jumping off a bridge in the Appalachian Mountains. As she was nearing the spot she planned to jump from, her coworker (the one from our church) called her.

Ginger took that as a sign from God, turned her car around, drove back to Raleigh and checked herself into a hospital. Several people from our church came to visit her, and one gave her a copy of a book I wrote called *Gospel*.

When her doctor walked in, he saw it on her table and told her that he had just finished reading my book. (He did not go to our church.) They talked for a long time about finding hope and, to make a long story short, Ginger found Jesus while lying in that hospital recovery room.

Just last week Ginger got back from her third mission trip to India. The next time, she told me, she may not come home! She believes God has called her to serve on one of our church planting teams overseas.

I love having large crowds at Easter, but to be honest, I love Ginger's story a thousand times more. Every time she reports to me the great things God is doing on these trips in India, I think about the spiritual children and grandchildren God is giving us through her. What we have put into her is being multiplied exponentially through her.

Every Christian Is Born to Reproduce

Trotman's booklet *Born to Reproduce* wrecked my life in college. It explains that every Christian, regardless of their personality or spiritual gift mix, is "born to reproduce." God did not design only *certain* humans for biological reproduction; it's inherent in being human. In the same way, all healthy Christians are designed for reproducing themselves.

Coleman says it this way:

A barren Christian is a contradiction. A tree is known by its fruit.... Fruitlessness was the thing lacking in the lives of the Sadducees and Pharisees which made them so wretched in his sight.[6]

Jesus said that he chose us "to bear fruit" and that if we are not producing fruit, we need to check our connection to the vine (John 15:1 – 16). Every believer has the capacity — and the responsibility — to reproduce.

Trotman says we cannot defer responsibility for spiritual reproduction to the corporate structures of church. The focal point of spiritual reproduction is the individual believer. Reproduction does not happen through programs, books, or experiences, he says, but when individual Christians accept their role in the Great Commission.

He also says, *"God works through men. I see nowhere in the Word where God picks an organization."* Programs, preaching, small groups, worship experiences — these can all *assist* in the discipleship process, but the most essential element is the relationships of individual believers with unsaved people. Around our church we say, "Discipleship happens only in relationships." (Another plumb line!)

That means that the ministries we pursue as a church should aim at assisting and facilitating our members in making disciples. Assisting members in making disciples is different than making disciples for them.

Our success as a church will never go beyond the commitment of individual members to make disciples:

> When will the church learn this lesson? Preaching to the masses, although necessary, will never suffice in the work of preparing leaders for evangelism. Nor can occasional prayer meetings and training classes for Christian workers do this job.... *Men are God's method.* God's plan for discipleship is not something, but someone.[7]

The success of the church in the next generation will not be found in better programs or better preaching, but in better men and women — Spirit-filled men and women who have taken up Jesus' call to make disciples. As Coleman says, *you* are God's method.

Trotman challenged his generation:

> In every Christian audience, I am sure there are men and women who have been Christians for five, ten and twenty years, but who do not know of one person who is living for Jesus Christ today because of them.
>
> Men, where is your man? Women, where is your woman? Where is your girl? Where is the one whom you led to Christ and who is now going on with him?
>
> There is a story in 1 Kings 20 about a man who gave a prisoner to a servant and instructed the servant to guard the prisoner well. But as the servant was busy here and there, the prisoner made his escape. The curse of today is that we are too busy. I am not talking about being busy earning money to buy food. I am talking about being busy doing Christian things. We have spiritual activity with little productivity.[8]

I can think of few challenges more pressing for our day.

"Yes, We Can"

We come up with all kinds of objections as to why this responsibility cannot possibly belong to us. As a pastor, I've heard my fair share of excuses for why people don't disciple others (and, to be honest, I've *made* my fair share as well). Let me address, briefly, a few of the more common ones.[9]

"I DON'T HAVE WHAT IT TAKES."

Yes, you do. You have the Spirit of God. As we learned in chapter 6, the Spirit of God in you gives you more potential in ministry than John the Baptist, the greatest prophet who ever lived. The Spirit has come upon you to do the "greater things."

In him, you have what it takes. The crucial factor is not your ability, but your availability for his use. "But I'm not an extrovert," you say. Evangelistic effectiveness comes not from an outgoing personality, but from the Spirit who resides in your heart and speaks through your mouth. He promises that the words you need to say will be given to you in the very moment you need them (Luke 12:12).

"EVANGELISM IS JUST NOT MY SPIRITUAL GIFT."

It is true that God has given some believers the "gift of the evangelist" (Eph. 4:11). But don't confuse a spiritual gift given to some with an assignment given to all. A spiritual *gift* is usually just a special empowerment — an unusual effectiveness — in an assignment given to all believers. For example, those believers who have the gifts of "service," "generosity," or "faith" are not the only ones who serve, share their stuff, or believe God's promises. God gives some Christians an *extraordinary* effectiveness in those things, but serving, being generous, and showing faith are the responsibility of all believers.

The same is true of evangelism. While the Spirit has made some believers especially effective in bringing others to Jesus, he empowers us all to testify, Peter declared (Acts 2:17). (And, by the way, there's nothing wrong with asking for a greater measure of that gift! If you've got to do it anyway, you might as well ask God to make you really effective at it!)

"I WITNESS WITH MY LIFE."

The sentiment behind this one is that demonstrating the love and generosity of the gospel through our lifestyle removes our responsibility to verbally explain it to others.

A generous lifestyle is great, but, as I noted before, the gospel is, in its essence, an *announcement* about what Jesus did to save people, not a presentation of what a good person you are. Sharing that announcement requires *words*. Trying to share the gospel without using words is like watching a newscast with the sound turned off: I might recognize that the newscaster is agitated about something, but I won't know why. And if he's telling me about a tornado headed my direction, I need to know exactly what he is saying.

The announcement of the gospel must be communicated in words. A generous, humble, gracious, sacrificial, holy life can complement gospel proclamation, but never replace it.

"I DON'T HAVE TIME."

You might say, "When would I possibly have time to go out and 'evangelize'? I barely have enough time to be a good husband, father, and employee. I definitely don't have time to *add* a program of evangelism."

We are a culture of busy people, that's for sure. But the answer is simple: Be busy *with* people. Jesus accomplished a lot in the three years of his ministry — saving the human race and everything. But he still managed to disciple twelve men along the way. Everything he did, he did *with* the disciples. The Great Commission is not an addition to your life, but an essential component of every other part of it. The Spirit fills you to testify as you go throughout life.

I once heard a lady lament that she couldn't take her kids to soccer practice because she had too much ministry activity at her church. Why not look at soccer practice *as* a place of ministry? There are more "lost" people in the crowd of parents at soccer practice than there are at the church!

In Acts, the Spirit of God takes believers *outside* the church more than he keeps them in it. So if you're walking with the Spirit, you will probably be connecting with lost people at soccer practice more than attending meetings *about* ministry at the church. British pastor Tim Chester says that evangelism is "doing normal life with gospel intentionality." As we go through our lives, we are aware that people all around us are in need of the gospel, and we look and pray for ways to share it with them.

"TALKING TO OTHER PEOPLE ABOUT JESUS MAKES ME FEEL WEIRD."

Well, of course it does. I've heard evangelism defined as "two nervous people talking to each other." But here's the thing: *Isn't the message important enough for a little awkwardness?*

I heard a story several years ago about a man who was driving his car down an interstate highway outside of Los Angeles very late one evening. A significant earthquake rumbled through the region, and the man immediately pulled his car over to the side of the road to wait it out. The severe earthquake lasted just a few seconds, then ended. After the shaking stopped, the man pulled his car back onto the road and took a left to cross a bridge over a river.

As he began driving across the bridge, he noticed the taillights of the car in front of him suddenly just disappear. He stopped his car, got out, and realized that a section of the bridge had fallen into the river. The car in front of him had driven off a newly created cliff, at full speed, plunging nearly seventy-five feet into the water below.

The man turned around and saw several more cars headed toward the break. He began to wave his arms frantically, but people driving across a bridge outside of Los Angeles at 3 a.m. are not likely to stop for what looks like a crazy person on the side of the road. He watched as four cars drove right past him, their drivers plunging to their deaths below.

He saw a large bus coming toward the break. He made up his mind that if that bus went off the bridge, it would have to take him with it. So he stood in the bus's path and waved his arms to get the driver to stop. The bus honked its horn and flashed it lights, but he would not move. The bus driver got out, saw the danger, and angled the bus so no more cars would go over.

What would you have done had you been the first one to see the collapse of the bridge? I assume you would have done just what that man did. Would you have cared that observers thought you had lost your mind? Probably not. You know something they don't, which makes their ridicule irrelevant to you.

How much more important is *the gospel*? Isn't it worth the occasional awkwardness, or even the outright persecution, that might come along with sharing it? How are people supposed to believe that we have an urgent, life or-death message if we share it only with casual diffidence?

Recently I have become friends with a very prominent imam (Islamic religious leader) in our area. We both have young families, so one night we had his family over for dinner. As we gathered around the table, I wondered about the appropriate thing to do regarding the meal blessing. Usually, when just he and I got together for lunch, I would bow my head and do my thing while he did his. So I said, "Should I just pray for my family, and you for yours?" He thought for a moment and said, "Why don't we have our daughters do it for us?" His oldest daughter was eleven; mine was seven. I said, "Okay, are you up to it, Kharis?" She stared at me for a moment, and then my brave little seven-year-old said, "Okay!"

His daughter bowed her head and began to pray in Arabic. For something like a minute — which may not seem like a long time, but when it's all in Arabic and you have four kids under the age of seven, it feels like a long time. She finally said something that sounded like "Amen," followed by a dead space of silence. It was Kharis's turn. I looked up out of the corner of my eye, just in time to see my seven-year-old daughter lift her head toward heaven and say, "Dear God. Thank you for sending your Son, Jesus, to die on a cross for our sins so we could be saved, and thank you for leaving us your Holy Word so we could all know about it. And thanks for this food. In Jesus' name, Amen."

I have never been prouder — or more mortified — as a parent than I was at that moment. Proud because she's brave. Mortified because I was sure the imam believed I had put her up to that. But in a seven-year-old's mind, the message is important enough to take any opportunity to share it.

The message is worth the awkwardness. It's worth *anything*.

Our future success resides in our ability to raise up disciples who can make disciples. When a church is filled with disciple-makers, sending happens naturally. Disciple-makers, you see, gravitate toward unreached fields. And if a church is *not* filled with disciple-makers, then sending does no good — because even if we convince people to go, we're just shuffling around and are high-maintenance, high-cost professional Christians with no capacity to reproduce.

The next great missional expansion will occur when the church refocuses itself on making disciples who make disciples.

What about you? Are you good at making disciples?

What a tragedy if we spend our whole life busy in ministry but overlook *the one thing* Jesus told us to do, the one thing Jesus said would advance the mission.

My least favorite days are those when I feel as if I am getting slammed in the face, from the moment I wake up, with stuff other people need me to do, and I never actually get to the things that day that I wanted to do. I wake to the kids standing at my bedside demanding that I find the hamsters that have escaped from their cages. During breakfast, someone from my medical insurance company calls me to tell me that I have an issue with payment that I need to resolve that takes four hours on the phone. The car has a flat tire. Three or four unexpected situations arise at work that I have to address. By the time I get to the end of my day, I feel exhausted, but I can't really tell you anything I actually did that day, at least anything that mattered.

I don't want to get to the end of my life and feel that I spent my life crazy busy, doing a lot of ministry stuff, but never accomplishing the one thing Jesus said I *must* do, the one thing that advanced the Great Commission: *making disciples*.

CHAPTER 9

Your Church Doesn't Need a Missions Pastor

PLUMB LINE:

"Every Pastor Is Our Missions Pastor."

While I lived in Southeast Asia, an older man there told me about an incident that took place when he was young. A group of Japanese fishermen, he said, had been found floating off one of the islands in the Pacific Ocean, clinging to the debris of their small, wrecked fishing vessel. When questioned, they claimed that "a cow had attacked them from heaven." The authorities assumed they were smugglers of some kind who had had their ship destroyed in an altercation, so they held them in prison pending further investigation.

A week later a group of American servicemen rather sheepishly came forward and explained that they had been guiding their B–24 bomber down the airstrip of a small nearby island when a cow meandered across the runway. They thought, "Free steak tonight!" and loaded the cow into the bomb bay. After the plane took off, however, the cow began rampaging and kicking around the plane. They couldn't calm it down, so they assumed it had mad cow disease or something. So they placed it over the bomb doors and pressed the little red button.

You can probably figure out the rest of the story.

I cannot verify the authenticity of that story, although the old man who told it to me swore that it was true. Regardless, I have often thought of that cow as a picture of what it's like to get swept up into the mission of God. There you are, a normal ol' rambling cow, thinking only about where to get your next bite of grass, when you get whisked up into something that takes you high up into a new world with a force you never even knew existed. When you become a follower of Jesus, God sends you back into the world immediately with a mission.

Disinfecting Versus Discipling

Jesus launched a *global* mission, and when he saves a person, he sweeps them up immediately into that mission, global dimensions and all. He doesn't just sanitize us and put us on his sanctified shelf; he sends us on his saving mission. Or, as David Platt says, the goal is not to disinfect Christians and separate them *from the world* but to disciple them and send them back *into the world*:

> Whereas disinfecting Christians involves isolating them and teaching them to be good, discipling Christians involves propelling Christians into the world to risk their lives for the sake of others. Now the world is our focus, and we gauge success *in the* church not on the hundreds or thousands whom we can get into our buildings but on the hundreds or thousands who are leaving our buildings to take on the world with the disciples they are making.[1]

Discipleship is going from "mission field" to "missionary."

In the Bible we find no gap between the call to follow Jesus and the call to engage in mission. God's promise to bless Abram included the promise to make him a blessing to *all nations* on the earth as well (Gen. 12:1–3). When God called Paul, he commissioned him to be a messenger *to the nations* at the very moment he called him to faith (Acts 26:16).

Follow me, Jesus said, *and I will make you fishers of men* (Matt. 4:19 ESV). To follow Jesus *means* to become a fisherman.

As I said at the beginning of this book, God is like a spiritual cyclone: he never pulls you into himself without hurling you back out into mission. Jesus doesn't pull you in to stay and soak; he pulls you into salvation to send you out as a part of his global mission. When Jesus sent the Holy Spirit, as told in Acts 2, he filled *every believer* in the room. The Holy Spirit came into the room like a mighty, rushing wind — blowing each believer out to the uttermost parts of the earth.

In this chapter, I want to discuss why that coming of the Spirit in

Acts 2 ought to reshape every ministry of the church. Specifically, I want to show you that your church doesn't need a slate of full-time mission pastors in order to be effective in the mission, because every pastor is your "missions pastor." Every ministry is a "missions" ministry.

The Light That Shines the Farthest ...

Early in my pastorate, a well-meaning pastor told me that we should not think that much about international missions during our first ten years of ministry; we should focus on building up our church locally. I know he meant well, but I have come to see this as very bad advice. Inherent in the call to follow Jesus is a call to the nations. The Great Commission, given to every disciple says:

"Therefore go and make disciples of all nations...." (Matt. 28:19)

Some have said that this commission was given to the apostles and is not the prerogative of "normal" Christians. But consider the verse that follows the Great Commission:

"And surely I am with you always, to the very end of the age." (Matt. 28:20)

I have yet to meet a Christian who hesitates claiming *that* part of Jesus' statement. But how do we claim the promise in 28:20 and ignore the command in 28:19?

Furthermore, Jesus commanded his first disciples to teach others *"everything"* that he had commanded (Matt. 28:20). *Everything* would include the command to make disciples of all nations. Jesus did not say, "Teach them all that I have commanded, except this command to make disciples internationally ... that's only for you."[2]

In *The Mission of God*, Christopher Wright points out that God's promise to use Abraham and his descendants to bless the nations rushes like a river through every chapter of the Bible. Scripture, he says, is not just a collection of theological truths to learn and moral lessons to master. Scripture is an announcement about a rescue mission God has come on for us, and an invitation to join that rescue mission (2 Cor. 5:14–20).

God formed the church *for* mission, Wright says. He didn't come up with a mission for his church as much as he formed a church for his mission.[3] Thus, to separate any teaching of Scripture from its context of global mission is to misinterpret it. In other words, you can't teach any text of Scripture properly if you don't teach global missions out of it. Any ministry that is not formed in light of the Great Commission is erred from the start.

If a church is not engaging in mission, it really has no point in existing. And if a church has not embraced the global dimensions of the Great Commission, it has not understood the mission of Jesus. John Piper says that God creates a yearning in every believing person to see the nations worship. We want to see God's glory extend wherever there are sons of Adam.[4] Some of us may never be able to go to foreign lands ourselves, but deep in our hearts is a desire to see his glory cover the earth the way the waters cover the ocean floor (Hab. 2:14).

Can an emphasis on global missions unhelpfully distract a church from its local responsibilities? It can, and I have seen that happen sometimes. More often, however, a focus on the nations *increases* passion for mission at home. When believers are exposed to another culture, their myopic view of the world is exploded. If God is doing this around the world, they ask, why is he not doing it among my friends? Why would I be passionate about God's work here and not at home? Furthermore, they see how transient and small their "kingdom" is in light of God's.

Every dollar you spend getting your members engaged in overseas missions will return to you fourfold. When believers see with their own eyes what God is doing around the world, their hearts open, and so do their pocketbooks. The first year I was pastor we sent forty people to care for missionary families in Asia. All told, the trip cost nearly $100,000. The next year, however, we gave an astounding and unprecedented amount in our annual Christmas missions offering. The International Mission Board told us we were the "highest missions giving church per capita" that year in the Southern Baptist Convention. The money we spent on the trip generated new money for missions.

Going overseas helped teach our people that multiplying and sending is what we do, even when it's inconvenient and involves leaving a place you're comfortable with to set up chairs in an elementary school gym across town. This past year we gave a half-million-dollar gift to start a new urban city center that will reach at-risk teens in our city. Giving money has become part of our DNA, and that happened as we exposed ourselves to what God was doing around the world. As Keith Eitel, my seminary missions professor, used to say: *"The light that shines the farthest will also shine the brightest at home."*

The Heresy of Sequentialism

David Garrison, who served for many years as a church planting catalyzer for the Asian world, talks about "the heresy of sequentialism." Sequentialism is separating into components what really ought to be embraced all at once.[5] You shouldn't eat a cake, for example, one element at a time: flour, eggs, vanilla, and then baking soda. The real enjoyment occurs when every element is present in every bite. Global missions is part of God's essential recipe for discipleship, not something you get to only in Christianity 401. It ought to be present in the first bite.

On the local front, a new convert's most evangelistically effective season is usually their first year post-conversion. That's typically when they know the most unbelieving people and when their friends are most aware of the change that is happening. When Jesus cast the demon out of a man, the man wanted to join Jesus' band and "do seminary" with him. Jesus would not let him, but said:

> "Go home to your own people and tell them how much the Lord has done for you, and how he has had mercy on you." (Mark 5:19)

Thus, from the very beginning, new believers should be taught to engage their neighbors and the nations in the mission. To that end, every ministry in the church — and not just the "missions department" — must ask: *"How is our ministry leading people into God's global mission?"*

Global Missions as a Goal for Every Ministry

Larger churches often hire a "missions pastor" to spearhead the missions thrust of the church, and that is fine, but quite often the presence of a pastor "responsible" for the missions of the church can distract from the fact that *every pastor is a "missions" pastor, every ministry a global missions ministry.* We should not confine "missions education" to a single program; it must saturate every facet of every ministry, just as it saturates every chapter of the Bible.

No blessing that God gives his people is separated from the responsibility to become a blessing to the nations. For example, at the Summit church we build a global missions thrust into the first stages of our family ministries. Psalm 127 teaches us that our kids are given to us "like arrows in the hands of a warrior" (v. 4), and (to use the words of Jim Elliot), what are arrows for but to be pulled back on the bowstring of faith to be launched into God's global battle?[6] We quit doing "baby dedications" and now hold "parent commissionings," in which parents covenant with the church to raise up their children for the mission of God and to release them freely into that mission whenever and wherever God calls them. I make the parents promise, "If God calls my child one day to a difficult mission field, I promise not to stand in the way, but to bless and encourage my child to follow God." We don't need to dedicate a baby — the baby already belongs to God. It is the parents who need to dedicate *themselves* to raise up the child for the mission of God.

We have mapped out for parents a "family ministry plan" that identifies key milestones in their kids' lives and explains how to engage them in mission during those times. Ideas, for example, about how to serve together as a family among the underprivileged in our city, or how to take a short-term mission trip together as a family.

Reggie Joiner, in the book *Parenting Beyond Your Capacity*, talks about how crucial it is for kids to encounter mission early, otherwise they adopt a warped view of the gospel or are discouraged from faith altogether. He tells the story of a dad concerned as his daughter cooled toward the faith in her early teen years. She began to date a boy the dad described as "bad news," started to dress Goth, and showed a general disdain for church. He confided to a pastor, "I just don't know what I am doing wrong! We have always been faithful at church, making it a priority. We've had her memorize the verses. We've sent her on the youth activities."

"What ministries is your family involved in?" replied the pastor. The father couldn't name any. "That might be your problem," said the pastor. "The world is offering your daughter a more compelling story than you are. In the world she sees adventure and purpose. Here at church you have treated her as a receptacle of information."

The father found a small orphanage in Central America that his family could adopt. After dinner one night he pulled out a white board and asked the family to brainstorm how they might bless the orphanage. Ideas began to flow, and even his daughter got involved. The family began taking trips to this orphanage, raising money together, and praying together for the children. Soon, Joiner says, the bad-news-boy had faded from the picture, and his daughter's dress and demeanor had changed.

Joiner says, "When there is nothing challenging or adventurous about your style of faith, you begin to drift toward other things that seem more interesting and meaningful. Mission helps your faith."[7]

When God has designed kids to be arrows, and instead we treat them like pieces of art to decorate our home, we are not only stunting their development but discouraging them from faith altogether.

We challenge our high school students to serve for one month of one summer on one of our global mission teams, and we encourage all students to give one entire summer of their college career to serve in one of our mission projects around the world. That's how our kids' pastors, student pastors, and even parents are our "missions pastors."

We encourage each small group to adopt both a city service-evangelism project and an international missionary. We urge them to go on mission together — taking short-term international trips to see their missionary. Small groups are the frontline prayer, supply, and support teams for each missionary. A couple of times we have seen entire small groups move together to plant a church — to new cities in the United States and even a few times overseas. Sometimes small groups are even formed *for that purpose* — that is, rather than being a group that goes on mission, they come together for mission and form a group. Sometimes it's better to send people and group them rather than group them and send them.

We foster church planting multiplication principles in the way we start new small groups. Each year we encourage small groups to identify a prospective leader in their midst and to ask that leader to pray about starting his or her own group. When it's time, that small group "sends out" the new leader. In our opinion, that's better than the church always recruiting new leaders to start independent new groups, because in that model, existing small groups never think about mission. They become cliques instead of multiplying small groups.

This approach is also better, in our view, than the "cell" model — in which a group gets to 16 and then divides into two smaller groups of 8, which again grow to two groups of 16, and splits again, and so on. (That *model* works in some places — but we decided it was a bad idea for us. We had encouraged our people to work hard at establishing enough trust to really open up to each other, and just about the time they were starting to do that, we would tell them they have to split into two. They felt that they had been sucker punched!)

Sending out a new leader from the group to start a new one is painful, of course, too, but it feels more like birthing than forced division. Birthing is a more joyous — and frankly, a more biblical — process. Furthermore, such a multiplication process inculcates the principles of multiplication, the core competency of any sending church, into the smallest organized unit in the church. Small groups should be taught to understand, by their very design, that they are born to reproduce. This is how our small groups pastor is our missions pastor; and, for that matter, how *every small group leader* is *our missions* pastor, too.

I am not against a designated "missions pastor." We have a few of them, actually. But their jobs are primarily to catalyze the other pastors to lead in global mission through their ministries. Our missions pastors should not do missions *for* the church; they should catalyze missions *in* the church. Big difference. They should not be *leading* in missions as much as creating opportunities for *others to lead* in missions.

Building a Mission Ethos That Pervades the Church

We want excitement about global missions to pervade the very air that we breathe. New people should not have to wait for the "annual missions series" to know that the Great Commission defines who we are and what we do. They should sense this from the first time they step foot on one of our campuses.

Here is a handful of ways (in addition to the examples above) by which we attempt to infuse this global missions ethos into the air that we breath:

- In **every sermon** I preach, I ask myself, "Have I connected this text to God's global mission? How does this passage advance that mission?" If God's promise to make Abraham a blessing pervades every chapter of the Bible, I want it to feature prominently in my preaching. Preaching is not merely bringing a refreshing cup of water of life to people, by which they slake their thirst and go back to the pastures of their self-centeredness; good preaching shoves people into a rushing river that not only quenches their thirst, but carries them to the nations.

- We **decorate our campuses** to communicate the value we place on mission. The pictures in our lobbies and the verses we put up on our walls emphasize the Great Commission. We designed the kids' area at our main campus like our local airport. At one point we only served coffee from regions in the world where we had planted churches, with a little coffee coozie that said, "Like this coffee? Want to see where it's grown? Sign up today for a mission trip to (*wherever that coffee was from*)."

  We have designed our facilities to feel "minimalistic." This is not just to save money; it is to communicate a message. At the time of this writing, our largest ("main") facility is a flat-floored, renovated warehouse with a concrete floor and metal roof. We may get into something more substantial one day, but it will never be anything grandiose. We want our facilities to communicate that Jesus' commission was not to build a gigantic monument to him made out of bricks and mortar. He commissioned us to reach the world. Buildings are only *facilities*. Facilities *facilitate* the mission. They are only tools — means to the end — not the end itself. We have no problem with facilities being spacious, functional, comfortable, and even attractive, but we insist they be *facilities* and nothing more.

- We **highlight mission testimonies** in our services, on our websites, and in our publications. As I said earlier, what you celebrate, you replicate, so we choose to celebrate mission advance. Any chance we have to platform a missionary or church planter, we do it. When they return home, we greet them with a standing ovation.

- During the offering, we often **explain how giving is connected to mission**. If you ask us how much of our budget is dedicated to missions, we'll say "the whole thing." Every penny of our offering goes to advance the mission. I want the church to know that everything they give goes to advance a mission.

- We build sending into our **baptismal confession**. We ask each person before they are baptized: "Are you willing to go wherever he sends you, and do whatever he asks you?" Sometimes we show baptism video-testimonies from our church planting teams during our baptisms.

- We **"preach" the announcements**. Church announcements ought to offer specific ways by which people can engage in the mission. In many churches, the announcements only inform. We want our announcements to provide ways to apply the sermon. We try to find other ways besides "church announcements" to communicate information that doesn't serve a missional purpose.

- We **end every service with the phrase, "You are Sent."** We call it our "missional blessing." We got this idea from two places in the Bible. First, in Psalm 67, Asaph takes the traditional priestly blessing of Moses:

> The LORD bless you and keep you; the LORD make his face to shine upon you and be gracious to you; the LORD lift up his countenance upon you and give you peace. (Num. 6:24–26 ESV)

and transforms it into a missional prayer:

> May God be gracious to us and bless us and make his face to shine upon us, that your way may be known on earth, your saving power among all nations. (Ps. 67:1–2 ESV)

Second, at the end of Luke's gospel, Jesus gives what we see as a pattern for worship services, and it includes commissioning. He celebrates Communion with his disciples, expounds the Word to them, raises his hands, bestows on them the power of the Holy Spirit — and then commissions them to reach the nations (Luke 24:35 – 52). What better pattern for our worship services?

Most church services end with simply "You are dismissed." But does the church ever really "dismiss"? Don't we just gather for a few hours on the weekend so that we can scatter for mission throughout the week? In our view, "You are sent" communicates that better than "You are dismissed."

- We often get **international church planters to lead us in Communion** (via video), or get them to record a "You are sent" missional blessing that we show at the end of a service. Sometimes we flash up shots of our church plants doing Communion during the worship songs we sing while we are doing Communion. It helps our church connect what we are doing here to what they are doing there.

Missions is not a 401 class for mature saints ready for premium membership in Club Jesus. Missions is the very substance of our call to follow. When we separate mission from discipleship, not only do we thwart the mission, but we keep some from faith altogether.

If you are a pastor or church leader, I explain a little bit more in appendix 1 how you can set up an international missions strategy in your church. But the big takeaway in this chapter is this: *If we want to be sending churches, we cannot relegate "missions" to a specific department in the church.* Being a disciple means being sent; so sending should pervade every aspect of discipleship development. Everything we do and learn in the Christian faith ought to be in the context of the Great Commission.

CHAPTER 10

Racial Reconciliation as a Fruit of the Sending Culture

PLUMB LINE:

"We Seek to Live Multicultural Lives, Not Just Host Multicultural Events."

"If I could do it over again, I would pursue a racially diverse church even if it meant Willow Creek became only half the size it is today."

I heard Bill Hybels make that rather shocking statement at a breakfast I shared with him and some fellow Raleigh-Durham pastors back in 2006. It is quite a statement, considering that Hybels was a pioneer of the modern megachurch movement, practically inventing the "seeker service." Hybels built Willow Creek, a congregation that exceeds 25,000 weekend attenders, on the "homogeneity principle," which is the idea that you can reach more people if you package your "product" for a particular slice of society — in his case, professional, middle- to upper-class white people in the suburbs of Chicago.

Knowing his heart for evangelism, I pressed him: "So you would be willing to reach fewer people just so your church could be culturally diverse? Greater diversity outweighs total number of conversions?"

Without skipping a beat, Hybels replied, "Yes, but that's a false dichotomy. The corporate witness of racially diverse churches in America would be more powerful, and result in greater total number of conversions, than a numbers surge in any one congregation."

In this chapter I want to press home Hybels's point by arguing that the diversity of the church, reflecting the multiethnic nature of the body

---

161

of Christ, will be a powerful witness in today's world, one that is timely and prophetic for our generation. Our world knows that multicultural diversity is beautiful, but try as it may, seems unable to achieve it. We in the church have an opportunity to show that the gospel can accomplish what the world is incapable of. And, in line with the dominant theme of this book, I want to show you that the real potential for a multiethnic movement lies in the creation of a sending culture at your church.

Along the way I will share with you some things we, a historically white church, have learned as we have pursued multicultural diversification — insights that I hope both excite you about the possibilities as well as temper your expectations.

Why Even Try?

The first thing anyone who has tried to live multiculturally will tell you is that the novelty of being "multicolored" quickly wears off. It starts with an inspiring blog post and some token friends of color and a lot of "Hey, aren't we neat?" kinds of pleasantries. But that sentimentality quickly fades, and people go back to preferring friends more like them.

At some point, if you're serious about this, you'll ask, "Is it even worth the effort? Is this just the fad *de jour* of the contemporary church?"

But reflect on this: The author of multiculturalism is God, and he declared his desire for it in his church from the very beginning.

From Genesis 12 onward, we see a subplot at work in the unfolding story of redemption. God is not only bringing sinners back to himself, but is also bringing *together* the divergent ethnic and cultures that sin separated. The salvation that God promised to Abraham was not just an individual reconciliation with God; it is also an intercommunal, intercultural, and interracial reconciliation with one another.

On the day of Pentecost, the birth of the church, the author gives us a striking and *deliberate* picture of unity among ethnic diversity. The apostles, filled with the Holy Spirit, begin to preach the gospel in the languages of people from all around the world — languages they didn't speak and likely had never heard before — to a group of people from sixteen different geographical areas, ethnic groups, and racial categories (Acts 2:8–11). The significance of this cannot be overstated: The very first time the Holy Spirit preached the gospel, he *did* so in multiple languages simultaneously.

This wasn't a cool stunt or a one-time fluke. It flowed right out of the vision of the church that Jesus had painted for his disciples, a vision arising out of the ashes of God's purposes for the people of Israel: to be a light to the Gentiles (Isa. 49:6; Luke 2:32). Jesus viewed God's "house" as a place where people from every nation would come to pray (see Mark 11:17). In Revelation John sees believers from "every tribe and language and people and nation," united, in all their multicultural glory, in worship around Jesus' throne (Rev. 5:9; 21:26).

The church between Pentecost and Revelation is to be a "sign" of this coming kingdom, an "already/not yet" picture of what is to come. Paul explains that the unity in the church between people of diverse cultures and ethnic groups signifies to the world the multifaceted wisdom and power of God (Eph. 3:10–11). It is a sign of the coming age.

Think about that! According to Paul, the wisdom of God is most clearly demonstrated, not in eloquent, anointed preaching or exuberant, intense worship — but through racial and ethnic unity in the church.

In Acts 13:1–2, Luke takes special care to point out that the early church experienced this unity. In listing out the names of the church leaders in Antioch, he gives their nationalities, too. Paul and Barnabas were Jews, though neither of them was born in Israel. Manaen was from Herod's household, indicating a privileged Jewish upbringing. Simeon had the nickname "Niger" (which literally meant "black"), because he was from the region of sub-Saharan Africa. Lucius was from Cyrene, modern-day Libya. Of the five leaders mentioned, one was from the Middle East, one from Asia, one from the Mediterranean, and two were from Africa.

Why does Luke take the time to tell us the backgrounds and races of these church leaders? We don't hear anything about most of these leaders ever again. The only reason I can come up with is that Luke wanted to show us that the leadership in Antioch was multicultural. And is it a coincidence, then, that it is there in Antioch that the followers of Jesus are first called "Christians"? It was there, in their *unity*-in-diversity, that *they* came to be known *by the name of "Christ"* — *because no other factor could explain their amazing unity.*

It's About More Than Not Being a Racist

When you bring up the topic of racial diversity in most churches, many people think to themselves, "Well, I'm not a racist. So, I'm good!" But God's goal is not simply to have us stop looking down on other races. God wants unity, not just a ceasing of hostilities. He wants the very makeup of his church to preach the gospel: that despite our racial variants, we are united under one ancestor, Adam; we had one problem, sin; and one hope, salvation in Christ. He wants us to demonstrate to the world that this unity in Christ is weightier than anything that might divide us. When the Holy Spirit confronted Peter's racism, he didn't just command him to quit looking down on other races. He commanded Peter to *embrace* Cornelius, to go in and eat with him. Peter did not go from "racist" to "non-racist"; he went from "racist" to "gracist."

Thus, if your metric for success is only "have ceased to be racist," you haven't fully realized the gospel's goal. Christ is not after racial neutrality; he wants multicultural unity.

Only 5.5 percent of American churches today qualify as "multicultural," which sociologists generally define as no one race making up more than 80 percent of the congregation.[1] Full disclosure: at the Summit Church, we are not quite at the 20 percent diverse marker yet (currently, we are at 15 percent), but by God's grace we are getting close. And we are tenfold farther along than we were five years ago!

Multicultural diversity is in the very DNA of the gospel, and a Spirit-filled church will naturally drift toward this diversification. We see this reflected even in how the gospel has spread down through history: Christianity has roughly 20 percent of its followers in Africa, 20 percent in Asia, 20 percent in Europe, 20 percent in North America, and 20 percent in South America. Every other major religion has at least 80 percent of its followers concentrated on one continent. Christianity, statistically speaking, has no dominant culture. It is the most diverse movement in history.

So the fact that the majority of churches in the United States are predominately one culture is an abnormality. Thus, how can a white — or black, Asian, Hispanic, or Arab — church achieve multicultural diversification in its local fellowship?

Elevating Our "Third Race"

To achieve unity-in-diversity, each member must elevate their "third race."[2] Think of your "first race" as whatever race or ethnicity you were born into, and a "second race" as all the races you are not. The third race is the new person that God has made you in Christ.

When you become a Christian, you don't cease to be your first race, nor do you assimilate into the second race of the people who brought you to Christ (if they were different from you). Instead, you become a part of a new race, a third race, though still maintaining your first race. In that third race you find a unity with other believers that supersedes any differences that come from distinctions in your first races. In Christ, Paul says, "there is neither Jew nor Greek, there is neither slave nor free, there is neither male nor female" (Gal. 3:28 ESV). He did not mean that we cease to be Jews or Greeks when we get saved any more than we cease to be male or female. Our race in Christ simply becomes *weightier* than any other distinctions — of gender, culture, or socioeconomic status.

God is not colorblind, and neither should we be. There's no bleach line in heaven where God makes us all the same. Revelation 21:26 says that God brings into heaven "the wealth and the honor" of the nations, which means he wants in heaven the rich varieties of culture. In that great throng of believers worshiping together around the Lamb's throne, we still have distinctions of race, culture, and language (Rev. 5:9–11). It will be beautiful.

When our third race becomes our weightiest identity, unity becomes a possibility. We will always have ethnic preferences, of course, and there is nothing wrong with having those. I don't need to hide the fact that I was born in West Virginia to a white family of Dutch and Scottish descent. I grew up in central North Carolina, and that shaped my tastes in music, food, clothing, and what I see as proper etiquette. I can appreciate those things without letting them become more defining for me than being "in Christ."

The apostle Paul, a "Jew of the Jews," was thoroughly Jewish, but he wore his Jewishness lightly. In 1 Corinthians he said, in fact, that to the Jews he "became like a Jew" (9:20). *Wasn't Paul already a Jew?* Why would he need to become like a Jew if he already was one? Evidently, Paul no longer saw his ethnicity as *primary* to his identity. He was still Jewish, of course — and would never deny that — but his Jewishness was something so "light" to him that he could take it on and off like a garment. His *third race* — being in Christ — was more permanent, more central, and weightier to him than even his Jewish racial, ethnic, and cultural identity.

Recently a nonwhite friend and member of our church told me that our music, service length, and behavior in church are much different from what he is accustomed to, "but I so resonate with the gospel and mission here that all those other distinctions don't seem that important anymore." His *third race* hasn't eliminated his first preferences; it has overshadowed them, however, and given him unity with a group of people he wouldn't otherwise choose to hang out with.

We Must Balance Multiculturalism with the Need to Reach Whatever Majority Culture Is Around Us

Multiculturalism is a wonderful and inevitable product of the gospel, but it is not the only assignment, or even primary assignment, given to the church. Jesus identified "making disciples" as the core of the Great Commission. Thus, we must balance our efforts at diversification with the need to reach the entire community around us. To do that, Paul says, we must adopt the cultural patterns of those around us, becoming "a Greek to the Greeks." It makes sense, then, that a lot of our cultural adaptation would be weighted toward the majority culture around us.

You reach Greeks best when you put the gospel into Greek clothes, Greek expressions, and Greek styles (1 Cor. 9:19–21). Paul didn't expect the lost Greeks to become multicultural appreciators of Jewish or Ethiopian culture before they were saved, so he said he would adapt himself as closely as he could to the culture of the Greeks in order to reach those Greeks.

Certain outreaches are best done on homogenous grounds — athletes typically reach athletes best, professors often reach professors best, and yes, one ethnic group is typically most effective at reaching those of their own group. *That's not wrong*. It is recognizing a characteristic of human nature and accommodating yourself to it, just as Paul did.

So we must balance our pursuit of multicultural unity with God's command to make disciples of as many people as possible as fast as possible. It seems that some ministries put so much emphasis on a good thing (multiculturalism) that it has distracted them from the chief thing: making disciples. This is not to say we don't lead disciples toward multiculturalism (that's part of what it means to be a disciple), just that we can't always start there.

Furthermore, local churches this side of heaven will only be a pale reflection of the multicultural unity we will one day experience in heaven; only a *sign*, and not the fulfillment, of the coming kingdom. At our very best, our reflection will be partial and distorted. This side of heaven, diversification has limits — if for no other reason than we don't all speak the same language! Language is the most basic element of a culture, and church services, for the most part, can only be conducted in one language.

Furthermore, geography makes certain kinds of multiculturalism impractical. To judge a church in Northern Ireland for not being multicultural when their entire community for miles around is white would be unfair. Only in heaven will we experience the fulfillment of multiculturalism. Can *any* church on earth say it truly "looks like heaven" yet? I know several multicultural churches that have achieved remarkable diversity, but no one church has the rich diversity or absolute unity we see in Revelation 5:9–11, where even language distinctions don't seem to be a problem.

I personally don't know any churches that feature *both* Arabic and Inuit music in their services, even though both of those groups will be worshiping side by side around God's throne one day. Maybe such a church does exist, and I suspect someday I'll get a note from a reader telling me they attend that very church, but you get the point: While churches can be a reflection of the coming unity, we will not experience its fulfillment until Jesus returns. Even though all the different nationalities in Acts 2 heard Peter preaching in their own tongues, that has never happened to local Hispanic or Chinese residents around here while I preached. So we have separate services for them in which they can hear a preacher preach in their native tongue.

Thus we must balance our pursuit of multiculturalism with the need to adapt our message into the cultural forms of the community around us. Here is an example of how we are trying to pursue both unity and effective outreach at the same time: We have a Hispanic campus at our church that reaches hundreds of Hispanics. These Hispanic brothers and sisters don't join in with the English speakers for most of our services, because they wouldn't be edified by a message they can't understand. But the Hispanic leadership in our church has chosen *not* to launch out as their own church (even though we gave them that option), because they want to remain in corporate unity with their English-speaking brothers and sisters as a sign to our community of our unity in the gospel. So each week our Hispanic pastor takes whatever text I am preaching and preaches it to our Hispanic congregation in Spanish. We are one body, under one government, meeting in the same facility, but worshiping in two different rooms and in two different languages.

Some churches seem to confuse multiculturalism with the gospel itself. I've even heard some talk about "the gospel of racial reconciliation." While I understand their heart, I think that's deadly dangerous nomenclature. The gospel is fundamentally about God's reconciliation of us to himself in Christ (a vertical reconciliation), and the *fruit* of that reconciliation is reconciliation with everything else (horizontal reconciliations), including racial reconciliation. (As a general rule of thumb, anytime you hear "the gospel of . . ." and what follows is something other than *Christ's* finished work on the cross, chances are a fruit of salvation is being substituted for its means!)

Majority Cultures Must Give and Adapt, Too

Many majority culture believers *say* they want a multicultural church, but when you get down to it, they really don't. They want a group of people of different races coming together to worship in *their* style. You might say they want a *multicolored* church, not a *multicultural* one.[3]

"Do you want to know how you know you are in a multicultural church?" a friend of mine asks. "Frequently you feel uncomfortable." If you're not feeling uncomfortable, he says, chances are you are in a church still dominated by your own cultural preferences. I once had a white college student tell me that he wished our church were more multicultural. I told him to keep praying with me about that. A few weeks later he told me that he didn't like how one of our worship leaders jumped around on stage and told everyone to raise their hands, and he wanted to know if I would tell that leader to back off a little. I suggested to him that maybe he didn't really want a multicultural church after all, just a bunch of different-colored people worshiping in his preferred style.

The majority culture must learn to sacrifice its preferences, too. In fact, they should lead the way, because that is the way of the gospel. Those in a position of "strength," Paul says, are to serve those in a position of weakness. Paul tells the Philippians to follow the example of Christ in considering others' preferences more important than their own (2:1–5). Certainly that would have included their preferences of culture. Christians in positions of strength, including cultural strength, are to leverage that to serve not themselves, but those in positions of weakness. Majority cultures in churches may not have to give up their cultural preferences in order to grow numerically, but if they want to serve the minority cultures around them, they will elevate some of that culture's preferences above their own.

Does that sound like I am contradicting my previous point about a church needing to weigh its adaptation to the majority culture around it? Maybe I am, a little. You have to balance these two principles.

It Is About the Music. It Isn't About the Music.

On that note, let me address what is probably the thorniest issue Western churches deal with as they pursue diversification: conflicting preferences in music and worship styles. Here is something important I have had to learn about diversification, in all its contradictory glory:

1. DIVERSITY IS NOT JUST ABOUT THE MUSIC.

Some people say, "You want black people in your church? Play gospel music. Want Latinos? Play salsa music. Want rural people? Play bluegrass. Want them all? Play a little of each."

That rarely works. If anything, it just reinforces the differences between us.

Gospel unity is about something far beyond uniformity on what constitutes good music and good worship experiences. Gospel unity is primarily about intentional relationships and a disposition of humility toward others.

2. AT THE SAME TIME, DIVERSITY IS ABOUT THE MUSIC.

There's just no getting around this: Musical style seems to be the biggest practical sticking point churches encounter as they pursue multiculturalism. *Everybody* loves their preferred worship expression, and they can't understand people who don't like what they like.

We have some traditional Southern Baptists at our church, and during the musical portion of the service, they sing boisterously while keeping their hands firmly glued to their sides. Occasionally one puts up a hand shoulder high or, during a reflective song, they put out both hands in front of them as if they are trying to carry a TV set. But that is about it. When I stand up to preach, they pull out notebooks and feverishly take notes as if they are writing down directions for a recipe, slipping in an occasional, rousing "Amen!," especially when I alliterate a point.

We also have some black members who jump and dance (and occasionally run) during worship, and some often attempt to carry on full conversations with me while I am preaching (not "Amens," but sentences with subjects and verbs and adverbs).

There are also Korean believers who sing so energetically during worship that I sometimes wonder if someone is going to get hurt. They yell (not sing, but *yell*) the songs, and sometimes I think they are trying to jump up to heaven to give Jesus a high-five. During the preaching, however, they sit back and don't make a sound. (I asked one why they are so demonstrative in singing and so demur during the preaching, and they said that in their culture it is rude to talk while someone else is talking, particularly when someone is teaching. So their silence is reflective of respect.)

Which of those behaviors is "best practice" in worship?

Well, Amen.

Some of the more expressive cultures in our church look with consternation at believers who remain unemotional in the presence of so great a God. They point out that we scream our heads off at basketball games, but we won't do the same for the God of the universe? Why would King James (LeBron James) deserve a more rousing response than King Jesus?

On the other side, there are those who feel that aggressively "charismatic" worship leaders play on emotion, building crowd dynamics, and then unjustifiably labelling that "the Spirit." Loud music, shouting, and a charismatic leader, they say, can get a crowd worked up regardless of the subject matter. Furthermore, unbelievers in the Western context are *very* skeptical of emotional moments they perceive as contrived — especially when you label those moments "the Spirit of God." So if you want to reach unchurched Western people, you must guard against "emotionalism."

Which culture's concerns are more valid?

Umm ... Well, again, *Amen.*

Both sides bring truths that need to be heard. What is wrong is for either side to declare the other's concerns *invalid*. We must study our Bibles, analyze our given contexts, and be open to worshiping together with others who express themselves in different ways than we do. Again, the sign of being in a multicultural church is that sometimes you feel uncomfortable, because in a multicultural church there's a strong chance that the person beside you, or on the stage in front of you, might be doing things differently from how you do them.

We sometimes use the analogy of beef stew to illustrate how we think racial diversity will play out in our church. We don't want to be a bag of marbles, where each culture exists side by side in a congregation but with interpenetration with the others. We also don't want to be a melting pot, however, where each culture loses its distinctive flavor. If you mix a hundred different paint colors together, you end up with a dull gray. We want the church to be like beef stew, where each element retains its basic consistency but "flavors" the others, too. That's cheeky, for sure, but it helps us picture what racial diversification might look like in a local body.

The Staff Should Stay "Ahead" of the Congregation in Diversity

If we want to see multiculturalism take root in our churches, we must prioritize diversity in our leadership. Leadership sets the tone for the congregation to follow. The church in Acts 13 seems to have prioritized — and prized — diverse leadership, elevating and celebrating it. Eventually, the rest of the church followed suit.

Some people object, "But isn't prioritizing diversity in leadership just tokenism?" Tokenism, as I understand it, is when either (1) you have no intention of *actually* giving away authority and just want a different colored face up front to make it look as if your leadership is diverse; or (2) you put an unqualified person in a position of leadership *simply* because of their skin color.

Tokenism is insincere, but intentionally pursuing diversity in leadership is different. Pursuing diversity deliberately in your leadership sends a signal about your intentions: "We may not yet be as diverse as we want to be, but this is where we want to go." I once visited a large, all-black church with a white friend. I think my friend and I were the only white people in the whole place, and I felt like everyone was looking at us, wondering, "Why are you here?" They were extremely friendly to us, but I still felt out of place.

If just one white person had walked across the stage, I would have felt, "Oh, I belong here. He's like me." Maybe I shouldn't have felt the way I did, but the fact is, I did. That experience helped me understand how blacks, Hispanics, Asians, or Arabs must feel when they step into our church and see nothing but a sea of white.

We try to have minority presence in positions of leadership in every service at the Summit Church, and we have elevated several new pastors and elders of color into senior leadership positions on our team. We have begun training numerous others for future leadership positions. We have seen the number of qualified pastors and leaders of color multiply as we do so. As of this writing, 60 percent of our central worship staff is black, and four of our eight campus pastors are nonwhite.

The point of pursuing diverse leadership is not to present an image, but to actually bring a diversity of backgrounds and perspectives to the table. This kind of cultural diversification will rarely happen without intentionality. Left to ourselves, we veer back to the ditch of homogeneity. Achieving diversity takes intentional, diligent gospel leadership.

Live Multicultural Lives, Not Multicultural Events

Gospel multiculturalism is not a weekend show; it is a way of life.

Before you bemoan the lack of diversity in your church, ask yourself: Are *you* pursuing intentional friendships with people of other races?

This interpersonal connection is more important than finding a worship style that white, black, and Hispanic people all like. God did not call us to put on a multicultural display on the weekend; he called us to live out a multicultural wonder the whole week. When we begin to live multicultural lives, our events will naturally take on a multicultural flavor.

Some of us should consider cross-cultural engagement in our own communities a "calling." Multicultural engagement within your city, like international missions, is something that *all* believers are expected to participate in, but that God moves certain believers to pursue with focused intentionality. The apostle Paul was in that category. Some of us (under the leadership of the Spirit) need to make this cause *our* cause. After all, it makes no sense to send people 10,000 miles across the globe to reach people of other cultures when we won't send people ten miles across our own city to reach people in different neighborhoods. Why would we cross the seas but not the tracks?

Earlier in this book I brought up our "Dwell" initiative, in which singles and families from our church have intentionally moved into a different, less culturally familiar neighborhood for the purpose of integrating their lives and living out the gospel there. It has turned out to be a powerful testimony to our community. Perhaps you should pray about God sending you, or a group of friends from your church, into another part of your own community to live out the gospel this way.

Even if you're not specially "called" to focus on this, however, we are all commanded to *intentionally* form relationships with people outside of our comfort zones. In that way, Paul said, we model Christ (Phil. 2:1–5) and declare the multifaceted, richly beautiful wisdom of God (Eph. 3:10–11). Following Jesus means going "outside the camp," even in your own city or school (Heb. 13:13).

We Are at a *Kairos* Moment Regarding Race

The Declaration of Independence of the United States made the greatest statement about the equality of races ever put forward in a secular government document: *"We hold these truths to be self-evident, that all men are created equal."* Yet, before the ink on the page was dry, many of its framers had returned home to their slaves.

Our country has always had the highest aspirations on this issue, but we have never been able to achieve the racial harmonization we desire. Even today.

I saw a recent article in *The Atlantic* magazine that showed how even those individuals who say they *prefer* mixed-race neighborhoods still gravitate toward neighbors of their own race once they have moved into those neighborhoods.[4] Racial integration works better as a theory than as a sociological reality.

What the world wants, the gospel accomplishes. Paul said, "For what the law was powerless to do because it was weakened by the flesh, God did by sending his own Son ..." (Rom. 8:3). The United States Constitution, like all *laws*, is sufficient to tell us how we *should* be, but insufficient to *make* us that way. For fallen human nature, laws function like railroad tracks: they lay out the path we *ought* to travel on, but are powerless to move us along the tracks.

The gospel is the engine that moves us toward fulfillment of the law. African-American pastor Tony Evans says,

> Our racial divide is a disease. Over-the-counter human remedies won't fix it; they merely mask the symptoms for a season. What we need is a prescription from the Creator to destroy this cancer before it destroys us. It is my contention that if the church can ever get this issue of oneness right, then we can help America to finally become the 'one nation under God' that we declare ourselves to be.[5]

That prescription is the gospel. Evans continues,

> The reason we haven't solved the race problem in America after hundreds of years is that people apart from God are trying to create unity, while people under God who already have unity are not living out the unity we possess. The result of both of these conditions is disastrous for

America. Our failure to find cultural unity as a nation is directly related to the church's failure to preserve our spiritual unity. The church has already been given unity because we've been made part of the same family.[6]

When the church demonstrates the unity between races that our society yearns for, we will show that there is only one God who can save, only one God who accomplishes that for which our hearts yearn.

Sadly, however, it seems like the majority of the Western church is still *behind* the world in racial integration. We all know Martin Luther King Jr.'s famous quip, *"Eleven o'clock on Sunday morning is the most segregated hour in America."* Movies frequently depict churches as racist and bigoted. While some of that depiction may be unwarranted, much of it is based in truth.

The racial unity our nation thinks it is achieving, however, frequently reveals itself to be an illusion, and most sociologists recognize that. In the last decade, numerous events have revealed the deep divide remaining between whites and blacks in the United States: the Duke Lacrosse case; the Trayvon Martin shooting; and the death of Michael Brown in Ferguson, Missouri, being recent examples. Recent discoveries of email correspondence between Hollywood executives reveal a deep racial divide among the people who often fulminate the loudest against racial injustice.[7]

That's why I say we, in the church, are at a *kairos* moment regarding race. *Kairos* is a Greek word for time that implies a specially appointed moment. I believe that God has appointed this moment for the church in the West to demonstrate a unity in Christ that the world yearns for but has yet been unable to obtain. What the flesh is unable to do through the law, God does by his Spirit through the gospel.

Rodney Stark, in *The Rise of Christianity*, points to the multicultural unity of the early church as among the primary factors that led to its growth explosion. The Roman Empire, he says, brought various cultures into close proximity in megacities for the first time in human history. Unprecedented racial strife plagued these cities. Local churches, Stark says, were the one place in the Roman Empire where races got along without social hierarchies.[8] As the Roman world watched in amazement, these Christians explained that their unity came from the fact that Jesus was not raised from the dead for their sins as a Jew, or a Greek, or a Roman, but as the Lord of *all* humanity and the Savior of *all* races.

I believe we are in just such a *kairos* moment today. Humanity has a common problem, sin, and a common Savior, Jesus. Multiculturalism in the church puts on display our common humanity and common salvation and glorifies the Firstborn of *all* creation.

The great news is that the Spirit of God really wants to do this, so we have to just stay out of his way. The apostle Paul charged the Ephesians to "preserve" the unity of the church (4:3). *Preserve* means he didn't expect the Ephesians to create it — the gospel and the Spirit would do that. They just needed to cultivate and protect it. The Spirit does the heavy lifting.

If we will step back, I believe the Spirit will do a marvelous work of unification in our generation.

Multiculturalism 2.0: Church Planting

Maybe you are wondering how all this applies to the theme of this book: *The future belongs to churches that send.*

It does in at least three ways: First, as Bill Hybels said, you may sometimes have to choose (temporarily, at least) between a numbers surge you can achieve through homogenous ministry and building a multicultural community of faith.

Like Hybels, I believe the long-term evangelistic effectiveness of a multicultural church will be greater than the temporary jolt of a numbers surge brought on a homogenous ministry. A group of 25,000 white people gathering to listen to great music and an entertaining speaker is not really a demonstration of the power of God. It happens in a Justin Bieber concert. By contrast, a group of people who come together around Christ when they have little else in common declares that God has the power to save.

Second, in order to achieve multicultural unity, churches and individual believers are going to have to learn to live "sent" to the other cultures right in their own cities, cultures distant and unfamiliar to them right in their backyards. If churches continue to coast along, simply watching to see who shows up in church each week, in five years the Christian society will be no more multicultural than it is today.

Third, the greatest displays of multicultural unity will probably happen in the churches we plant, churches that write this into their DNA from the beginning.

Civil rights activist John Perkins, after preaching at our church, said to me,

> The American church will probably soon achieve the levels of diversity many of us have always yearned for, and always knew were possible ... but mostly likely not through majority churches diversifying themselves — though they should pursue that. It will come through the planting of new, deliberately multicultural churches.

As many parents realize, our "children" can be greater than us. They can learn from our mistakes and stand on our shoulders to achieve heights we have only dreamed of.

This is not to say we established churches should not be pursuing diversity, too, just that it will come more naturally to our "children." As I noted, the Summit Church is a large, majority-white church that has been pursuing cultural diversification, and by God's grace, we are making progress. But we are excited to see what God does through churches we plant that establish this as one of their values from the beginning.

So, even in this, the future belongs to churches that send.

CHAPTER 11

There's More Than
One Way to Be Wicked

PLUMB LINE:

"Risk Is Right."

During my first year of college, a group of us traveled out to a box canyon called "Split Rock" about an hour away from our campus. The
canyon was hard to find — you had to park your car at an unmarked spot
on the highway and walk about a hundred yards into the woods, where
you would hear the unmistakable sounds of a pounding waterfall. When
you heard that sound, you had to pay attention because, almost without
warning, the ground at your feet dropped away, and 40 feet below you
lay the pool basin of a waterfall.

I'm not sure who figured this out first, but if you got a slight run, you
could jump off of the cliff and plunge into the pool. But here was the
thing: The distance you had to cover horizontally to clear the slightly
sloping canyon walls was longer than you could clear in a broad jump
(about 10 feet). Because you were in the air for so long, however, if
you jumped hard, your forward momentum would enable you to clear
(pretty easily) that horizontal distance, plunging safely into the waterfall
pool basin below, which was more than 30 feet deep.

Was I one of the ones who jumped? Well, since my mother may read
this book some day, and maybe my son when he grows up, I will take
the Fifth. But I will tell you, what an exhilarating experience it was as
your feet left the side of that cliff and you sliced through the air to the
icy water below.

Taking risks is always frightening, yet few of life's rewards come without them. (And, to note, I am not saying that this risk was a wise one or that the payoff was worth it ... and Adon, son, if you read this someday, you are NOT allowed to do this!)

For many of the most important things in life, you will never clear the distance unless you leap with abandon. That certainly is true if you're going to be a sending church, or sending parent, or sending person.

To All Would-Be Disciples: Risk Required

Jesus told a story about a rich boss who left behind sums of money for his servants to invest that established risk-taking as a necessary component of true discipleship. To one servant he gave five "talents," to another two, to another one. (A talent was a rather large unit of money: about twenty years' salary![1] So, to one man he gave twenty years' salary (on our terms, about a million dollars); to another, double that; and to another, a hundred years' worth.

> He who had received the five talents went at once and traded with them, and he made five talents more.
>
> So also he who had the two talents made two talents more. But he who had received the one talent went and dug in the ground and hid his master's money. (Matt. 25:16–18 ESV)

The man with two million turned it into four, and the man with five turned it into ten. When the master returned, he commended the first two servants for their wise investment of his resources. But to the one that sat on it, he said:

> "You *wicked* and *slothful* servant! You knew that I reap where I have not sowed and gather where I scattered no seed? Then you ought to have invested my money with the bankers, and at my coming I should have received what was my own with interest. So take the talent from him and give it to him who has the ten talents. For to everyone who has will more be given, and he will have an abundance. But from the one who has not, even what he has will be taken away. And cast the worthless servant into the outer darkness. In that place there will be weeping and gnashing of teeth." (Matt. 25:26–30 ESV)

Two things about that parable grip me. First, Jesus *commended* the first two servants for taking a risk with *his* money. Investing it means they could have lost it. That's the nature of investing: no guarantees! Yet, Jesus doesn't say, "What were you thinking? You could have lost all my money!" Instead, he commended them.

The second thing that stands out is even more startling, however: He called the one who did not take the risk "wicked."

Wicked?

What had he done? There seems to be no stealing, immorality, or even reckless irresponsibility involved. He didn't blow the master's money on partying, prostitutes, gambling, or first-class accommodations in the Caribbean. In fact, he had not spent a single penny on himself. He returned 100 percent of what he had been given to the master.

And for that, Jesus called him "wicked."

Most of us tend to think about wickedness only in terms of bad things that we *do*. But according to this parable, "wicked" can apply as much to what we *don't do* as to what we do. Failure to risk our lives to the fullest potential for the kingdom of God is as wicked as the most egregious violations of the laws of God.

Let that sink in for a minute.

The question is not just whether you have done bad things; the question is whether you have done the right things with the good things God has given you.

Growing, But Wicked, Churches?

Typically, we apply this parable to individuals, but I want to encourage local churches to apply it to themselves as a whole.

As we have discussed throughout this book, most churches tend to judge their success only by their size, so they spend the lion's share of their resources on growing their congregation. Of course, growing a church and reaching the community can be a wise investment of kingdom resources. But what if Jesus saw our reticence to *send out* some of our best leaders and resources as an attempt to sit on his blessings to us, to safely guard them instead of scattering them into the harvest so they could multiply? *Might he also call us "wicked"?* If we only spend money to bring in people who will enhance our bottom line, we are not being risky in our investment at all. When you spend money on things that grow your attendance, you experience the reward of your "investments" immediately.

Might Jesus say to church leaders who have devoted all their resources to things that increase their own comfort and prestige in this world what he, in essence, said to the Pharisees: "You already have your reward" (see Matt. 6:2–4)?

As I have explained throughout this book, sending is both costly and risky. You give up some of your best people, divest yourself of precious resources, and exert emotional energy to see something flourish somewhere else. But we do so because the Master has told us to invest what he gave us, to send it out into the field so that it can multiply. Jesus gave us what he gave us so that we could create greater return for his kingdom, not so we could have more to sit on for ourselves.

Each May we commission teams going out from our church to plant churches that fall. Each domestic plant is led by at least one resident planter who has spent nine months on our staff preparing for the plant, recruiting other Summit members to go with them. As these teams stretch across the stage, I typically see leaders who have led vital ministries in our church. I see friends. I see faithful volunteers and big givers — because people missional enough to join a church planting team are usually the kind that are sacrificially generous. I told one church planter that my name for his team is "a new sound system," and another "that high-tech lighting package." Looking across that stage I see a lot of "things" I would like to keep at our church. But I know that those rewards do not compare to the reward the Master will one day give us if we have invested faithfully.

Yet, still … I feel the fear. What happens if the 160 we sent out this past year aren't replaced? What if no one steps up to fill the gaps they leave? What if new givers don't rise up to replace the money these 160 will no longer give to us?

Well… that's just a risk we have to take. To not take those kinds of risks would be wicked.

The Guaranteed Bankruptcy of Not Taking Risks

What is more: Not taking those risks *ensures* our decline. The servant who refused to risk had even the one talent he held onto taken away from him.

The nation of Israel in the time of Moses did not take the risks God laid out for them. Ten of the twelve spies Moses sent out to survey the Promised Land came back and said, "The land is good ... but there are giants, and we are like nothing but grasshoppers to them!" Only two of the spies, Joshua and Caleb, countered: "Yes, but what are the giants to God? He promised us victory. It's worth the risk!" (see Num. 13:26–33).

God called the report of those ten spies "evil" (Num. 13:32), even though every word of their report was true.[2]

Risking for God is dangerous; but *not* risking is *more* dangerous.

When Jesus taught the principle of the harvest in John 12:24, he said that those who "hold on" to their lives surely will lose them. That means if we hold on to our resources, our leaders, or our power, we surely will lose them. In the kingdom of God, what you hold on to, you lose, and what you give away, you keep. What Jim Elliott, martyred missionary in Ecuador, said is as applicable to pastors and churches as it is to individual believers: "He is no fool who gives up what he cannot keep to gain that which he cannot lose."[3]

God has blessed our church so much since we began to devote ourselves to sending. Every dollar we have put into church planting has multiplied at least ten times in terms of how much these churches now gather for the kingdom. And I believe God "credits" their success to our account. The joy we have watching our plants baptize people exceeds even the joy we have baptizing people of our own. Like the first and second servant in Jesus' parable, we have the joy of knowing we have placed the resources of our church in his hands and that we have all of eternity to share in the ROI. God really is "enriching us in every way" as we leverage our resources for his kingdom (2 Cor. 9:11). But every time we give something significant away, we face the fear that this time it will not work out.

Blessed Are the Aggressive

Throughout Scripture, we see the kingdom of God advancing through risk — risk with no guarantee the gamble will pay off. When David took on Goliath, he took a risk. We don't see anywhere in Scripture that God *told* David to fight Goliath or verbally assured him he would get the victory. David simply found himself in a place with a defiant giant, whereupon he picked up some rocks and trusted that God would knock him down (see 1 Sam. 17).

King David's best friend, Jonathan, *took a risk* against an entire garrison of Philistine soldiers when he had only one companion (1 Sam. 14:1 – 6). Jonathan was out in the wilderness with only his armor bearer and a couple of swords when he encountered the hiding Philistine platoon. Rather than do the smart thing and wait for backup, he and the armor bearer decided to take on the entire garrison by themselves. More accurately, *Jonathan* decided to do it. Listen to how he invited his armor bearer to join him:

> "Come, let's go over to the outpost of those uncircumcised men. *Perhaps* the LORD will act in our behalf. Nothing can hinder the LORD from saving, whether by many or by few." (1 Sam. 14:6)

Uhhh … *perhaps*? I'm sorry, bro, but if you are inviting me to take on an entire, fortified garrison of trained Philistine soldiers, then I'm going to need more than your "perhaps." Yet, they took the risk, and God gave the victory (1 Sam. 14:11 – 15).

Shadrach, Meshach, and Abednego *took a risk* in defying King Nebuchadnezzar. We see no place in Daniel 3 where God told the three college-aged young men that he would deliver them from Nebuchadnezzar's fiery furnace. In fact, in their response to the king I hear a curious mixture of certainty and uncertainty:

> "The God we serve is able to deliver us from [the blazing furnace], and he will deliver us from Your Majesty's hand." (Dan. 3:17)

That sounds like certainty, but then they turn around and say,

> "But even if he does not, we want you to know, Your Majesty, that we will not serve your gods or worship the image of gold you have set up." (v. 18)

If not …? Why the sudden flash of uncertainty? Because God had given them no assurance they would walk out of the furnace unscathed. Going into the fiery furnace was a risk they had to take. And God delivered.

Esther *took a risk* when she appealed the fate of the Jews before loony King Artaxerxes. She had no idea what his response would be. We know this, because she said to her Uncle Mordecai before she went, "If I perish, I perish" (Est. 4:15 – 16).

Paul's entire life was *one risk after another* (Acts 20:23; 2 Cor. 11:24 – 28). John Piper, who wrote a book called *Risk Is Right*, says of Paul,

> [He] never knew where the next blow would come from. Every day he risked his life for the cause of God. The roads weren't safe. The rivers weren't safe. His own people, the Jews, weren't safe. The Gentiles weren't safe. The cities weren't safe. The wilderness wasn't safe. The sea wasn't safe. Even the so-called Christian brothers weren't safe. Safety was a mirage. It simply didn't exist for the apostle Paul.[4]

Piper concludes: *"The Christian life is a call to risk. You either live with risk or waste your life."*

We say, "God, I want some kind of guarantee!" He doesn't give one. Planting, sending, investing, going — all take leaps of faith. Yet without risk, the kingdom of God does not advance.

Piper says, "It is the will of God that we be uncertain about how life on earth will turn out for us, and … that we take risks for the cause of God."[5]

Paul: *My* Ambition

I am certainly not saying that every desire to risk is from God. Sometimes the wise thing to do is hide in the woods and wait to fight another day. King David walked away from quite a few fights, and Paul had himself smuggled out of a city to avoid a confrontation (Acts 9:25).

Following Jesus means asking the Holy Spirit what risks he wants you to take for his kingdom. The whole of the Great Commission is too big for any one person, so the Holy Spirit narrows it into specific assignments for you. You are not called to take every risk — as Larry Osborne once explained to me, "Not everything that comes from heaven has your name on it." Something does, however, and we are responsible to find the garrisons of Philistines that God has for us — and then take the risks in pursuit of them.

At the end of the book of Romans the apostle Paul reveals a narrowing of his ministry focus he experienced toward the end of his life. "*My* ambition," he says, is to preach Christ where he has never been named (Rom. 15:20 ESV). His ministry focus, you see, had started really wide: he debated Jews in the synagogue, helped build up the first churches, and preached to Jews and Gentiles alike. But as his life progressed, God narrowed his focus onto one thing — preaching Christ where he had never been named — and Paul made that his *personal* ambition. He was willing to take whatever risks necessary to fulfill that ambition (see, for example, Rom. 15:31; Acts 20:22–24).

God does that for each of his followers. What part of the mission has the Holy Spirit elevated to be your "personal ambition"? Maybe God is calling you to start a Bible study in your workplace, to get involved in your church's ministry to children, to start the process of fostering or adoption, or to pursue a career field that lacks a gospel presence. Maybe he is leading you to move to an under-resourced part of your city or putting it into your heart to live out the gospel in an unreached people group. Maybe he is urging your church to give away more money for church planting next year than you have ever dreamed possible, or maybe to start the process of planting your first church.

Those are things the Holy Spirit will have to show you himself. But whatever it is, I can assure you it will involve risk.

A Certain Savior for an Uncertain Risk

To return to our parable, do you ever wonder what character quality separated the first two servants in Jesus' parable from the third? In other words, *why* were they able to risk for the master when the third one couldn't?

I think we find a clue in how the third servant responded to the master:

"Master, I knew you to be a hard man, reaping where you did not sow, and gathering where you scattered no seed, so I was afraid, and I went and hid your talent in the ground. Here you have what is yours." (Matt. 25:24–25 ESV)

The third servant did not trust his master's goodness. Apparently, the other two servants knew that their master was gracious — and also competent enough to handle any mistakes they made in pursuit of their risk.

Every great risk in God's name begins with *confidence in the goodness and trustworthiness of God*. The woman who touched Jesus' garment received healing from him because she believed in his goodness (Luke 8:45–46). The Gentile woman who coerced Jesus to heal her daughter did so because she knew there was so much grace in Jesus' heart that "even the little dogs," like her,[6] could have some (Matt. 15:27 NKJV).

The story is told that Alexander the Great had a general who approached him after many years of service to ask if he would pay for the wedding of his daughter. Alexander agreed and told him to obtain the funds needed from the treasurer. Soon thereafter the treasurer came to Alexander, complaining that this general was taking advantage of Alexander's generosity. He was asking for an exorbitant amount of money, enough to host the largest wedding Greece had ever seen.

Alexander thought about the situation for a moment, then waved his hand dismissively and said, "Grant him his request in full." The treasurer looked bewildered. Alexander continued, "My general pays me two compliments: He believes that I am rich enough to afford his request and that I am generous enough to grant it. In assuming these two things, he honors me."

Our God is so good, gracious, and powerful that we can never ask or assume too much of him. We don't offend him with large requests; we offend him with small ones! John Newton said it this way in his hymn "Come, My Soul, Thy Suit Prepare":

Thou art coming to a King, large petitions with thee bring!

For his grace and power are such, none can ever ask too much.

Any worthwhile kingdom attempt involves risk. C. S. Lewis said that the way to know you are living by faith is that what you are doing for

God *scares* you. If it doesn't, he said, there is no faith involved.[7] So get comfortable with being scared. We have a Master who not only has commanded us to risk, but also has promised us that as we do so, led by his Spirit, he will multiply our investments in the harvest of his kingdom.

Our church has asked God to allow us to plant 1,000 churches and bless 1,000 cities by 2050. We want to send out 5,000 people as a part of those church planting teams. We have started a pastor training school that will train pastors and church leaders. We have asked God to let us baptize 50,000 people in the Raleigh-Durham area. We have asked him to let us be part of major awakenings in Muslim and European nations. Each year we try to give away more money and send out more leaders than we feel we can afford. Only when our giving scares us do we know we are getting close to target.

Some well-meaning people have called our vision "grandiose"; others, "foolish." We believe, however, it is the required faithfulness to a Master who entrusted us with a small pile of talents to invest until he returns. He is gracious and powerful enough to compensate for our incompetence and would rather have us risk too much than play it too safe.

Where do *you* need to take a risk? Is the Spirit of God leading you to start the application process, or write the check, or walk across the street to knock on the neighbor's door?

You will clear the rocks below if you jump with all your might and trust that the God who walks on water can get you to exactly the place you need to be.

One important word of counsel, however: Every risk you take should be done in submission to wise counsel from your local church and under the clear direction of the Scripture. I am not advocating reckless foolishness, and the Spirit of God *never* leads us do anything that contradicts his Word. I know of a man, for example, who felt that God was leading him to leave his family to devote more time to the ministry. I can assure you that whatever he was feeling was *not* the Spirit of God (see 1 Tim. 5:8). Furthermore, God wants us to submit what we sense the Spirit is saying to the counsel of the local church (see Acts 13:2). If you feel God moving you toward a risk, get the counsel of your pastors and other Spirit-filled brothers and sisters before you do anything.

For what it's worth, I wrote *Jesus Continued...: Why the Spirit Inside You Is Better Than Jesus Beside You* to help believers discern what particular risks the Spirit is calling them toward. In that book I explore the various ways the Spirit moves and speaks in our lives and how to tell the difference between his voice and, say ... indigestion. Pardon the shameless book plug, but if you're looking to delve into that question more deeply, that book may provide a good starting place.

Do I Really Believe This?

Just to be clear: I haven't mastered this "risk" thing yet. I am always surprised at how much of a fight I put up when the Spirit of God moves me to a new venture.

In fact, recently I sat in a room asking myself if I really believe all of that stuff I just wrote above.

I was sitting around a table listening to our four church planters for the year give their report on whom they were taking with them to launch. One is planting in Washington, DC; another in Wilmington, NC; and two are planting locally, both less than twenty minutes from our home campus. One is taking 15 of our members; another, 23; another, 20; and one, more than 50. As they went through their lists of Summit-member recruits, I heard the names of elders, big givers, key volunteers, skilled musicians, and personal friends.

As the third planter started on his list, a small lump formed in my throat. I honestly couldn't tell if it was a lump of sadness or of joy. I think it was panic. Had we *really* committed to this? When each of the first two planters had gone over their lists, it had felt like two punches in the gut. Now this third guy was winding up for the knockout blow.

"Sending" preaches more easily than it is executed, you see. Our church will look different next year when these men and their teams leave. Their absence will leave significant gaps.

As I sat listening to them, I put my hands under the table and forced myself to open them to God. Opened in surrender. Taking my hands off of one of the most precious earthly things to me — my church. Opened as an offering of praise to Jesus and faith in his promise. Opened in the belief that God will build *his* kingdom if I let go of mine.

CHAPTER 12

Never Give Up

PLUMB LINE:

"When You're Sick of Saying It, They've Just Heard It."

Antwain was the first black man we ever baptized at our church. I had gotten to know him through a basketball ministry I had started. He was six-foot-four and an incredible player. His friends called him "Air" because of how well he could jump. (We all had court nicknames, such as "Money" and "Butter." Antwain called me, "No, Don't Shoot." Not kidding!) But God gave me favor with him, and Antwain and I began studying the Bible together.

He had had a rough past, to put it mildly: gang activity, violence, and crime. After several months of Bible study and friendship, the light of grace finally broke through to him, and Antwain broke down in tears, got on his knees, and gave his heart to Christ. Immediately he began bringing other friends to church with him. Soon after that I led his girlfriend to Christ. A short time later I performed their marriage.

As Antwain stood before our church the Sunday morning of his baptism, he looked out at our congregation and said, "Some of my friends ask me why I go over to 'that white church.' [At this point, we were still an almost all-white congregation.] But I tell them, 'It's not a white church. The bricks are red and the interior is mauve, in fact. This church is where I met Jesus, and he's the Savior of whatever color." Then I baptized him.

After the service an older gentleman in our church came up to me and said, "Son, you know I don't like some of these changes that you are making in our church...." Then he got choked up and said, "But if that right there is what we're getting [referring to Antwain's baptism], you can count me in for every single one."

The slightest glimpse of what "can be" creates more willingness to change than any sermons we can preach. If you want a ministry filled with people coming up with mission ideas faster than you can facilitate them, give people a glimpse of what can be and help them *feel* what God wants it to be. You don't have to give them a detailed blueprint, just a taste of what you know God wants.

Business guru John Kotter says that the place most leaders fail in effecting change is in assuming their people understand the need for change more than they actually do. By the time the leader suggests a change, he or she has spent months thinking about why the particular change is necessary. Others in the organization, however, haven't felt these things yet; all they feel is the pain associated with leaving the familiar. What looks to the leader like a no-brainer seems to the employees like unnecessary inconvenience.

Chip and Dan Heath call this "the curse of the knowledge gap."[1] They say leaders fail to appreciate how far behind their people are from them in understanding. To happily put up with the discomforts required for change necessitates feeling the disadvantages of the current situation as keenly as the leader does.

Help Them See the Rabbit

I once heard a story about an old grandfather sitting lazily on the porch of his country home with his grandson, his six dogs lying underneath the porch. About a hundred yards across the field a rabbit darted out of a bush, stared back at the house for just a second, and then disappeared into the undergrowth. One of the dogs perked up, let out a short bark, and took off across the field. Immediately, the other five dogs jumped to their feet, yapping excitedly, in hot pursuit of the first dog.

The grandfather said to his grandson, "Son, let me tell you what is about to happen. In about ten minutes, them other five dogs are going to come back, one by one, heads hung and tongues out. In about thirty minutes, that first dog will come back with the rabbit in his mouth."

Sure enough, that's what happened. The grandson asked, "How did you know?"

The grandfather replied, "'Cause that first dog, you see, is the only one who actually saw the rabbit. The others were just running and yapping because there was some excitement."

Like those first five dogs, a lot of people in the church get swept up in the passion of a good sermon and start to yap and run ... one by one, however, they come back, heads hung low, tongues out, clamoring for the way things used to be. Only those who have really "seen the rabbit" keep running until they catch him.

The only thing that enables members to push through the weariness of the constant inconvenience required for change — the only thing that sustains the motivation to sacrifice again and again — is glimpsing the vision of what God wants to give.

The Gospel

Coming up with a compelling vision is only half the battle. Helping the people you lead see it and feel it the way you do is the other — and more difficult — half.

So how can you birth in the people that you lead this passion to sacrifice whatever is necessary to win the lost?

We return now to where we started this book: the gospel.

Gospel-saturated people become visionaries. The gospel shows us the compassion of God for the world and his willingness to change it. The gospel is the single greatest catalyst for innovation in mission.

William Carey, the father of the modern missionary movement, famously declared to an English church resistant to send missionaries to foreign lands,

Expect great things of God, and then attempt great things for God!

The order of the phrases in Carey's statement is important. Great expectations come first; great attempts grow out of great expectations. Great expectations come from understanding the gospel. In the gospel we see God's willingness to save. That moves us to ask him to do it in our generation.

Every morning I try to pray through the gospel in four phrases. They are:

- *In Christ, there is nothing I can do that would make you love me more; nothing I have done that makes you love me less.* In the gospel, I receive full access to God and all of his blessings as a free, unmerited gift earned by Christ for me.
- *You are all I need for everlasting joy.* In Christ I have all I need for a life of joy and purpose. I don't need the praise of men or the accumulation of riches or anything else. So, in Christ, I can give up all that I have, because in Christ I have all that I need.
- *As you have been to me, so I will be to others.* What I have, I have because Christ gave up everything for me. He was rich and for my sake became poor. We who live by his death should therefore no longer live for ourselves, but should lay down our lives and resources for others as he laid down his for us.
- *As I pray, I will measure your compassion by the cross and your power by the resurrection.* What will I attempt for God as I view the world through the lens of his compassion (as measured in the cross) and his power to save (as measured by the resurrection)?[2]

These four gospel summaries help me "see the rabbit" each morning. Andrew Murray, the great nineteenth-century spiritual giant of prayer, said,

> Each time, before you intercede, be quiet first, and worship God in his glory. Think of what he can do, and how he delights to hear the prayers of his redeemed people. Think of your place and privilege in Christ, and expect great things![3]

A true glimpse of the gospel creates faith, and that faith creates vision for mission and the confidence to risk for the kingdom of God. As we discussed in chapter 3, keeping people saturated in the gospel is the single greatest thing you can do to birth and sustain vision in them.

Here are some other things you can do to cultivate the vision God births in your and your people's hearts through the gospel.

Corporate Prayer

God the Father revealed to Jesus after an all-night prayer meeting which twelve men were to become his disciples and subsequent leaders of the Christian movement (Luke 6:12–16). It was during a focused time of corporate prayer that God revealed his plan to send out Paul and Barnabas on the first, official missionary trip from the Antioch church (Acts 13:2).

One "God idea" in ministry is better than a thousand good ideas. Quite often, as he did with Jesus and the apostles, God reveals those "God ideas" to us through prayer.

When the Holy Spirit reveals an idea to a congregation through prayer, the whole congregation feels that they own that vision. When I read Acts 13, I don't get the impression that a few leaders decided Paul and Barnabas should be sent out and then asked the church for money to make it happen; rather, the Holy Spirit spoke to the whole church, and they responded together. This was *their* vision; their assignment from the Spirit. As a result, they were willing to give sacrificially to make it happen.

The great Protestant mission movement of the nineteenth century can be traced back to an impromptu prayer meeting that took place under the shelter of a haystack. A group of five students from Williams College in Massachusetts had been sitting out under a tree in a field discussing theology and the fate of unreached peoples when a sudden thunderstorm forced them to seek refuge. Then they spent the next several hours in a haystack praying for the conversion of those lost nations.

Out of this prayer meeting would come the American Bible Society and the United Foreign Missionary Society, which combined to launch the mission movement in the United States that sent out more than 1,250 missionaries over the next fifty years. For two generations leaders would trace the origins of that movement back to an impromptu prayer meeting in which the Holy Spirit revealed his intentions for the church in America.

John Wesley, a leader in America's first "Great Awakening" and the catalyst of one of the greatest church planting movements in history, said,

God does nothing except in response to believing prayer.[4]

Every year our pastoral team takes several days to get alone with God to hear what the Holy Spirit has to say about his plans for our future. We want prayer to be a core source of our ideas. Some of our planning meetings ought to look more like "prayer with a little discussion mixed in" rather than "brainstorming with a little prayer mixed in."

If you want to see vision and mission birthed among your people, get them on their faces to pray together. Mission advance grows out of the church together on its knees. Andrew Murray, whose ministry was characterized by continuous miraculous provisions, said,

> The man who mobilizes the Christian church to pray will make the greatest contribution to world evangelization in history.

Repetition Ad Nauseum

Bill Hybels says that the problem with great vision is that it leaks. Simply filling up the vision bucket once cannot sustain it, because over a relatively short time all the delicious vision seeps out the cracks. Hybels says,

> Whatever the value, if it's alive and well in a local church today, it's not by accident. It's only because of intentional, committed, dedicated effort.[5]

Visions needs "heat," he says, not just light. If light is the brilliance of the idea, heat is the energy the leader puts behind spreading that idea. You not only have to articulate your vision well, but have to repeat it a lot.

Biographers say that early in his career British Prime Minister Winston Churchill's impressive oratorical abilities actually *hindered* his leadership power. Churchill felt so confident of the "light" in his speeches — which were fantastic — that he failed to do the hard work of personal follow-up (the heat) required to effect the changes he argued for. By that, I mean he did not meet face-to-face with key leaders, patiently answer objections, or build personal loyalties. He assumed that once he had presented the case winsomely, with enough light, people would get on board. He was wrong. Eventually he learned to add heat to his light and became one of the twentieth century's greatest leaders.

U.S. President Lyndon Johnson, by contrast, was not a particularly great orator, but he was a very effective leader. Johnson's speeches, his biographers say, were merely introductions to the myriad personal conversations he would have one-on-one with members of Congress, in which he would repeat to their faces the key elements of his position and press them for response.

Repetition of the vision, in multiple mouths and multiple levels, is crucial to effecting change. Among our staff, we often repeat this plumb line: *"When you are sick of saying it, the leaders in your ministry have probably just heard it. When your leaders are sick of hearing it, then everyone else has heard it for the first time."*

I want new people at our church to be able to tell what is important to us within six weeks of coming to our church. That should be long enough for them to be able to figure out that we are passionately devoted to building community, loving our city, affirming the centrality of the gospel, caring for our families, making disciples, and planting churches around the world. As I described in chapter 9, we literally write our vision on the walls, repeat our values in sermons and announcements, and saturate each ministry with the essential elements of our mission and vision. We don't bury our vision in an obscure page on our website. We make it the air we breathe.

To use a cliché, vision is caught more than it is taught. Passion is contagious, and genuine passion is better than a hundred articulate explanations. An old lawyer once said to his apprentice: "If the facts are on your side; hammer the facts; if precedent is on your side, hammer precedent; if compassion is on your side, hammer compassion; and if none of these things are on your side.... Well, hammer the table, because people will just as often follow enthusiasm as anything."

The Momentum New Life Creates

Nothing motivates a believer to go to great extremes like seeing, up close, someone's life changed by the gospel. Every time I get a letter in which someone tells me how God used our church to introduce them to Jesus, I feel a surge of energy I can't get from anywhere else.

It was seeing Antwain's story firsthand that motivated the gentleman in the church to put up with the uncomfortable changes I was bringing to his church. So tell stories of the harvest as often as you possibly can — from the ministries of your church, from the successes of people you have sent out, and from your own personal life.

My wife, Veronica, and I were talking the other day about how different those first days of our service at the Summit Church seem to us now — when the church was a traditional Baptist church of 350 meeting in a small auditorium in one location. It almost seems as if it is a completely different church that we could go back to now and visit, as if that same group of people is still sitting together somewhere in that same old auditorium. But that church has become a congregation of 9,000 people in eight locations across Raleigh-Durham.

My mind spins when I think about how much has changed in our church in these last twelve years. Our doctrine is the same, but our church government, constitution, music style, ministry philosophy, and just about everything else have evolved. Yet — and this is the weird thing — at no point did it feel as if we introduced a *big* change to the church. We changed, gradually, whatever we needed to change to reach more people the next year. We have never had less than a 96 percent affirmative vote on any change we have introduced. Excitement over the harvest has created willingness and enthusiasm within the congregation to change whatever is necessary to reach more people.

One of my favorite all-time leadership books is Sun Tzu's *Art of War*. Momentum, Sun Tzu says, is a general's most valuable ally. With momentum, a smaller army can win battles against a much larger one. The question is not just *what* battles need to be fought, he says, but *when* they need to be fought. Winning a small succession of battles can create the momentum that enables you to win much larger ones. Many battles can be won bloodlessly, he says, if you fight them at the right time and in the right order.[6]

When I first came to the Summit Church, there were a number of things I wanted to change, a number of "battles" in which I wanted to engage. But we postponed discussion about most them, and instead focused on changing only what was necessary to reach people. We set the audacious goal of having 1,000 people at Easter services that year, only three months away. This seemed outrageous to people, as there was not a single church in our city of more than 800 in weekly attendance.

On that Easter Sunday, one of our leaders came up with tears in his eyes to tell me we had 1,122 people in attendance. He too had not been excited about some of the changes we were discussing, but he told me he was ready to go wherever God would lead us. Meeting that outrageous goal created the momentum for us to make our next round of changes — and we did so with little to no opposition.

Maybe you are in a church of 35 and at Easter you hope to bring in 50. That's nothing to be discouraged about. In that additional 15 are probably enough stories to ignite the passions of your people. Tell those stories.

If you are in a church resistant to new ideas, change only what you need to in order to reach a few new people, and then, as you do, celebrate those stories. That will help get you the capital you need to "purchase" the next round of changes.

Nothing's Gonna Stop Us Now

Early in the nineteenth century, an old man stood at a newly constructed railway station watching as the giant locomotive started to shoot puffs of steam up into the air. He had heard of these new steel machines, but seeing the monstrosity in person overwhelmed him. He muttered under his breath, "They'll never get it started, I tell you.... They'll never get it started."

Then the whistle blew, and the powerful engine began to turn the wheels. The seemingly immovable fortress began to edge forward, picking up speed. Soon the only evidence of its existence was the billowing puffs of smoke receding into the distance.

The old man then muttered, "They'll never get it stopped. I tell you.... They'll never get it stopped."

Saturation in the gospel, strong times of corporate prayer, repetition ad nauseum, and letting people feel the momentum of the harvest births a vision in them that is hard to stop. Once that momentum gets going, you won't need to drag them along into mission. They'll be dragging you.

The Spirit moves the church. He is the mighty rushing wind that filled the church in Acts 2, and his torrential gospel winds are still blowing today. We just have to put up the sail and keep our flesh out of the way. As Martin Luther said of the Reformation, we just preach the Word of God, yield to the Spirit, and let God do his work.

Our response to the Word and the Spirit takes three primary forms, and I share them by way of conclusion:

— **Faith and obedience:** Born out of a confidence in the goodness of God.
— **A love for God's kingdom, not our own:** Souls are precious. They are more valuable than our tiny kingdoms. God's glory is more important than our reputation. When we are lifted up, people admire us for a moment and then they forget us. When Jesus is lifted up, people get saved for eternity. The "talents" we invest in Jesus' kingdom may never come back to us in this life, but we will reap the rewards of them for eternity. At that point, we'll have no regrets. We will wish we would have given away more.
— **The courage to risk:** God rewards those who, in submission to his Word and under the direction of his Spirit, make great attempts in his name.

As we embrace these things personally and hold them up before whatever people we lead, there will be no stopping the sending church. With the Spirit of God in our hearts and the promises of Jesus at our backs, even the gates of hell will not prevail against us.

Jesus has placed the seed in your hand. You can either hang on to it, or you can sow it. There is only one wise choice.

APPENDIX 1

Setting Up an International Missions Strategy

J.D. Greear (Pastor) and Will Toburen
(Executive Pastor of Ministries, the Summit Church)

In this appendix we want to suggest eleven building blocks for setting up an "international missions strategy" at your church. These eleven elements form the core of our approach to international engagement. Perhaps not all these elements will transfer to your context, but these should get you started in thinking about how your church (or ministry) can effectively engage the nations.

1. The Priority and Urgency of Unreached People Groups (UPGs)

God's expressed plan for history is to create a thriving church in every people group on the planet. We see that vision culminate in Revelation 5 with people from every tribe and language and nation crying out to God, "Worthy is the Lamb, who was slain!"

History cannot end until we see members of every people group come to know the Lamb that was slain for them. So we are not *just* after the greatest number of people saved; we are also pursuing the *particular shape* Christ has declared he wants for his body — people of every tribe and tongue. That's why some people, like the apostle Paul, Adoniram Judson, and Jim Elliot, have left places where they were seeing great numbers saved to go to places where Christ had yet to be named.

Here's the point on which a lot of leaders stumble: We don't pursue international missions just because it's the fastest way to add to the ranks of heaven. Justification for the endeavor doesn't depend on massive numbers of people saved (though you hope for that, of course!). We do it because God has declared that he wants heaven to consist of people of every tribe and tongue, and that history cannot end until that happens (Matt. 24:14). In Acts, we see men like Philip move from places where they are experiencing large numbers of conversions to places where they experience relatively few, because the Spirit of God is pursuing that end (Acts 8:1–39; cf. 1:8).

Even with the technological advances of the twenty-first century, there remain thousands of unreached people groups throughout the world, distinct ethnic groups in which there are no known believers and no churches among them. Sadly, for many of these unreached people groups there are no current plans for missionaries to bring them the gospel. This is wholly unacceptable, especially considering that two thousand years have transpired since Jesus first gave the Great Commission.

Christ has done the work to save them, but they have to hear about it before it can benefit them. As Carl F. H. Henry was reputed to say, "The gospel is only good news if it gets there in time." It is our responsibility to get it to them.

Many of the most unreached places are unreached for a reason. They are hard to get to, not really touristy, and can be downright unfriendly to Christians. Jesus has declared, however, that members of those groups will be represented around his throne. We go in response to that promise.

Just a few years before the horrendous tsunami that devastated Southeast Asia, I stood on the very beach where the destructive wave would first strike land. I was with Paige Patterson, then president of the Southern Baptist Convention. As we stood there, he said something to me that has stuck with me ever since: "All over the world, we've seen remarkable breakthroughs of the gospel, with people from nearly every background. And yet there still isn't a breakthrough, a truly great movement of the gospel among Muslims. Where is that chapter of the church's history?"

Muslims make up most of the 10/40 window, the most unreached part of our world. I know many of us feel *needed* where we are, but why stay where you're needed when there are places where you would be irreplaceable?[1]

I have a friend who served in an unreached city in Central Asia. Recently he was offered an incredible position at a large Christian university in the United States to be their missions mobilizer. The president of the university called my friend and said, "I literally have 100 resumes on my desk of people that want this job, but I think you are the guy for it." My friend told me, "I know his goal was to affirm me, but what I heard was, 'There are 100 other people who are ready to take this job if I don't.' But if I left my post here in Central Asia, there is literally no one on the planet in line to take my place, and if someone decided today they would do it, it would take them at least five years to learn the language and culture well enough to take my place. I thanked the president for his kind words but told him, 'No, I will turn down where I am needed to stay where I am irreplaceable.'"

Yes, there are lots of needs everywhere. But there are thousands of unreached people groups around the world where no one has yet gone, and no one is in line to go. God has promised to pour out his power in those places if someone will be his conduit there. We just have to go.

I often tell our church we are going to be like the proverbial woodpecker tapping away faithfully on a telephone pole when a bolt of lightning suddenly splits it in two. The woodpecker, dazed, regains his composure and promptly flies off to gather a few of his friends. He brings them to the pole and says, "There she is, boys. Look at it!" When that happens in the people group we are ministering in, we'll stagger backwards, saying, "I knew it would happen! He told me it would." And he will get all the glory.

I have tried, personally, to be obedient to that call, doing my doctoral studies on new trends in Muslim evangelism and authoring a book called *Breaking the Islam Code: Answering the Soul Questions of Every Muslim.*

The encouraging news is this: Ralph Winter notes that when Paul died, there were 12 UPGs for every one church; now there are *6413* churches for every one UPG. There are 60 U.S. churches alone for every one UPG.[2] That means if just *one* out of every 60 U.S. churches took responsibility to bring the gospel to a UPG, every tribe and tongue would receive a witness to Christ's name in our generation (and that's not even to factor in the impressive work being done among UPGs by believers in other nations). God has placed the completion of this assignment within our grasp.

2. Create a Portfolio That Engages All Gifts in the Body of Christ and Believers at Various Stages of Maturity

We should prioritize reaching UPGs with an urgency befitting the reality that many people have never heard the name of Jesus or seen a copy of the Scripture in their language. But we also need to recognize that if we focus only on the difficult and unengaged unreached parts of the world, many of the people in our churches simply won't be able to be personally involved. Not everybody can go and live in Somalia.

God puts multiple gifts into his body, which means not everyone is assigned to the same thing. Many in our congregations have a heart for poverty relief, orphan care, and medical relief ministries. *We therefore need a portfolio of missions options that engages all of giftings and Spirit-birthed passions in the body.* God put those gifts into his church, and we need to create outlets for their use.

There's nothing wrong with creating "easy" on-ramps for people going into missions. A trip to Central America or the Caribbean can be a cheaper, more accessible venture for people who may not be able to afford the money or time required to take a month-long trip to Afghanistan. Some may not be ready for the dangers required to get the gospel into the hardest-to-reach areas. And that's okay. In John 6 Jesus withheld certain things from some he said were just not ready for them. If *he* did that, we can allow for that kind of discernment in how we set up our missions programs, too.

Churches often go to one extreme or the other — too shotgun in their focus or too laser pointed. The "shotgun" approach simply disperses people out wherever those people want to go, scattering them throughout the world without much intentionality — a couple missionaries in China, some in Sweden, one in Egypt, another in Peru. It's hard for the local church to feel like they "own" a given field, which discourages focused prayer and emotional investment in those areas. On the other end, "laser-pointed" approaches often fail to engage the vast majority of people in the church. Their "Sudan or bust" approach leaves many willing participants standing on the sidelines.

What we need is a balance between the two approaches, so that we gain the benefit of the laser-focused intentionality while giving people the freedom to explore God's particular calling on them. Through mentorship books and classes we capitalize on the opportunities provided by short-term trips to "easy" places to impart vision for the most unreached UPGs.

3. Set Goals, But Talk Mostly About Vision

Number goals can be good, and they can be abused. Often, number goals imply, "This is what *we* plan to accomplish." We can't guarantee that God will move a certain way just because we declared our goal. God's Spirit moves like the wind: There are times when our faithfulness yields less than we want, and times when he does exceedingly abundantly above all we had even asked or dreamed.

At the same time, actual number goals can be energizing. They can serve as a tangible way for people to dream about actual things God might do through them. At our church, for instance, we set number goals for the amount of people involved in short-term (terms up to a month), mid-term (terms up to two years), and long-term missions. This year we are aiming to send 1,000 people on short-term trips, and we hope over a lifetime to send 5,000 people long-term. We have set out the goal of planting 1,000 churches in our lifetime.

When I introduced these real number goals to our church, I saw a new fervency grip our staff and leaders. Plant 1,000 churches? Send out 5,000 people? What if we really could leave that legacy behind us? With the number goal, we could measure our progress and inspire one another to work harder in pursuit of it.

This anonymous quote captures well the balance between number goals and vision:

> Goals can be energizing ... when you win. But a vision is more powerful than a goal. A vision is enlivening, it's spirit giving, it's the guiding

force behind all great human endeavors. Vision is about shared energy, a sense of awe, a sense of responsibility.

So use goals, but major on vision.

4. Create an Ethos

We covered this in chapter 9, but for a missions strategy to be effective, it has to appear more often than in a sermon series every year or two. It must saturate the air you breathe in your church, something so integral to your church's DNA that even anyone who visits for a couple of weeks immediately knows that this matters to you. Missions needs to find its way into every facet of ministry — frequent in the examples used in sermons, the curriculum of your small groups or Sunday school classes, the content of your prayers, even the pictures on your walls.

International missions should color into every dimension of the ministry. When you cordon off missions into a department, you separate church ministries from God's master plan and indirectly communicate to people that missions is only something done by a select few. The truth is, missions is what every follower of Jesus gets swept up into.

Infusing missions into the DNA of our church means engaging children and families early on. As we discussed in chapter 9, parents should rear their children with the knowledge that God gives children to believers for the furtherance of his mission. As King Solomon said, "Like arrows in the hands of a warrior are children born in one's youth" (Ps. 127:4). This priority informs everything from the environments our children meet in, to the curriculum we teach, to the mission trips and service opportunities we offer for families.[3]

This continues in our student ministry, as we encourage all high school students to spend four weeks of one of their high school summers to live and serve with one of our church planting projects overseas. For our college students, we ask them to give us at least one entire summer to serve in missions. During that summer we send them on three mission trips and fill their summer with classes that teach them what God is doing in the world and how they can be part of it. From top to bottom, every ministry in our church aims to encourage people to find their place in God's global mission. Missions isn't just something we do; it is who we, as the people of God, are.

5. Design Initiatives Around Specific Gifts and Talents

Early on in our recruitment of people into mission engagement, I got extremely frustrated at our lack of volunteers. During one season, when we had 1,000 people at our church, I couldn't get twenty for a particular trip. For over a month I kept inviting people: *"Come on, Summit! We need only fourteen more to get the twenty we need!"* But one Sunday I changed my tactic and said, "We need five dentists, five doctors, and five nurse practitioners." We had more than twenty volunteers by the end of that service.

People respond more readily to a call when they feel that they have a particular role to play. When people know that they have some asset that will be specifically helpful on the field, their excitement level goes up. Most believers, I have found, are actually longing to know how they can leverage their life for the kingdom. No one has ever told them how or where. Many people are simply waiting to be presented with an opportunity to use their specific skill or passion in the mission!

They say that when you are recruiting volunteers, it is easier to get one volunteer out of three than 3,000. When you address 3,000, everyone assumes that you are talking to someone else. When you direct your appeal toward three, they know you are talking to them. So when you address 3,000, help the three know you are talking specifically to them. Help people know that God is calling *them* to missions by providing specific opportunities that engage their particular skills.

One of the ways we do this is by identifying the "domains" of cities we are trying to reach. "Domains" are those dimensions that make up the character of the region — things like education, medicine, agriculture, government, business, and recreation.[4] Come up with a strategy to engage those domains.

For example, in our own city we have identified business, medicine, and education as the three biggest areas that define Raleigh-Durham. Many of our ministries therefore focus on discipling believers to live out Christianity in those arenas. We have also identified five broken areas in our city — the homeless, orphans, prisoners, unwed mothers, and high school dropouts. We are developing ministries (or catalyzing our members to do so) for each of these areas.

Teach your people to view the cities you engage through this lens, and you will have no shortage of opportunities to get people involved.

Most church people assume that *real* mission work is the sort of thing only professional Christians can do. "Regular people" only tag along, prayer walk, occasionally put roofs on church buildings, and most of all, give money. However (as we saw in chapter 6), gospel writer Luke presents "ordinary" Christians as the tip of the gospel spear. Countries closed to gospel work are open to development in education, business, sports, and medicine. Help your people see that, and your church can go from "sending" missionaries to "being" the missionary.

6. Short-Term Mission Trips Are Not a Waste of Time

We ask every pastor to take a short-term overseas trip every two years and give them the funds to do so. It is extremely important for pastors and church leaders to see what God is doing in the nations firsthand, for nothing creates zeal for missions like seeing it. We also are committed to covering a percentage of the trip cost for each Summit member who goes on one of our trips.

Much has been written over the years disputing the value of short-term missions: Are they a big waste of money, gobbling up resources that could just be given to indigenous church planters directly? Don't a lot of church people use them to scratch their "foreign travel itch" — i.e., "vacationaries"? Aren't a lot of short-term trips unhelpful to the work on the field — forcing church planters to take time from real ministry to serve as tour guides and babysitters for curious Christians? And why would we go overseas to help there, when our communities are in such need here — isn't that arrogant?

These critiques should be taken very seriously, so let me address them briefly and show why I am, despite the truth in some of them, still a very firm believer in short-term trips.

"SHORT-TERM TRIPS ARE A WASTE OF MONEY."

Dollars spent on short-term trips are not zero-sum — that is, every dollar spent on a mission trip is not one less dollar you can give to people serving permanently on the field. Quite the opposite: people who see mission firsthand typically give more in missions offerings. In other words, money spent on short-term trips multiplies itself by creating greater willingness to give in the future among those who go.

In chapter 9 I explained that a rather costly mission trip involving several of our members so inspired our people that the next year our missions giving was the "highest per capita" in the Southern Baptist Convention. The $100,000 our members spent on the trip resulted in them giving twice that amount directly to missions the next year. (And it's not as if members would have given the money they spent on the mission trip directly to missions had they not gone. They would have found another use for the money!)

Last year we sent 39 members on a trip to Central Asia. This year, 8 of those 39 are leading their own short-term trip. And in the last two years we have directed 6.2 million dollars to missions, giving 2.1 million of that to groups such as the International Mission Board.

Furthermore, an extraordinary number of mid-term (one year or longer) and career missionaries trace their call, in part, back to a short-term mission trip. God often uses what we see and experience on a trip like that to shape the rest of our lives.

Finally, let us never forget that the first time God sent the gospel outside of Jerusalem, it was in the mouth of layman on a short-term trip (Acts 8:26–39). Philip met the Ethiopian eunuch 165 miles from Philip's home, led him to Christ, and helped equip him to be the first national church planter in Ethiopia. Short-term trips are God's idea.

We say, *"Short-term trips create lifetime missionaries."* God sends his people to the nations, not just so they can change the nations, but so the nations can change *them*, too. Sometimes God has to send us over *there* to change how we live *here*. One of our missions pastors says, "I guarantee you that once your feet touch foreign soil, you will never be the same."

"SHORT-TERM TRIPS ARE REALLY JUST EXOTIC VACATIONS FOR CURIOUS CHRISTIANS: VACATIONARIES."

Unfortunately, for some Christians this is true. Despite our best efforts, we are always going to have people who see short-term mission trips as church-sponsored vacations. But we do all we can to discourage this. Some of our short-term destinations are exotic and fun, but many others are physically uncomfortable, not the sort of places that people would choose if they wanted to get away and relax. We also make it clear as we recruit and advertise that the purpose of the trip is to *serve* those on the field, not to fill up a scrapbook.

We also use the lead-up to a mission trip as an intense discipleship experience. In preparing for a short-term trip, members read books, memorize verses of Scripture, keep a prayer journal, and share their faith. Ironically enough, many who enter the process with a motivation of simply seeing the world have their hearts changed along the way. I've seen it time and time again: potential "vacationaries" have their hearts touched by the global need for the gospel and return with new eyes and fresh vision.

"SHORT-TERM TRIPS DON'T MAKE SENSE WHEN THERE IS SO MUCH NEED HERE."

What business do we have going around the world when there is so much need here? Recently a church leader explained to me that the reason his church is not involved in global mission is that their local community had so much need, and it seems arrogant to go and try to "fix" someone else's culture when his own is in such bad shape. My question back to him was, "If the people who shared the gospel with our culture had waited until their culture was gospel saturated before coming to us, would they ever have come? Did Paul go to the Gentiles because the Jews had all become Christians?"

We don't go overseas because there is no work left to do here; we go because God gives to every believer the capacity and the responsibility to carry the gospel to the nations. As we discussed in chapter 9, we must avoid the error of "sequentialism." Overseas engagement should be in our portfolio of mission from the very beginning, just as it is in the call to discipleship from the very beginning.

Believers who want to possess the heart of God for the world have to create space in it — a large space — for the nations. Churches that want to be filled with the Spirit of God must collectively join in his mission to witness to the gospel "in all Judaea and Samaria, and to the end of the earth" (Acts 1:8 NKJV).

"SHORT-TERM TRIPS ARE MORE HARMFUL TO THE FIELD WORK THAN HELPFUL."

Unfortunately, this is often accurate. Well-meaning mission trips can not only eat up valuable time of resident missionaries, who end up serving as babysitters and tour guides for traveling church groups, but can also set the work back through poorly administered aid or sloppy evangelism. One mission agency leader told me that there is a city in Mexico that is a popular destination for American church mission trips, and the number of conversions reported in one year for that city was three times the population of that city. Not helpful.

An indispensable resource to counteract this problem is Steve Corbett and Brian Fikkert's helpful and provocative book, *When Helping Hurts: How to Alleviate Poverty Without Hurting the Poor*. The authors show that much of the "helping" that we do actually ends up being harmful to those we intended to help. When we do for people what they can (and should) do for themselves, it may make us feel good, but it can hinder those groups from developing the leadership skills necessary to meet their own needs. God has put as much leadership capacity in them as he has in us. We don't serve them well by leading in their place.

For example, we don't send groups to construct churches that local believers can and should construct for themselves. It ends up being a really inefficient, and ineffective use of resources. It costs us ten times as much to do the work that it would cost them, and quite often it discourages, rather than empowers, local engagement. We try to use short-term trips to serve and empower local believers, not to come in with any sense that we need to rescue them.[5] They are more capable of leading their movement than we are. We go to catalyze, assist, and empower.

Short-term mission trips *can* be more harmful than they are helpful. But they don't need to be. Which leads us to our next point.

7. Let Indigenous Leaders Set the Agenda

In their book *Helping Without Hurting in Short-Term Missions*, Corbett and Fikkert help us see short-term trips from the perspective of national pastors in the countries receiving the teams. Imagine, they say, you are an American pastor who receives a call from a Thai pastor who wants to bring a team of twenty-five people to your church, about half of them in high school, to conduct Vacation Bible Schools (VBS's) in the neighborhoods around your church. He tells you they can only come during your peak ministry season, but not to worry because they have prepared a number of excellent lessons, skits, and games to use in the VBS's. They are also bringing gifts from Thailand to entice neighborhood kids to come. Oh, and on the team, he says, is an electrician who would love to do some work in the church.

They will, of course, need rides to and from the airport, which is about two hours away from your church. And they will need to be housed and fed three meals a day with food not too unusual for them. He says that he knows you Americans love casseroles, but the Thai probably won't enjoy that very much. So fix food they'll like. Furthermore, most of those coming on the trip speak little to no English, so you will need to arrange translators to accompany them everywhere they go. They would also like to visit some of your famous landmarks while they are there, and go on a couple of shopping trips to the malls in your city. Then consider:

> Meanwhile, your church members have spent the past three years gradually developing relationships with the apartment residents and building their trust. The apartment residents are mostly low-income families, and it has taken time for them to feel comfortable with your church's presence in their neighborhood.
>
> While you consider the pros and cons of this offer, the voice continues: "We are just so excited about this opportunity to sacrifice for the sake of the gospel. Our church members are ready and willing to raise $40,000 to come." Your church could certainly use the money to purchase new AV equipment and refurbish its nursery. But at what cost? Housing, feeding, and supervising twenty-five people with limited English skills? And what about the relationships at the apartment

complex? How will the residents respond to a group of Thais passing out candy and leading VBS sessions?

"Do unto others as you would have them do unto you." It sounds so simple. Until it isn't.[6]

At our church, we are nigh unto fanatical about letting indigenous leaders and resident missionaries set both the priorities and the rules of engagement for any short-term trips we bring there. We make clear to them that we are there to serve them, not have them serve us. So instead of setting an agenda based on what we feel is necessary, we let them tell us what we can do that would help them. And if they tell us a trip itself would not be helpful (which sometimes is true), we find other ways to support them besides coming. We should not be going on mission trips just to help us feel good about ourselves or to give us cool stories to tell later.

Corbett and Fikkert explain that short-term trips are effective when (1) the agenda is set by local, indigenous leadership, (2) those coming from abroad have as their focus the empowerment and support of local leadership, and (3) the short-term missionaries develop a long-term relationship with the people they are serving in which they give and pray faithfully for a lifetime.

Westerners who go in to "save the day" for poor, underprivileged people make a fatal philosophical mistake that undermines all their well-intentioned offers to help: They assume they are somehow different from the people they are trying to save — as if there is something fundamentally different about *them* that makes *them* able to thrive in the world, whereas the people in these poor countries cannot. Each person on the planet is made in the image of God, which means each has the potential to thrive. Our task is not to do things for them so much as help them realize the potential God has given them to meet their own needs.

Corbett and Fikkert say that rather than going into a community and asking, "What are the needs that I can meet?" we should ask, "How can we help you meet your own needs?" or "What assets do you have that I can help you capitalize on?" The nationals are the leaders; we visitors are the servants. They are the need-providers and problem-solvers; we are merely the catalysts. And we want to do the hard work of pursuing long-term relationships with them, even after the trip is over. It takes more humility and diligence to maintain a friendship than to dig a well, but the benefits to the people of that country last much longer.

8. Small Groups Are the Best Organizing Units for Mission

A small group or a Sunday school class is usually the perfect size for a mission trip. So why not transfer the responsibility for short-term trips to those groups, letting them come up with the funds, organize them, and take the lead in planning the trip? It is much more efficient for a church to *catalyze* small groups for mission rather than *owning* the entire process. (Remember the Own, Bless, and Catalyze taxonomy on pages 110–11? Churches that catalyze mission leaders, rather than "own" all mission trips, will be more effective in mission mobilization.)

As I mentioned, one of our greatest joys is to see small groups not only take mission trips together, but move to strategic areas together to help plant churches there. We pretty regularly have small groups move together to North American cities as part of our church planting efforts there. I even know of a church plant in Central Asia that met together as a small group in the United States for three years. God called the whole group to go live overseas together! By that point they already had a lot of their relationship kinks worked out. That's a big deal, because (as is often pointed out) the number one reason people come back from the field is that they can't get along with each other. A small group has already had several years' practice learning to get along and had to work through some of these interrelational issues. Forming small groups for the purpose of church planting and sending them out together might be the thing we are most excited about in our mission future.

9. Preparation for Mission Trips Provides an Ideal Forum for Discipling Believers

Most pastors face the enduring problem of how to get people engaged in "normal" Christian disciplines such as Scripture memorization, evangelism training, prayer, and Bible study. Mission trip preparation provides an ideal situation to kick-start those disciplines. We have found there is nothing that so effectively engages people in Christian disciplines as preparing for a mission.

So, as I mentioned, we fill the lead-up to the mission trip with a list of books to read, verses to memorize, and prayer journals to keep. We establish accountability partners. Many people learn to share their faith for the first time on a mission trip. Others begin the daily habit of a quiet time.

I suppose it is sad that we have to spend $2,500 and send people 7,000 miles away to learn to do what they really *should* be doing here, but there's something about a cross-cultural experience that goads people into stepping up their game. That's especially true for high school and college students.

Short-term trips give people a taste of what God is doing in the world that helps them better understand what they are doing *here*. On nearly every mission trip we have people return and say, "I asked myself, 'Why aren't I living this way back in my neighborhood? Why am I not prayer-walking, sharing my faith, and meeting needs here?'" I've heard it said, "The best cure for a sick church is a missionary diet."

Mission trips may be an expensive discipleship program, but, it turns out, a very effective one. On the whole, I would consider money spent with those kinds of results in discipleship to be *very* well spent.

As we said, the light that shines the farthest will also shine the brightest at home!

10. The Greatest Missionaries to Foreign Lands Are Studying in Your Community's Backyard

No foreigner will ever be able to work as effectively in an unreached people group as a native believer. What many of us may not think about, however, is that globalization has brought the nations *to us*. For perhaps the first time in history, God has given us a chance to equip natives to fulfill the Great Commission around the world ... without even leaving our city.

Data from the 2010 census indicates that more than 1 in every 10 people in the counties surrounding our church (Wake, Durham, and

Orange) is foreign-born. There are large populations of international students on our college campuses, as well as numerous refugee communities from North Africa, Central Asia, and the Middle East comprised of families from some of the most unreached people groups in the world.

Sadly, many of these students and refugees will never develop friendships with an American. An estimated 80 percent of college international students spend their entire academic career without even setting foot in an American home![7] When we consider that approximately 300 current and former world leaders studied at American universities, isn't this an enormous missed opportunity?[8] The best and brightest from "closed" countries come to live within mere miles of us. We need to recognize this as the God-ordained opportunity that it is.

When I was in college, all the international students met together at a special student center. I got to know a few of them, and the first time I ventured down to their student center, I was told I was the first American to visit that year! My heart broke. They graciously invited me into their world. I invited some of them home with me at Thanksgiving, I stayed in their dorm, and I hung out with them at a break. That Christmas they threw me a Christmas party, even though none of them were Christians. Engaging with them was one of the most enriching experiences of my college life, and I was able to lead a few of them to Christ. I continued to get letters from one years later, telling me how she was sharing Christ with family and friends in her home country!

As hundreds of thousands of individuals from unreached people groups stream into your neighborhoods, you have three options: You can view it as an inconvenience; you can ignore it; or you can seize the moment that God has given us. How tragically ironic would it be to overlook the world coming to us while we spend billions of dollars to go to the world?

11. Denominations Are Helpful, But God Gave the Great Commission to Local Churches

Perhaps you have a denomination or a parachurch organization (parachurch means "coming alongside the church") that you work with. We do. We partner heavily with the International Mission Board, Cru, and Pioneers, to name a few. We value those partnerships. We can do more together than we can do alone, and denominational structures provide specialized help that far exceeds the abilities of our congregation to work on its own.

Furthermore, denominational structures provide a staying power that individual churches or movements lack. Individual churches can have boom seasons and lean ones. Institutions develop funding mechanisms and training programs that generate stable, perpetual activity.

Tim Keller notes that movements and institutions need each other. (By "movement," he means large groups of people energized around a mission, usually involving the leadership of charismatic individuals.) Institutions without movements, he says, are lifeless and dead; but movements without institutions lack staying power.[9]

That said, God gave the Great Commission to local churches. In Acts, you won't find a lot of highly organized mission boards or seminaries, just local churches sending out people to plant churches. This is not to say there is not a place for mission boards, or that we don't see them in "seed" form in Acts, just that we must not let those things eclipse the responsibility that has been given to *local churches*. The local church is God's "plan A." Everything else we design should be done with the centrality of the local church in mind.

To that end, let me offer a couple of thoughts as you seek to craft out a partnership with your denomination or parachurch affiliate.

A. YOU CAN'T FARM OUT OBEDIENCE TO THE GREAT COMMISSION.

There's good parachurch and bad parachurch. "Good parachurch" seeks to assist the local church in accomplishing her mission; "bad parachurch" seeks to take the mission from the church and do it for her.

It's great that we have so many organizations to assist in the task of fulfilling the Great Commission, but the local church must not abdicate its responsibility. You can't farm out obedience to this command any more than you can farm out obedience to the Ten Commandments! "I don't feel like being truthful. Will you do that for me?" In the same way, a local church can't give away the responsibility to do missions by giving money to a group to do it for them. They can *partner* with others to help them do it better, but they can never release responsibility for that mission.

What churches need most is for their denominations to empower them to fulfill that mission.

Thus, parachurch ministries and denominational structures should not celebrate how many churches they plant; they should celebrate how many churches they help local churches to plant. That may sound like a subtle distinction, but it would represent a cataclysmic change for many parachurch and mission organizations today.

In my denomination, there has been, in the last few years, a wonderful restoration of local church planting as the *goal* of our missions. I think there now needs to be corresponding revitalization of local churches as the *means* of accomplishing that mission. It is not enough for our convention to value church planting; we have to establish local churches as the means for accomplishing that mission. Local churches should lead; denominations should facilitate and assist. Put simply, the local church is not just the *goal* of missions; it should be the *means* as well.

B. DENOMINATIONAL STRUCTURES NEED TO BROADEN THEIR APPROACH TO MISSION EMPOWERMENT.

Many denominations have a "one-size fits all" approach to missions. You send your people and money to the board, and they turn those people into international missionaries for you. But as I argued in chapter 6, the frontier work of missions is being done, in large part, by believers whose "secular" vocations taken them into the most hard-to-reach areas.

I pointed out that there are 2 million Americans working in the 10/40 window under secular employment. If just 10 percent of those were living as disciple-making Christians, the number of "missionaries" would swell by 500 percent, *with no additional cost.* Shouldn't denominational structures be helping churches identify people like these and helping to train, network, and care for them?

Denominations and parachurch groups have accomplished much through their traditional sending mechanisms. We don't need a decrease in that at all. But we need these agencies to expand the scope of what they do to include empowering local churches to better equip and send out their people. So ask them to help *you* recruit, train, and send out teams. Tell them, for example, that you would like them to help you form the team within your church and train them together, as a small group, for a couple of years before the board sends them out. Or tell them you would like for them to work with you to train business leaders whose jobs are already carrying them around the world to be disciple-makers as they go, and show them how to funnel the people they win to Christ into indigenous church planting movements within the country.

Conclusion

Hopefully these eleven principles give you some handles for building an international missions program into your own ministry.

Some may be more applicable to you than others. Seek the guidance of the Holy Spirit as you design a program for your church or your ministry, and as you do, realize that Jesus, the Shepherd who came to seek and save the lost, has promised to help you in this if you simply yield yourself to him. *"Follow me,"* he says, *"and I will make you* fishers of men" (Matt. 4:19 ESV). If you will simply follow and believe, he will impart all the instruction and skill you will need: *"I will build my church,"* he says, *"and the gates of hell shall not prevail against it ..."* (Matt. 16:18 ESV). *"Ask of me,"* he says, *"and I will give you the nations for your inheritance"* (Ps. 2:8 NKJV).

Why not stop right now and ask him that?

APPENDIX 2

Developing a Domestic Church Planting Strategy

J.D. Greear (Pastor) and Mike McDaniel
(Director of Domestic Church Planting, the Summit Church)

In this appendix we want to lay out some ideas for developing a domestic church planting strategy in your church. I (J.D.) have maintained throughout this book that more important than a church planting strategy is a church planting *culture*. Strategy without culture yields fatigue, frustration, and failure. The late Peter Drucker said, "Culture eats strategy for breakfast."[1]

If sending does not pervade our culture, very few of our efforts take root in the hearts of our people. Tim Keller says that if the sending culture is absent, church planting remains infrequent, exceptional, and usually traumatic.[2] On the other hand, in the right culture, church planting comes as naturally to the church as apples do to an apple tree.

Therefore, in this appendix we are not trying to give you a program to add to your church, but to demonstrate how you can ingrain church planting into the programs you already have. We assume that you already value sending and are inculcating that value into your people — by means already described throughout this book. If so, use of the suggestions in this appendix might help you articulate your strategy better, streamline your efforts, and make church planting feel more natural and less exceptional.

Before we jump into the "how," however, we need to address an important question that pops up in the mind of pastors and members alike when we talk about *church planting*: Aren't there already enough churches in the United States? Why spend time starting new ones when so many old ones are in need of help? Won't the mission be better served by focusing on evangelism and discipleship initiatives that serve existing churches?

Why Church Planting Is Paramount in the Mission

Obviously, church planting does not exclude the need to revitalize and assist existing churches. Our church, the Summit Church, is a revitalization, not a plant. Here are five reasons, however, we believe church planting must remain paramount in any mission strategy.

1. PLANTING CHURCHES IS THE PRIMARY NEW TESTAMENT STRATEGY FOR FULFILLING THE GREAT COMMISSION.

You can sum up Paul's entire evangelistic strategy in Acts as identifying the biggest, most influential cities in his region and going to plant churches there.[3] This is not to say that we don't also plant rurally, just that things tend to flow into the country from the cities, so in a completely unevangelized area, the city is typically the best place to start.

Tim Keller points out that we can only fulfill Jesus' Great Commission by planting churches, because he told us to "teach them all things" and "baptize them," and baptism implies incorporation into a covenant community. In other words, Jesus did not intend his disciples to go about haphazardly evangelizing; he instructed them to gather these new converts into new churches. So Paul tells Titus: "The reason I left you in Crete was that you might put in order what was left unfinished and appoint elders in every town, as I directed you" (Titus 1:5). The appointment of elders implies organized churches. Evangelism is not enough. We need to plant churches.

2. EVEN IN THE UNITED STATES, PLANTING CHURCHES IS THE GREATEST NEED.

You may say, "Well, 'planting churches' makes sense in unreached places, but what about here in America? Our community has a church on every corner!"

Consider this: Statisticians say that in 1900, there were 28 churches for every 10,000 Americans. By 2004, that number had dropped to 11 for every 10,000 — and it continues to decrease. In fact, studies show that just to keep pace with population growth, we need to double the rate at which we are currently planting new churches.[4] Did you catch that? We need to plant over 7,200 new churches every year just to keep pace with population growth — let alone advance against lostness in America!

Even the Southeast, where the Summit Church is located — the Bible Belt, to be exact — is no exception. This map gives you a glimpse of the progress of Christianity in America — the darker states representing areas of growth and the lighter ones areas of decline:

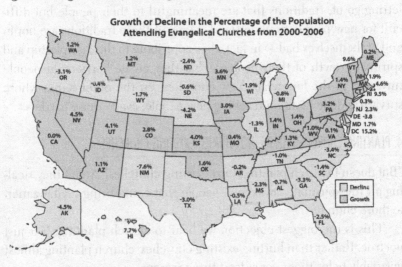

Growth or Decline in the Percentage of the Population Attending Evangelical Churches from 2000–2006

As you can see, many of states experiencing the highest drops in evangelical church attendance are found in the South.[5] Our state, North Carolina, right on the edge of the Bible Belt, has experienced the fourth greatest drop in evangelical church attendance in the nation.

3. PLANTING CHURCHES IS OUR MOST EVANGELISTICALLY EFFECTIVE OUTREACH.

"But why not," you say, "just revitalize existing churches? Why spend all the money and effort planting new ones when so many are dying?"

Simply put, church planting is the most effective way to reach new people:

> Studies confirm that the average new church gains one-third to two-thirds of its new members from the ranks of people who are not attending any worshipping body, while churches over ten to fifteen years of age gain 80 to 90 percent of new members by transfer from other congregations.[6]

In other words, new churches are six to eight times more evangelistically effective than existing churches. Larry Kreider shows that in the average church plant, it takes three people to produce one baptism. At an existing church, it takes ninety-five.[7]

Why is this so? Kreider speculates that older, more established churches tend to have traditions they understandably have a hard time letting go of, traditions that are meaningful to their people but difficult for new people to understand. Many of those traditions are not in and of themselves bad — in fact, they contribute to the discipleship and spiritual growth of their people — but they create barriers for people unversed in the language. New churches, on the other hand, whose survival is dependent on reaching new people, evade those barriers.

4. PLANTING CHURCHES HELPS, NOT HURTS, EXISTING CHURCHES.

"But doesn't church planting hurt existing churches? Aren't they stealing all the spiritually awakened people that could bring revitalization to those churches?"

This is the biggest objection we hear to church planting. It is just not true. Rather than hurting existing churches, church planting almost invariably helps them, for at least three reasons.

First, *new churches raise the evangelistic climate in an area*. When the water in the harbor rises, all the boats rise, meaning that as church plants raise the spiritual temperature in a city, all the churches are positively affected. Here's how it happens: A new person in the church plant comes to Christ, and they begin to talk about that with their neighbors. Inspired by the newfound faith of their friend, some of those neighbors decide to get more involved in *their own* churches, where they have been only nominally involved. (This very thing happened in my [J.D.] neighborhood when we moved in. A couple we befriended, seeing our commitment to our church, resolved to get more involved in their own church.) New churches multiply followers of Jesus in an area, and there being more followers of Jesus increases the number of people sharing Christ in that area, which increases spiritual interest in the whole area, which results in more seekers going to various churches.

Second, *new churches feed back into existing churches*. I (J.D.) run into people all the time who came to the Summit Church for a season. After a while, they ended up going back to their churches where the majority of their family and friends were. That used to bother me, but now I recognize that God simply loaned them to us for a season so that he could use us to instill some things in them that he wanted taken back to their churches. Big churches are not for everyone, *and that's* ok.

In a similar way, the smallness and rawness of church plants are not for everyone. Church plants can't offer many of the resources or programs that existing churches can, so it's not unusual for people to come to Christ at a church plant and then move to an established church, where more services for their family are offered.[8]

Done the right way, church planting can be a great blessing to existing churches in a community.

Done right, church planting blesses the planting church, too. Sure, we know of horror stories where a bunch of people get mad and go start a church down the road and call that a "plant," but that really ought to called a "church split," not a "church plant." Healthy planting almost always benefits the sending church, because it helps focus the attention of their members outward, which invariably brings great benefit to the outreaches of the church. Studies bear this out: churches that plant other churches are much more likely to grow themselves.[9]

Third, *new churches generate new ideas in the body of Christ*. As Tim Keller notes, new churches are forced to figure out new ways to reach people in order to survive. Many established churches cannot get away with pioneering these new ideas — existing members aren't willing to change from what they believe is working to something unproven and uncomfortable — but once these new ideas have been "proven" elsewhere, established churches often adopt them.[10]

5. PLANTING CHURCHES "GROWS THE PIE" OF RESOURCES AVAILABLE FOR THE GREAT COMMISSION.

Some pastors feel that the expense of church planting saps money away from important, frontline ministries like evangelizing college students, feeding the poor, or developing the kids' ministry. It is true, church planting can be expensive, and there are methods of planting that are inefficient and financially unsustainable. But church planting done right yields the largest financial return available in kingdom investment. Planting new churches multiplies resources available in the kingdom of God by multiplying givers. Says Keller:

> A city needs many ministries — youth work, Christian schools, missions to new groups, and so on. All of them are charities that need to be supported from outside their own resources. They will require funding from Christian givers indefinitely. A new church, however, only requires outside start-up funding at its inception. Within a few years, it becomes the *source* of giving to other ministries, not its *target*. Because new churches bring in large numbers of non-churched people, church planting is by far the fastest way to grow the number of new givers in the kingdom work of a city.[11]

Four years ago we planted the Summit Church in Denver, Colorado. (The name "Summit" is much more appropriate for them since they actually have ... er ... *mountains* there.) We sent 25 people to start the church. By last year, the church had grown to over 150 people, and the opportunity arose for them to purchase the building where they were meeting. But because their building was large and located in an up-and-coming part of town, it was expensive. Bryan, the lead pastor, tells the story of what happened:

> Honestly, it made no sense for the owner to sell us the building. It was located in one of the most up-and-coming parts of the city, just a few blocks from Coors Field (where the Rockies play). New bars, restaurants, coffee shops were popping up on every corner. Property values were skyrocketing. On top of this, the owner was a hotshot investor known for getting his way. But one of our pastors, Andy, had gotten to know the owner, so he approached him to ask if he would sell us the building.
>
> Andy was a nervous wreck when he went to that meeting. He decided to walk around the building three times before going in, partly because he was nervous, partly because he had just read the story about Joshua walking around Jericho seven times before taking the city for God, and figured, it can't hurt.
>
> So Andy goes into the meeting and just lays out our vision — this is why God has called us here; this is how God has called us to love this

city. Then he says to the owner, "I want to tell you something, and I say this as a friend: 'You don't own this building.' The owner gives him this puzzled look. Andy says, "Your name may be on the piece of paper, but you don't own this building. God owns this building, and we think he wants you to sell it to us." Then Andy looks at him again and says, "I'm telling you this as a friend. If you don't sell this building, God is going to hold you accountable."

To note, I (J.D.) didn't authorize that last statement, and we didn't teach him to fundraise that way during his training. Nevertheless, the owner responded by agreeing to sell them the building at less than asking price. And then the story really gets good. Their lender called a few weeks later, telling Bryan that the owner had inserted a new clause in the contract, stipulating that they needed to bring $150,000 to closing. And closing was in ten days.

So Bryan called us, his sending church, to see if we would supply the $150,000. We agreed to help, but I challenged Bryan to take that need to his people first. Remember, this is a church of 150, and almost every member was young and/or a new Christian. Most of them were already tithing. But Bryan laid out the need and called on them to give sacrificially. He then directed them to get down on their faces and call out to God for help.

Bryan said his people prayed the hardest he had ever seen them pray. Many literally wept. The Spirit of God moved through the church, and many repented of things they had bought that they didn't really need. Some called friends and family and asked for Christmas presents to be diverted into this need.

Drew, a former member of our church, told his brother, a high school student, about their need. His brother called and said he was sending a check for $90. Then he called back two days later and said he had been convicted that he could do more. He was saving money for the new PS4, but he wanted to give that to the church instead. So on the day that every high school boy in America was buying a PS4, this kid sent $500 to a church plant in Denver.

What was the result? Well, they didn't raise $150,000 in ten days. They raised $250,000 in four days.

Church planting yields an outstanding kingdom return on investment. Our investment in Summit Denver yielded, in a space of four days, $250,000 that would not otherwise have been used for kingdom work. Church planting produces new disciples who become new givers. Thus, church planting does not eat up resources from a limited pie; it grows the pie. Many ministries make converts, of course, but the process of transforming them into giving church members takes years. *Church planting does that almost immediately.*

SUMMARY

For these reasons and more, we believe planting should occupy a large portion of our sending portfolio. Planting new churches is not only biblical, needed, and financially wise; it represents "the best way to increase the number of believers in a city, and one of the best ways to renew the whole body of Christ.... Nothing else has the consistent impact of dynamic, extensive church planting."[12] The best way for your church to make a lasting impact that meets *both* the physical and spiritual needs of a community is to plant a church.

How to Plant Churches

So that's *why* we should plant churches. Now let's talk about *how* a church can actually do this. As we've said, our goal at the Summit Church is to plant 1,000 churches by 2050. So far we have planted 113, and, by God's grace, all have survived and are growing.

Our plan to accomplish our 2050 goal is built on the following principles.

MULTIPLICATION BEATS ADDITION.

When our church set out on this mission to plant 1,000 churches, we soon recognized that one church could never achieve this goal alone. It would take a "movement" — not one church planting churches, but churches planting churches.

Church planting is kind of like investing. When you make an investment, the interest you earn on the investment starts to earn interest. It's called "compound interest," and multiplies your money.

When I (J.D.) threw out the "1,000 in 40 years" goal, a lot of people thought it wasn't possible, but that's because we tend to think only in terms of addition. Multiplication changes the equation. We have figured out that if we continue to plant at our current rate (four churches a year), and if each of those churches plants one church every five years, with an 80 percent success rate, the number of churches will increase like this:

Projected Number of Churches

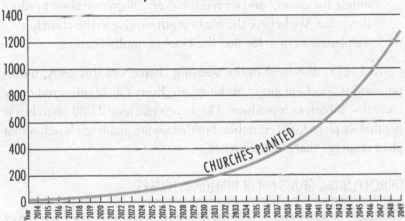

That is not even taking into account our international church plants. In China, it seems, you can plant one church in the morning and have 1,000 new churches by the afternoon. The power of multiplication brings the seemingly impossible into reach.

Our number goal may not be the same as yours. But here are three lessons we learned that we believe can be transferred into any context:

- **The most important factor in reaching our goal is the multiplication of the churches we plant.** Even if the Summit planted 5 churches a year until 2050, we would only have 200, or 20 percent of our goal. More than 80 percent of the churches we hope to plant will not be planted by us directly, but by our daughter churches.
- **Early investment amplifies exponential growth.** Again, church planting works like a retirement plan. The earlier you invest,

the bigger the yield in years to come. Or, as the proverb puts it, *"The best time to plant a tree was twenty years ago. The second best time is today."* The more churches we plant early (even if not all of those churches succeed!) and the quicker they attempt to plant, the greater our yield in the future.

- **The only way to reach 1,000 is by instilling the vision for multiplication deep into our "children."** It's vitally important that we not just plant churches, but that we pass on the vision of planting churches to our daughter churches. We call this "stewarding the vision," and we require every church we plant to adopt this value. We believe the greatest gift we give to the churches we plant is a vision for, and the DNA of, multiplication.

As I (J.D.) discussed in the opening chapters of this book, multiplication is how God grows his kingdom. Every Christian — and every church — is born to reproduce. The key to reaching 1,000 churches is not that *we* plant 1,000 churches, but that we are planting churches that plant churches that plant churches.

CHURCH PLANTING GROWS OUT OF DEVELOPING LEADERS.

Planting churches can be intimidating, especially if you have never planted a church yourself. If it makes you feel any better, neither of us (Mike or J.D.) has planted a church ourselves. (*Did we just put that in print?*) Yet our church has planted more than twenty successful churches in the United States alone — and by "planted" we mean (a) trained up the leader, (b) helped corral a core team of anywhere between a dozen and sixty people, and (c) provided the bulk of the funding for the first three years.

If you have never planted a church, the key to getting started is realizing that church planting is simply an application of the assignment given to all Christians: *make disciples and raise up new leaders.*

At its core, planting churches is really about developing leaders who make disciples. Good leaders plant healthy churches. Certainly there are some specific skills a planter needs to learn — such as how to do community research or how to launch an initial first service — but these can be gleaned through one of the many, well-written church planting manuals available, as well as from the abundance of supporting networks.[13] Nine times out of ten, what derails church planters has nothing to do with the particulars of how to *plant* the church. The planter fails in character or leadership or simply lacks the skill to grow a church. Planters face the same leadership challenges that all disciple-making pastors face.

Thus, if you are growing a vibrant church, you can plant a new church. Church planting is 45 percent disciple-making, 45 percent leadership development, and only 10 percent church planting skill (which you can get from manuals and networks). This realization gave us the confidence we needed to go all-in with planting. We had what it took. And so do you.

If you are pursuing the Great Commission, you will be raising up leaders. If you are not, can you really call yourself a fruitful church? In chapter 8 I lamented that many church planting organizations seem to rely more on recruiting leaders from the outside than raising them up internally. What does it say about a movement when it can't raise up its own leaders? If you are raising up leaders, church planting becomes an easy step.

Of course, leadership development takes intentionality. I (J.D.) started by simply mentoring young men on whom I saw the hand of God. Now, our church has developed an intentional training and support track for them. We launched a church planting residency called *The Summit Network*, in which we take 4–5 planters each year and work with them for eight months as they develop their vision and strategy, raise money, and build a team.

SUMMARY

Churches that want an exponential impact don't just send; they plant churches. And they don't just plant churches; they plant churches that plant churches. God gives the assignment to every church, not just large churches or pastors that have themselves planted. *Church planting is fundamentally about making disciples and raising up leaders, something all churches can do.* In order for a church to truly multiply, they have to raise up their own leaders, not recruit them from somewhere else. The real measure of multiplication is not how many churches we plant, but how many leaders we develop. After that, church planting becomes easy.

Five Elements of a Church Planting Strategy

Finally, we want to suggest five central elements upon which to build your church planting initiative. We believe your movement will be no stronger than the weakest of these five links. They are vision, assessment, recruiting, development, and support.

1. VISION: MULTIPLYING CHURCHES CAST A CLEAR AND COMPELLING VISION.

Hopefully, it has become clear by now that the greatest factor in creating a sending culture is a clear and compelling vision. Our church planted churches before we had any kind of church planting strategy, because we put forward a vision for multiplication. We simply said, "We want to be a sending church. God, show us how." People came forward, and we tried stuff.

The lead pastor has to champion that vision, or it will never gain traction. Congregants judge the value of something by how much the pastor talks about it from the pulpit. Unless the lead pastor completely buys in on the vision of planting churches, the people never will.

2. ASSESSMENT: MULTIPLYING CHURCHES SEND THEIR BEST.

The word "assessment" probably conjures up images of an exam or a job evaluation, but assessment simply means helping someone determine whether God has equipped them and called them to plant. You are doing no favors to someone by encouraging them to plant a church when God has not equipped them for it. Not every person who wants to be a heart surgeon is qualified to do so, and it can be an act of love, both for you and for your future patients, for a board of medical examiners to tell you that you are not qualified. Not every person who desires to plant a church is equipped to do so, regardless of how strongly the urge burns inside them.

In the New Testament, God confirms the internal call (the desire to do something) through an external validation by the church. In fact, in the case of Barnabas and Saul, Luke only mentions the external call to plant that came from the church, not any inward stirring of those two believers. Surely that call resonated with what they saw God doing in their own hearts, but Luke chose only to highlight the external call (Acts 13:2).

A number of tools exist for assessing church planters, but the best tool is involvement in the local church. As I asked in chapter 8, are these people making disciples? Are they faithful to the church? Are they multiplying small groups? Are they good with people? Do they get along well with peers? Do they start things and see them through to completion? We use online assessments, boot camps, and assessment retreats, but the best assessment is how they lead within our church. Typically, we don't have to ask if a guy will make a good planter. It is usually pretty obvious.

Don't outsource assessment entirely — own it. Be willing to ask the hard questions and then have the hard conversations. Sending out thirty people under the leadership of a poorly equipped planter not only wastes your money, but the lives of those thirty. Your willingness to do the uncomfortable work on the front end can save your people a great deal of pain on the back end.

3. RECRUITING: MULTIPLYING CHURCHES DON'T JUST CALL FOR, THEY CALL OUT.

Typically, we church leaders see our role in sending as putting forward the vision and then praying and waiting for people to respond. But in various stories throughout the Bible, the church initiated the call. Again, the call came *externally* (through someone else's mouth) before it was felt *internally* (that burning sense that God is calling you). For example, King David seems to have had little premonition of what was coming when Samuel showed up and told him that God was calling him to be king.

As I mentioned above, Acts 13:2 says that the Holy Spirit said *to the church*, "Separate for me Barnabas and Saul" for missionary work. This pattern continues throughout the book of Acts. In Acts 15:22, Luke records how the Jerusalem church recruited people to go on a mission trip to Antioch: "Then it seemed good to the apostles and the elders, with the whole church, to choose men from among them and send them to Antioch with Paul and Barnabas. They sent Judas called Barsabbas, and Silas, leading men among the brothers" (ESV). In 2 Timothy

4:11, Paul told Timothy to bring Mark to him, "because he is helpful to me in my ministry." That hardly sounds like passive leadership that says, "Just tell us when you feel called and we'll figure out how to pay the bills."[14] The early church did not wait for people to respond. They prayerfully approached people and asked them to consider going.

We need to recover this responsibility to actively recruit — not just calling for, but calling out. And we shouldn't limit this to just recruiting pastors. We have encouraged our church planters to recruit people from our church to go with them by spending a season in prayer, as Jesus did, and then to *ask* people to follow them in mission:

> One of those days Jesus went out to a mountainside to pray, and spent the night praying to God. When morning came, he called his disciples to him and chose twelve of them, whom he also designated apostles. (Luke 6:12–13)

How do you, as a church leader, facilitate this without depleting all your leaders? Won't the first few planters pick your leadership vineyard clean? Prospective church planters should be raising up new leaders within their own ministries (as in their small group), and those are the primary people they should be taking with them. If they are not doing that, they probably should not be planters! If we have a planter who identifies only existing church leaders (from other ministries) as his prospective recruits, we know he is not ready to be a planter. We do not want him merely poaching leaders from other existing churches where he plants (rather than raising up new leaders), so why allow him to build his planting team that way here?

God has gifted our church with many great leaders serving in areas of high capacity. There are just as many, however, with tremendous ability that have yet to be called out. Church planting provides an opportunity to call those people into the game. Each year we see leaders emerge in church planting teams who weren't doing much of anything in our church before that.

It's true, of course, that we have sent some of our best *existing* leaders with our plants. But usually they go because God has stirred them with a burden (independent of the planter's recruitment) or because they have been discipled by the prospective planter.

4. DEVELOPMENT: MULTIPLYING CHURCHES CULTIVATE PLANTERS FROM THE HARVEST.

A few years ago we stumbled on a secular leadership book that has proved immensely helpful in developing church planters. It is called *The Leadership Pipeline*,[15] and the premise is that organizations struggle to develop new leaders because they think of leadership development as a gradual incline rather than a journey with clear stages, turning points, and off-ramps. When we break leadership development down into small stages, certain people can grow from one leadership level to the next.

The leadership pipeline is not the same as the discipleship pipeline. The discipleship pipeline is one gradual ascent into Christlikeness. Maybe you would think of it something like this:

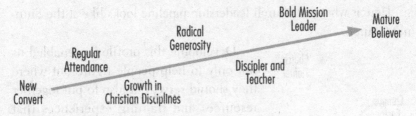

As you grow in Christ, you grow ever more generous, bolder, more loving, kinder, more knowledgeable, more Christlike — and you will never get to the top. You keep going "up" until the day you die. Both the new convert and the mature Christian have the same responsibilities; the mature Christian has simply grown more fruitful in them.

The leadership pipeline, however, is different. Completely new skills are required at each level. You move up the leadership pipeline in a zigzag formation, and there are off-ramps.

Certain people simply do not have the skills to grow past a certain level of leadership, and there's nothing wrong with that. It has nothing to do with spiritual maturity, but spiritual gifting. Ram Charan (writing not

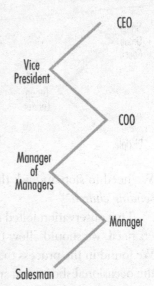

from the perspective of Christian ministry, but from business) uses the example of the salesman: A very effective salesman often gets promoted to lead other salespeople. But selling products and leading salespeople require two entirely different skill sets, and those who were incredibly successful salespeople sometimes make terrible managers of other salespeople. Their genius in selling does not always transfer to a genius in management. You should help that kind of salesman develop his selling capacity more, not saddle him with responsibilities outside his skill set.

Some disciples of Jesus will never become leaders of leaders because God just didn't gift them that way. They can grow infinitely more like Christ, but we are not doing them favors by pushing them into positions for which they are not gifted.

Here is what our church leadership pipeline looks like at the Summit Church:

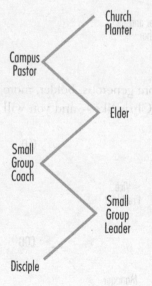

Developing this profile has enabled us not only to help people figure out where they should serve, but also to put together resources and training experiences that can help them become proficient at a given level and explore whether or not they are gifted to go on to the next.

5. SUPPORT: MULTIPLYING CHURCHES KEEP SENDING.

Recently we sat down with several of our planters to ask how we can better support them. One of them said, "Everyone complains about how often church plants fail, but they always put the blame on the plant. They never think about the sending church. We need to stop and ask the question, *what does it mean to be a good sending church?*"

That observation jolted us. Instead of assuming we know what planters need, we should allow them to help us understand what they need. We found in the process that while planters certainly need funding and the occasional short-term support trip, they really wanted ongoing relationship, brotherhood, and mentorship. They wanted to know that other churches, and other leaders, had their back.

Asking, "What do *you* need?" and "How can *we* help?" doesn't mean we become a giant Santa Claus. We have had to say no plenty of times, sometimes because we simply couldn't afford what the planters were asking and other times because we believed that giving them what they were asking for would not have been healthy for them. But through asking those questions they have helped us identify many new ways we can bless them — things we would never have figured out on our own. Furthermore, it has moved them from the position of "dependent child relying on daddy's wisdom to survive" to "captain of this mission who is responsible to enlist others for help."

Our sending doesn't end with commissioning the planting team. Like a good parent, we want to remain accessible and supportive to our "children" years after they have left the home. Paul didn't see his job as completed when he planted a church. He stayed connected to those churches. Supported them. Visited them. Collected money for them. Wrote angry or tearful letters to them on occasion. Paul empowered them into autonomy, but remained committed to seeing them finish as well as they had started. "It's not the getting out, but the coming home that determines the success of the sea voyage."

I (J.D.) think some of our most beneficial work in sending has taken place after the church plant walked out our doors. We believe our job is not finished when we launch that thousandth church, but when the thousandth one crosses the finish line.

Conclusion

Planting churches domestically is not something only megachurches can do. It's not the responsibility of your denomination. Nor do you have to have been a church planter yourself. Every Christian, and every church, was born to reproduce. Jesus wrote it into his disciples' DNA. And he gave such incredible promises of support if we would just try: He promised us that the gates of hell would not be able to prevent us. If we follow him, *he will* make us fishers of men. Our church planting efforts are built on those promises.

Not all of the principles we have introduced in this appendix will play out in your context in the same way they have played out in ours, but one thing you can be sure of: God intends for your church, or your ministry, to reproduce. As with all the promises of God, this one is yours for the asking. Take that first step out of the boat onto the fearful sea of church planting, and you will be amazed at how God's grace sustains you above the waves.

ACKNOWLEDGMENTS

I want to acknowledge the many who had a hand in shaping this book. God's greatest earthly gifts to me have usually taken the form of people. Specifically, in regards to this book, I am exceedingly grateful to:

... Sam James, who planted Homestead Heights Baptist Church in Durham, NC, in 1962. The church would in 2002 become the Summit Church. Sam birthed into this church the vision of being a church for the nations. He remains a dear friend and one of the most active octogenarians I know. When he preached at our church this year, he insisted on preaching all five services. A modern-day Caleb.

... Mike McDaniel, Curt Alan, and Bonnie Shrum, who have served beside me in making this dream of being a sending church into a reality.

... The people of the Summit Church, who give so generously and selflessly to see the kingdom of God grow in ways that do not directly benefit them. At every point in the growth of our church — from the decision to love and reach college students, to going multisite, to pursuing diversity, to planting churches — they have always prioritized the mission over personal comfort. I am especially thankful for the 300 who started with me. Gideon had his 300; you were mine.

... Veronica, my wife, who so generously shares our home and my time with the mission of church planting. There seems to be no inconvenience she won't suffer for the sake of the mission. No better word comes to my mind for her than "precious."

... Our first decade of domestic church planters (2005 – 15), who helped us figure out how to plant churches and then boldly took the first steps, going where no Summit member had gone before. Yours was perhaps the greatest leap of faith. We didn't know what we were doing — and you knew that — but you let us take your lives into our hands anyway. You are our inheritance.

... Ryan Pazdur and his excellent team at Zondervan — including the invaluable Jim Ruark — who pushed me to make this book 1,000 times better than when I first introduced it to them. And to Chris Pappalardo, my research partner, who works tirelessly behind the scenes to make sure we have our hands on the best, and most up-to-date, information. When he joined our team, I joked with him that his job description was, "Make me sound smarter." I'm not sure if he's done that, but anything in this book that sounds really smart probably originates from him.

NOTES

Introduction

1. http://www.english.illinois.edu/maps/depression/dustbowl.htm; http://www.pbs.org/wgbh/americanexperience/features/timeline/ dustbowl/ (accessed 5/13/2014). I first saw this story connected to kingdom giving in Andy Stanley, *Fields of Gold: A Place Beyond Your Deepest Fears, a Prize Beyond Your Wildest Imagination* (Carol Stream, IL: Tyndale House, 2004), 9–13.

2. Dietrich Bonhoeffer, *The Cost of Discipleship* (1959; New York: Touchstone, 1995).

3. I owe this analogy to Ann Voskamp. http://www.thehighcalling. org/reflection/building-platform-every-platform-altar#. VAtWGWSwKXI

Chapter 1: Aircraft Carriers, Cruise Liners, and Battleships

1. Undoubtedly, some of the details of that story have grown with Internet legend, but the core elements of Lawnchair Larry's escapade are documented. http://web.archive.org/ web/20070710212757/http://www.cnn.com/2007/US/07/10/flying. lawn.chair.ap/index.html

2. See David Olson, *The American Church in Crisis* (Grand Rapids: Zondervan, 2008), 176–80, and Pat Hood, *The Sending Church: The Church Must Leave the Building* (Nashville: B&H Publishers, 2013), 19.

3. Albert Mohler, "Life in Post-Denominational America" (September 22, 2012). http://www.albertmohler.com/2009/09/22/ life-in-post-denominational-america/ (accessed 1/15/2014).

4. Tim Chester and Steve Timmis, *Everyday Church: Gospel Communities on Mission* (Wheaton, IL: Crossway, 2012), 15.

5. "What If a Penny Was Doubled Every Day for a Year?" *Raivyn's Roost* (February 2, 2007). http://raivynnsroost.blogspot. com/2007/02/what-if-penny-was-doubled-every-day-for.html (accessed 1/15/2014).

6. Christopher J. H. Wright, *The Mission of God: Unlocking the Bible's Grand Narrative* (Downers Grove, IL: InterVarsity, 2006), 455.

7. Charles Spurgeon, "A Sermon and a Reminiscence," from *Sword and Trowel* magazine (March 1973). http://www.spurgeon.org/s_ and_t/srmn1873.htm (accessed 2/5/2015).

8. Timothy Keller, Sermon on Genesis 12:1–4, entitled "The Cost of Mission" (delivered October 30, 1994).

9. "Adoniram Judson, First Missionary from the United States," *Church History for Kids.* http://www.christianity.com/church/ church-history/church-history-for-kids/adoniram-judson-first-missionary-from-the-united-states-11635044.html

10. Rodney Stark, *The Rise of Christianity: How the Obscure, Marginal Jesus Movement Became the Dominant Religious Force in the Western World in a Few Centuries* (San Francisco: Harper Collins, 1996), 7.

11. Pat Hood, *The Sending Church* (Nashville: B&H Publishers, 2012).

12. This is a summary of Wright's primary thesis in his book *The Mission of God: Unlocking the Bible's Grand Narrative* (Wheaton, IL: InterVarsity, 2006).

Part 2: The Ten Sending Plumb Lines

1. I am indebted to Larry Osborne, a personal friend and pastor of North Coast Church in Vista, California, for this metaphor.

Chapter 3: Swimming in the Gospel

1. My paraphrase. Antoine's *Citadelle*, the source of this quote, was translated into English after his death and was published under the title *The Wisdom of the Sands*.

2. I owe this phrasing to my friend Tullian Tchividjian, who uses this line frequently in sermons and blogs.

3. Timothy Keller, *Center Church: Doing Balanced, Gospel-Centered Ministry in Your City* (Grand Rapids: Zondervan, 2012), 48.

4. For more on this, see my book *Gospel: Recovering the Power that Made Christianity Revolutionary* (Nashville: B&H Publishers, 2011).

5. See also Malachi 3:10–11.

6. Matthew 18:21–35.

7. A talent was about 6,000 denarii. The average wage back then was about 300 denarii per year. See Matthew–Luke, Volume 8 of *The Bible Expositor's Commentary* (Grand Rapids: Zondervan, 1984), 516.

Chapter 4: The Myth of Calling

1. Tony Campolo, *Let Me Tell You a Story: Life Lessons from Unexpected Places and Unlikely People* (Nashville: Thomas Nelson, 2000), 145.

2. For more on this, see Gene Edward Veith, *God at Work: Your Christian Vocation in All of Life* (Wheaton, IL: Crossway, 2002), 13–14.

3. http://www.travelkb.com/Uwe/Forum.aspx/air/2002/American-Airlines-Preaching-Pilot. Found in John Dickson, *The Best Kept Secret of Christian Mission* (Grand Rapids: Zondervan, 2010).

4. Stephen Neill, *A History of Christian Missions* (Harmondsworth, UK: Penguin Books, 1986), 22.

5. Patrick Lai, "The Business of Building Bridges," chapter 5 in Mike Barnett and Robin Martin, eds., *Discovering the Mission of God: Supplement* (Downers Grove, IL: InterVarsity Academic, 2012), via Kindle.

6. http://www.aaro.org/about-aaro/6m-americans-abroad. See also http://www.aboutmissions.org/statistics.html; http://www.christianitytoday.com/gleanings/2013/july/missionaries-countries-sent-received-csgc-gordon-conwell.html?paging=off; http://

conversation.lausanne.org/en/resources/detail/13027#article_
page_1 (all accessed 12/4/14).

7. I wrote *Jesus, Continued...: Why the Spirit Inside You Is Better Than Jesus Beside You* (Grand Rapids: Zondervan, 2014), in part to address this question. See also Kevin DeYoung, *Just Do Something: A Liberating Approach to Finding God's Will* (Chicago: Moody Publishers, 2009).

8. I found chapter 8 of Pastor Pat Hood's *The Sending Church: The Church Must Leave the Building* (Nashville: B&H Publishers, 2013) helpful in making this point, and I adopted some of the language he uses.

Chapter 5: Missional or Attractional? Yes.

1. Lesslie Newbigin, *One Body, One Gospel, One World: The Christian Mission Today* (London: Wm. Carling & Co. Ltd., 1958), 17–27. Newbigin himself did not use the term "missional," preferring to call the church "missionary" or to say that "the church is a mission." But the missional ideas are elaborated throughout his writings.

2. Alan Hirsch and Michael Frost, *The Shaping of Things to Come: Innovation and Mission for the 21st-Century Church* (Peabody, MA: Hendrickson, 2003), 9.

3. In the Old Testament the focus is on "come and see," although elements of "go and tell" are still evident. In the New Testament it is reversed; the focus shifts to "go and tell," but you can still find examples of "come and see."

4. From Lesslie Newbigin, *The Gospel in a Pluralist Society* (Grand Rapids: Eerdmans, 1989), 120, 133. See also Gary Tyra, *The Holy Spirit in Mission: Prophetic Speech and Action in Christian Witness* (Downers Grove, IL: InterVarsity Academic, 2011), 146.

5. "The installation of stalls for the sale of animals and of other requirements for the sacrifice such as wine, oil and salt had the effect of transforming the Court of the Gentiles into an oriental bazaar and

a cattle mart. Jesus was appalled at this disregard for the sanctity of an area consecrated for the use of Gentiles who had not yet become full proselytes to Judaism" (William Lane, *The Gospel According to Mark* [Grand Rapids: Eerdmans, 1974], 405–6). "The temple had been intended to symbolize God's dwelling with Israel for the sake of the world; the way Jesus' contemporaries had organized things, it had come to symbolize not God's welcome to the nations but God's exclusion of them" (Tom Wright, *Mark for Everyone* [Louisville, KY: Westminster John Knox Press, 2004], 152). See also F. F. Bruce, *The Gospel of John* (Grand Rapids: Eerdmans, 1983), 75.

6. For example, Andy Stanley's book *Deep and Wide: Creating Churches Unchurched People Love to Attend* (Grand Rapids: Zondervan, 2012) is immensely helpful for getting into the mind of the average visitor at your church. Stanley and I would think about church — and the purpose of, and proper content for, a worship service — quite differently, but it's still a helpful book for thinking about weekend outreach.

7. Thomas Hale, *On Being a Missionary* (Pasadena, CA: William Carey Library, 1995), 6.

8. Tim Chester and Steve Timmis, *Everyday Church: Gospel Communities on Mission* (Wheaton, IL: Crossway, 2012), 15.

9. Charles Spurgeon, *Lectures to My Students* (reprint, Grand Rapids: Zondervan, 1954), 343.

10. Charles Spurgeon, "How to Become Fishers of Men," Sermon (No. 1906). http://www.spurgeon.org/sermons/1906.htm (accessed 12/5/2014).

Chapter 6: How to Transform an Audience into an Army

1. Jim Collins, *Good to Great: Why Some Companies Make the Leap … and Others Don't* (New York: HarperBusiness, 2001).

2. Jack Welch, Interview with Piers Morgan on *Piers Morgan Tonight* (June 11, 2011). http://transcripts.cnn.com/TRANSCRIPTS/1106/11/pmt.01.html

3. Rowland Forman, Jeff Jones, and Bruce Miller, *The Leadership Baton: An Intentional Strategy for Developing Leaders in Your Church* (Grand Rapids: Zondervan, 2004), 24.

4. In addition to *The Leadership Baton*, I have found the books *Visioneering: God's Blueprint for Developing and Maintaining Vision* by Andy Stanley (Sisters, OR: Multnomah, 1999) and *Courageous Leadership: Field-Tested Strategy for the 360° Leader* by Bill Hybels (2002; reprint, Grand Rapids: Zondervan, 2012) to be helpful to this end.

5. Derek Lehmberg et al. "General Electric: An Outlier in CEO Talent Development," *Ivey Business Journal*. http://iveybusinessjournal.com/topics/leadership/general-electric-an-outlier-in-ceo-talent-development#.UwU0UkJdWDo (accessed 2/10/2014).

6. Liz Wiseman, *Multipliers: How the Best Leaders Make Everyone Smarter* (New York: Harper Collins, 2010), 37.

7. Kevin Nguyen, "Releasing Your Best for the Mission of God." http://sendnetwork.com/2014/05/12/releasing-your-best-for-the-mission-of-god/ (accessed 5/13/2014).

8. This quote is compiled from two places: (1) Comments to a GE corporate officer, Crotonville, NY (February 2, 1987). Cited in Janet Lowe, *Jack Welch Speaks: Wit and Wisdom from the World's Greatest Business Leader* (Hoboken, NJ: John Wiley & Sons, 2008), 87; (2) Interview with Reuters, "Jeremy Lin: Lessons from the Lin-sanity," (http://blogs.reuters.com/jack-and-suzy-welch/2012/02/24/jeremy-lin-lessons-from-the-lin-sanity).

9. John Calvin, *Commentary on the Epistle of Paul the Apostle to the Corinthians*, trans. John Pringles (Grand Rapids: Baker, 1981), 20:442–43.

Chapter 7: Painting the Invisible Man

1. I owe this great analogy to Mark Dever, from a talk he gave to the Summit Church staff.

2. Although I am paraphrasing her words here, this was her sentiment. She was first interviewed in the *Durham Herald-Sun*; see more of her actual words here: "Church Efforts Earn Family Status at Elementary School," *Biblical Recorder*, vol. 175, no. 19 (September 12, 2009), 7.

3. Timothy Keller, Sermon on Acts 3:2–8, 13–22, entitled "The First Miracle" (delivered January 6, 2013).

4. I borrow this phrase from N. T. Wright's book *Simply Christian* (San Francisco: HarperSanFrancisco, 2006).

5. Francis Schaeffer, *The Mark of the Christian* (Downers Grove, IL: InterVarsity, 1970), 29.

6. These insights from Acts 16 I first heard at least in seminal form from Tim Keller. Where his thinking stops and mine starts I can't always tell.

7. From Eberhard Arnold, *The Early Christians: In Their Own Words* (Farmington, PA: Plough Pub, 1997), 14.

8. Ibid., 16.

Chapter 8: Without This, You Fail

1. Robert Coleman, *The Master Plan of Evangelism* (Westwood, NJ: Revell, 1964), 104.

2. J. D. Payne, "Eleven Implications for the North American Church," in Mike Barnett and Robin Martin, eds., *Discovering the Mission of God: Supplement* (Downers Grove, IL: InterVarsity Academic, 2012), Loc. 2631.

3. Ibid.

4. Dawson Trotman, *Born to Reproduce* (pamphlet from Back to the Bible Publishers, 1957, now in public domain).

5. Coleman, *The Master Plan of Evangelism*, 43, 39.

6. Ibid., 107.

7. These are all Robert Coleman's words, but pieced together from various places in *The Master Plan of Evangelism*.

8. Trotman, *Born to Reproduce*.

9. I first introduced these objections and their answers in *Jesus, Continued...: Why the Spirit Inside You Is Better Than Jesus Beside You* (Grand Rapids: Zondervan, 2014), 56–60.

Chapter 9: Your Church Doesn't Need a Missions Pastor

1. David Platt, "The Multiplying Community," in *Radical* (Colorado Springs: Multnomah, 2010), chap. 5.

2. See D. A. Carson, "Ongoing Imperative for World Mission," in *The Great Commission: Evangelicals and the History of World Missions*, ed. by Martin I. Klauber and Scott M. Manetsch (Nashville: B&H Publishers, 2008), 179.

3. Christopher J. H. Wright, *The Mission of God: Unlocking the Bible's Grand Narrative* (Wheaton, IL: InterVarsity, 2006).

4. Sermon given by John Piper at the Advance National Conference (March 2009), called "Let the Nations Be Glad," held at the Durham Performing Arts Center in Durham, NC.

5. David Garrison, *Church Planting Movements* (Midlothian, VA: WIGTake Resources, 2004), 243.

6. See Elisabeth Elliot, *Shadow of the Almighty: The Life and Testament of Jim Elliot*, (New York: Harper & Brothers, 1958), 132.

7. Reggie Joiner and Carrie Neuwhof, *Parenting Beyond Your Capacity* (Colorado Springs: David Cook, 2010), 180–82.

Chapter 10: Racial Reconciliation as a Fruit of the Sending Culture

1. Curtiss Paul DeYoung et al., *United by Faith: The Multiracial Congregation as an Answer to the Problem of Race* (Oxford: Oxford University Press, 2003), 2.

2. Some refer to this concept as "transcultural." See, for example, Leonce Crump at http://www.desiringgod.org/blog/posts/tapestry-a-vision-for-trans-cultural-church.

3. I owe this phrasing to my good friend Vance Pitman, who pastors one of the most remarkable multicultural churches I have ever observed: Hope Baptist Church in Las Vegas, Nevada.

4. Jonathan Rauch, "Seeing Around Corners," *The Atlantic* (April 1, 2002). http://www.theatlantic.com/magazine/archive/2002/04/seeing-around-corners/302471/

5. Tony Evans, *Oneness Embraced — Through the Eyes of Tony Evans: A Fresh Look at Reconciliation, the Kingdom, and Justice* (Chicago: Moody Publishers, 2011), 22–23.

6. Ibid., 46.

7. http://www.washingtonpost.com/blogs/the-fix/wp/2014/12/11/sony-executive-on-obama-should-i-ask-him-if-he-liked-django/

8. Rodney Stark, *The Rise of Christianity: How the Obscure, Marginal Jesus Movement Became the Dominant Religious Force in the Western World in a Few Centuries* (San Francisco: HarperCollins, 1996), 161.

Chapter 11: There's More Than One Way to Be Wicked

1. See notations in chapter 3.

2. See John Piper, *Risk Is Right: Better to Lose Your Life Than to Waste It* (Wheaton, IL: Crossway, 2013), 34–35.

3. Elisabeth Elliot, *The Shadow of the Almighty* (New York: Harper & Row, 1958), 108.

4. Piper, *Risk Is Right*, 29.

5. Ibid., 30.

6. At this point in Jesus' life, his focus is on his people, the Jews, and he is not yet revealing himself to the Gentiles. The Jews are the children; the Gentiles are the "little dogs" that don't yet belong at the master's table. See Matthew 15:21–28.

7. See C. S. Lewis, *Mere Christianity* (New York: HarperCollins, 1952), 86.

Chapter 12: Never Give Up

1. See Chip Heath and Dan Heath, *Made to Stick* (New York: Random House, 2007).

2. For more on this, see my book *Gospel: Recovering the Power That Made Christianity Revolutionary* (Nashville: B&H Publishers, 2011).

3. Andrew Murray, *The Ministry of Intercession* (New Kensington, PA: Whitaker House, 1982), 189.

4. John Wesley, *How to Pray: The Best of John Wesley* (Uhrichsville, OH: Barbour Publishing, 2008), 25.

5. Bill Hybels, *Axiom: Powerful Leadership Proverbs* (Grand Rapids: Zondervan, 2008), 55.

6. Sun Tzu, *The Art of War* (Lindenhurst, NY: Tribeca Books, 2010).

Appendix 1: Setting Up an International Missions Strategy

1. For more on this, read John Piper's excellent book *Let the Nations Be Glad* (Grand Rapids: Baker Books, 1993). Piper explains why the cutting edge of God's work in every generation remains concentrated on unreached people groups.

2. http://joshuaproject.net/assets/media/assets/articles/amazing-countdown-facts.pdf. Winter, writing in 1980, said that there was one UPG for every 1,000 churches. By God's grace, much progress has been made since then! See also http://www.whatchristianswanttoknow.com/why-are-there-so-many-churches-why-are-there-so-many-denominations/ and http://hirr.hartsem.edu/research/fastfacts/fast_facts.html#numcong

3. For ideas on how to teach parents to do this, see our small group curriculum *Ready to Launch: Jesus-Centered Parenting in a Child-Centered World* by J.D. and Veronica Greear (Nashville: Lifeway, 2014).

4. I am indebted to Omar Reyes of Glocal.net for the concept of "domains." http://www.glocal.net/2014/06/05/blog-domains-key-transformation/

5. For another *great* resource on this, see Wayne Grudem and Barry Asmus *The Poverty of Nations: A Sustainable Solution* (Wheaton, IL: Crossway, 2013). (Foreword by Rick Warren.)

6. Steve Corbett and Brian Fikkert, *Helping Without Hurting in Short-Term Missions: Leader's Guide* (Chicago: Moody Publishers, 2014), 25.

7. http://www.bridgesinternational.com/

8. Ben Wolfgang, "Armed with U.S. education, many leaders take on world," *Washington Times* (August 19, 2012). http://www.washingtontimes.com/news/2012/aug/19/armed-with-us-education-many-leaders-take-on-world/?page=all (accessed 12/4/2014).

9. Tim Keller, *Center Church: Doing Balanced, Gospel-Centered Ministry in Your City* (Grand Rapids: Zondervan, 2012), 337–43.

Appendix 2: Developing a Domestic Church Planting Strategy

1. This quote is usually credited to Drucker, although it doesn't appear in any of his published writings.

2. Tim Keller, *Center Church: Doing Balanced, Gospel-Centered Ministry in Your City* (Grand Rapids: Zondervan, 2012), 355.

3. Tim Keller, "Why Plant Churches?" unpublished article. http://download.redeemer.com/pdf/learn/resources/Why–Plant–Churches-Keller.pdf (accessed 12/5/2014).

4. David T. Olson, *The American Church in Crisis* (Grand Rapids: Zondervan, 2008), 119–20.

5. Ibid., 43.

6. Keller, *Center Church*, 359.

7. Larry Kreider, *House Church Networks: A Church for a New Generation* (Lititz, PA: House to House Publications, 2001), 19.

8. Keller, *Center Church*, 360ff.

9. Ed Stetzer and Warren Bird, *Viral Churches: Helping Church Planters Become Movement Makers* (San Francisco: Jossey-Bass, 2010), 31. Stetzer cites a national research project called

FACT2008, which surveyed thousands of American churches. Among their results they found that churches that promoted leadership development and evangelism — including church planting — were the healthiest and most likely to grow.

10. Keller, *Center Church*, 360.

11. Ibid., 362.

12. Ibid., 365.

13. We have found Redeemer Presbyterian Church of Manhattan's manual to be particularly helpful, as well as resources provided by the North American Mission Board of the Southern Baptist Convention or networks such as Acts 29 or Launch.

14. See also 2 Timothy 2:2.

15. Ram Charan, *The Leadership Pipeline* (San Francisco: Jossey-Bass, 2011).

Jesus, Continued...

Why the Spirit Inside You Is Better Than Jesus Beside You

J.D. Greear

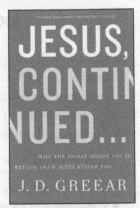

Encounter the presence of the Holy Spirit within you

Jesus gave his disciples the audacious promise that the Spirit he would send to live inside them would be even better than if he himself remained beside them. Yet how many of us consider our connection to the Holy Spirit so strong that we would call his presence in us better than Jesus himself walking by our side?

J.D. Greear was the pastor of a rapidly growing church who still felt that he didn't know how to relate to God *personally*. Though he knew a lot about God, he wasn't as sure about how to walk *with* God. Furthermore, he felt overwhelmed by the size of the mission left for his church. In a world of so much need, what difference could he possibly make? Learning how God dwells in us and empowers us in the Holy Spirit redefined his life and ministry. Ministry became less about working for God and more about letting God work through him. Drudgery was replaced by delight; helplessness was replaced by empowerment.

In *Jesus, Continued...* Greear explores — in clear and practical language — questions such as, "What does it mean to have a relationship with the Holy Spirit?" "How can we tell when the Spirit is speaking to us?" And, "What do you do when God feels absent?"

If you are longing to know God in a vibrant way, *Jesus, Continued...* has good news for you: That's exactly what God wants for you, too. His Spirit stands ready to guide you, empower you, and use you.

Tired of feeling burned out? Try being on fire.

Available in stores and online!

About the Exponential Series

The interest in church planting has grown significantly in recent years. The need for new churches has never been greater. At the same time, the number of models and approaches are expanding. To address the unique opportunities in this exciting time, Exponential, in partnership with Zondervan, launched the Exponential Series.

Books in this series:

- Tell the reproducing church story
- Celebrate the diversity of models and approaches God is using to reproduce healthy congregations
- Highlight the innovative and pioneering practices of healthy reproducing churches
- Equip, inspire and challenge Kingdom-minded leaders with the tools they need in their journey of becoming multiplying churches

Exponential exists to equip movement makers with actionable principles, ideas and solutions for the accelerated multiplication of healthy, reproducing faith communities. We provide a national voice for this movement through:

- The Annual Exponential Conference (exponential.org/events)
- Exponential Regional Conferences (exponential.org/events)
- Exponential Multiplication Assessment Tool (becomingfive.org)
- Exponential Resources, including free audio & video training, free eBooks and more (exponential.org)

CPSIA information can be obtained
at www.ICGtesting.com
Printed in the USA
LVHW030526230921
698504LV00003B/7